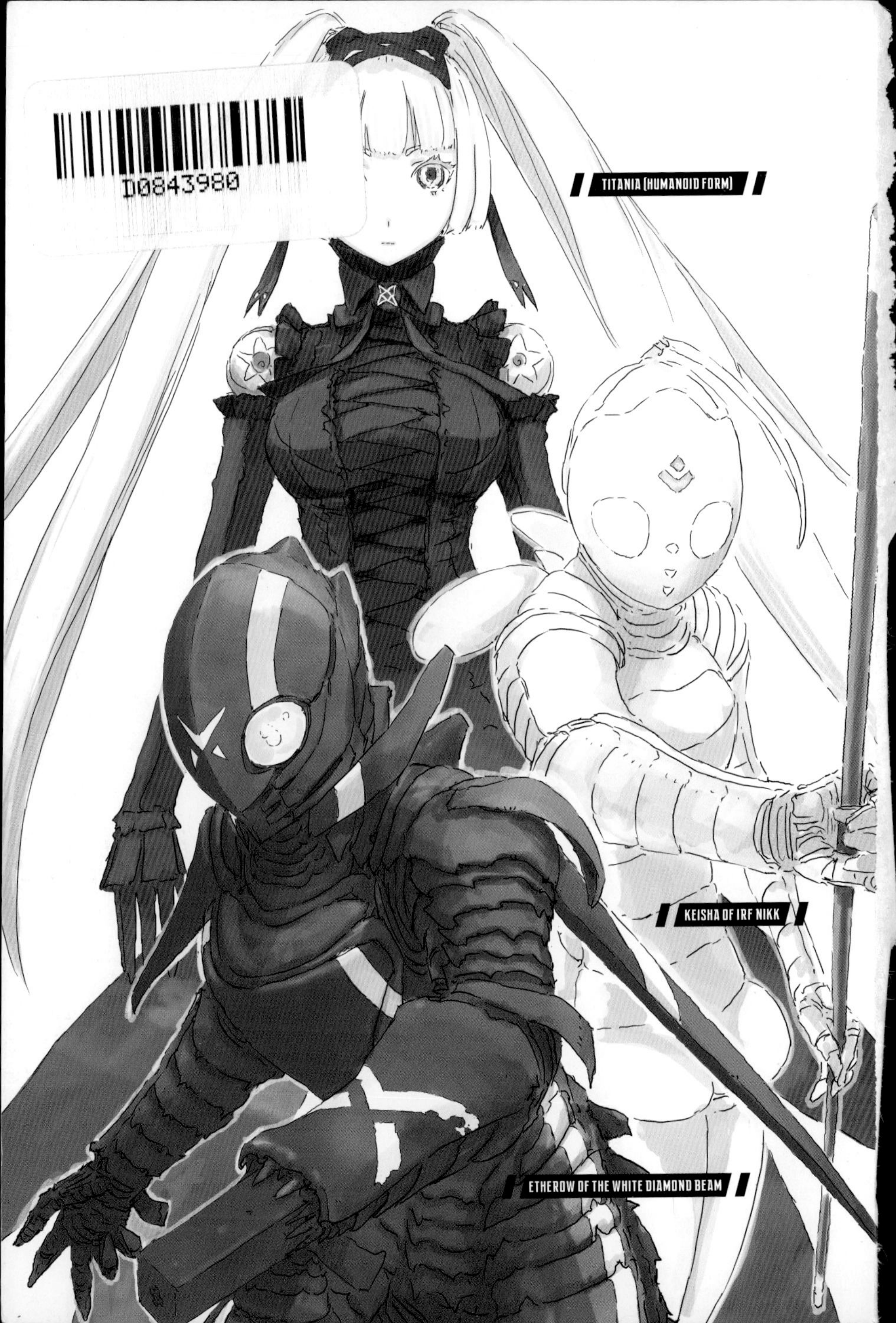
TITANIA (HUMANOID FORM)
KEISHA OF IRF NIKK
ETHEROW OF THE WHITE DIAMOND BEAM

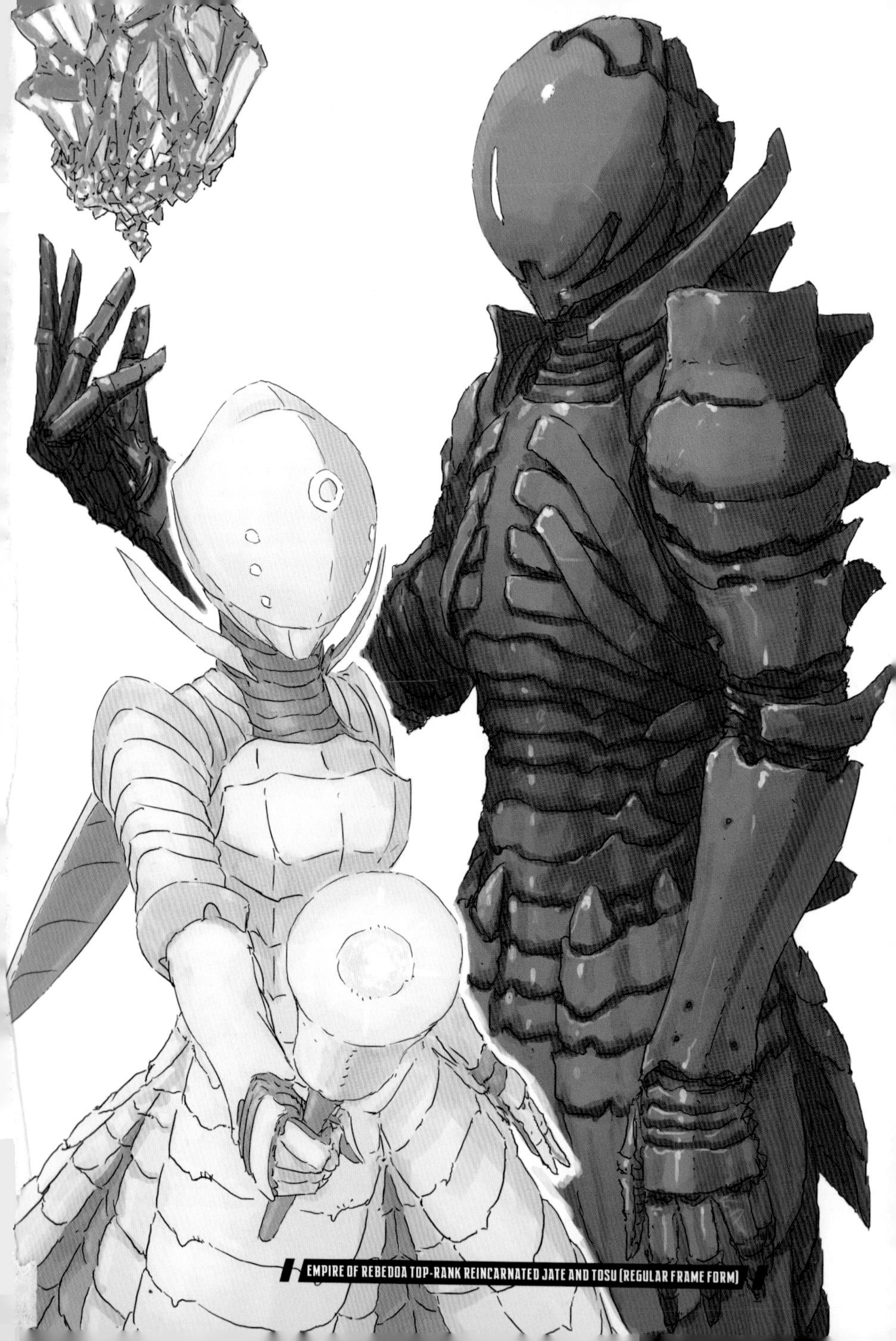

EMPIRE OF REBEDOA TOP-RANK REINCARNATED JATE AND TOSU (REGULAR FRAME FORM)

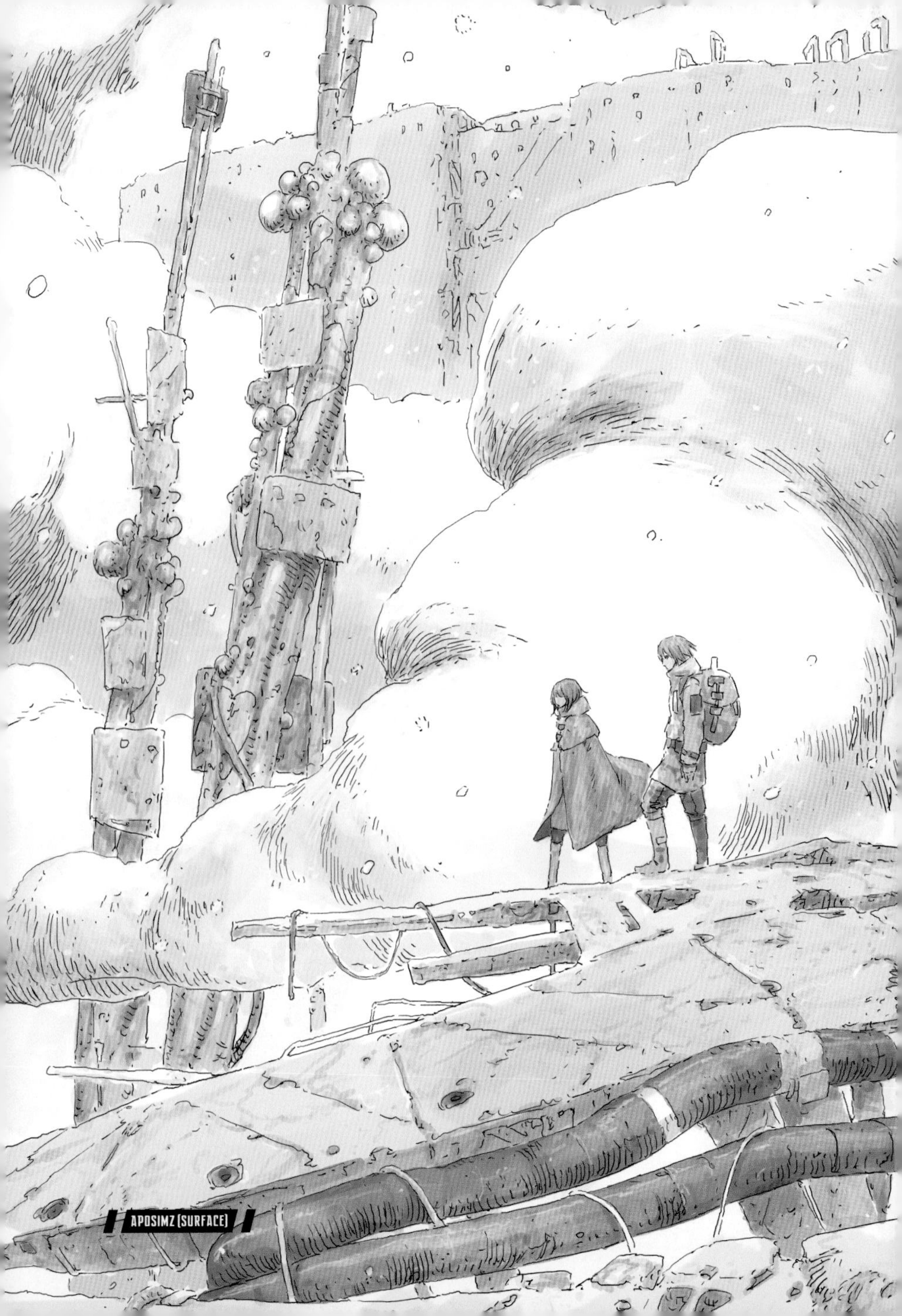
APOSIMZ (SURFACE)

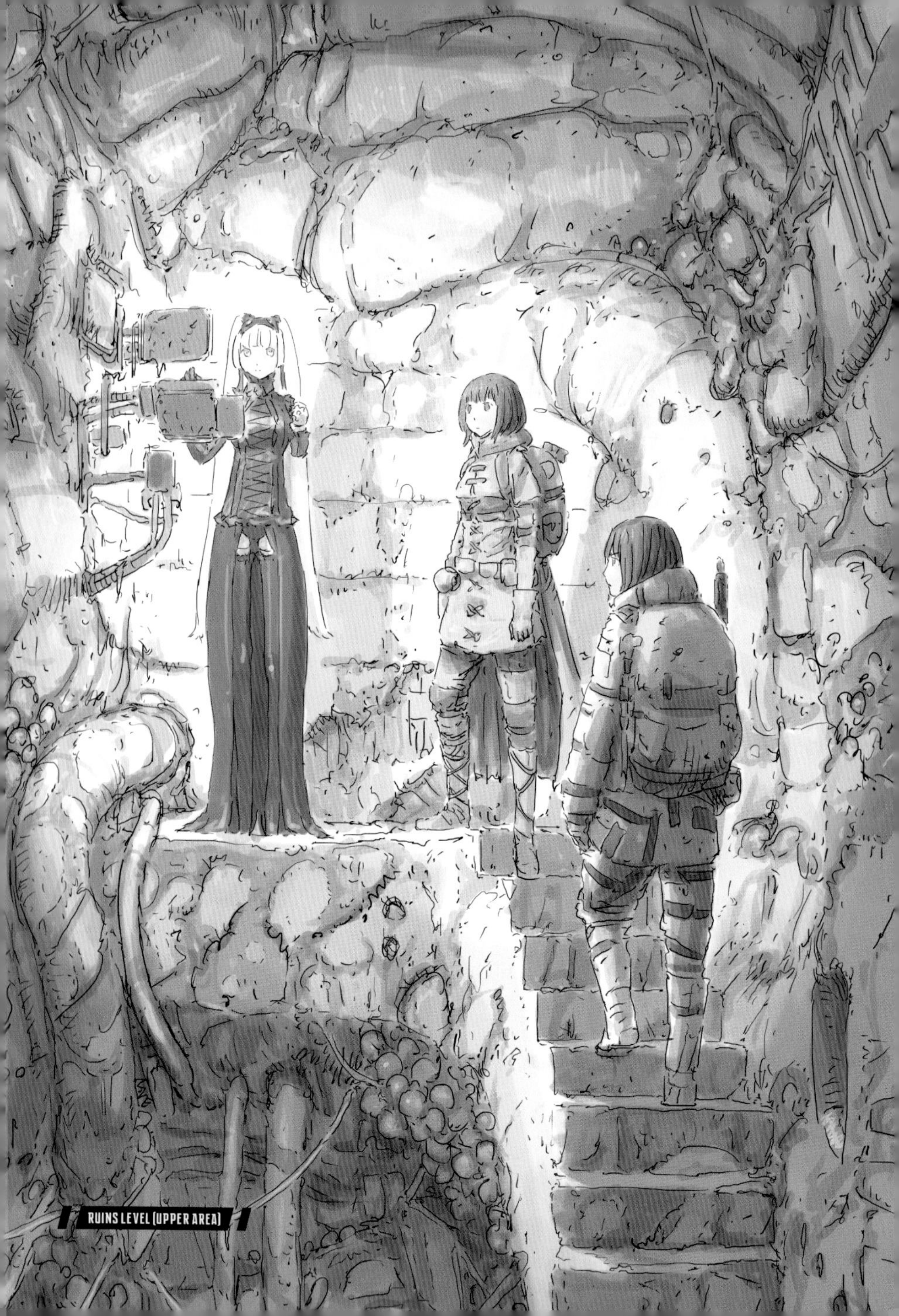
RUINS LEVEL (UPPER AREA)

APOSIMZ

04

TSUTOMU NIHEI

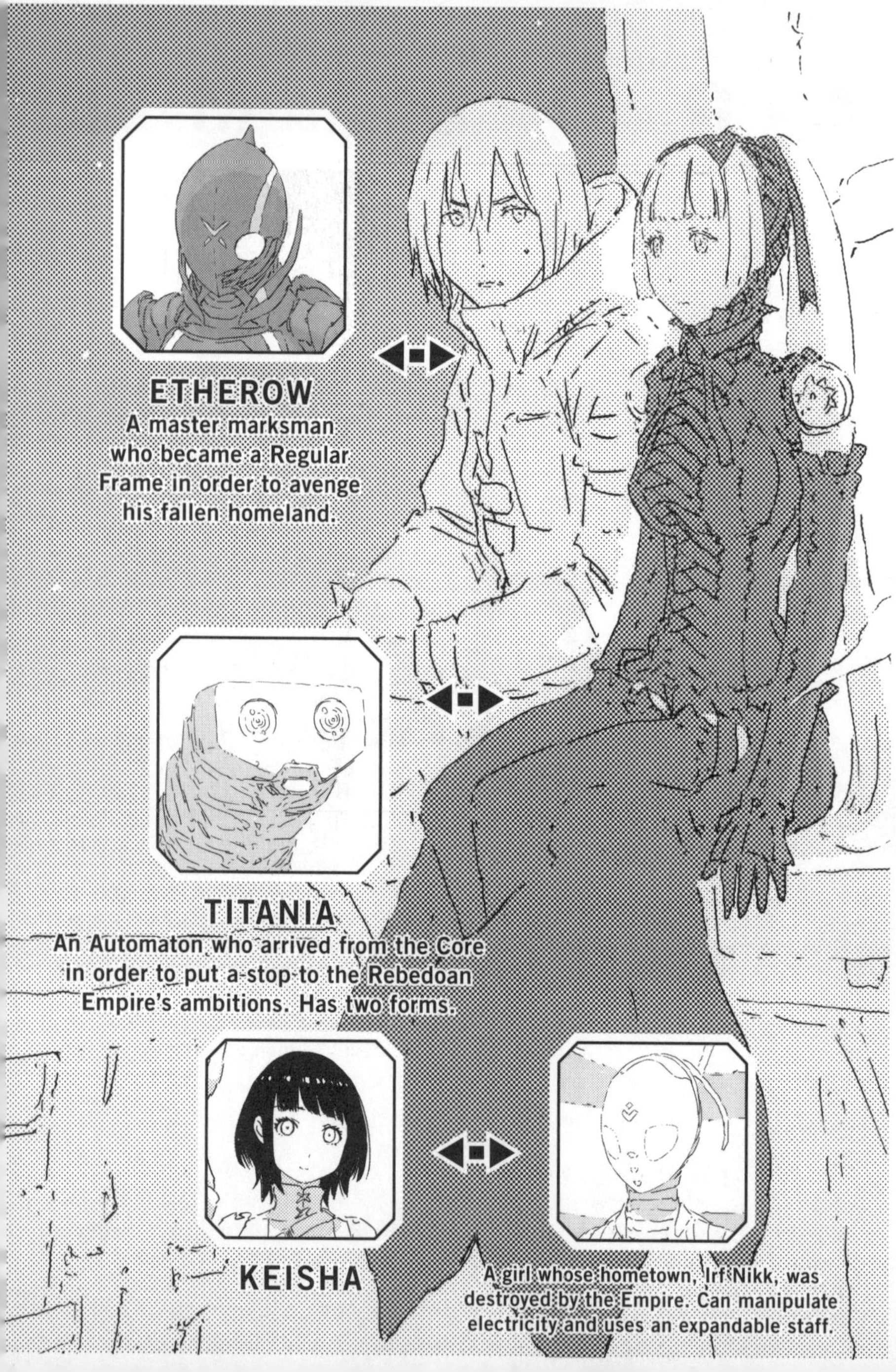
ETHEROW
A master marksman who became a Regular Frame in order to avenge his fallen homeland.
TITANIA
An Automaton who arrived from the Core in order to put a stop to the Rebedoan Empire's ambitions. Has two forms.
KEISHA
A girl whose hometown, Irf Nikk, was destroyed by the Empire. Can manipulate electricity and uses an expandable staff.

PLOT AND CHARACTER INTRO

NICHIKO SUOU

The Emperor of Rebedoa. He is currently creating powerful, high-level Regular Frames.

KAJIWAN

The King of Irf Nikk and Keisha's elder brother. After their hidden village was destroyed, he absconded in order to fulfill his own ambition.

JATE

A high-level Reincarnated of the Rebedoan Empire. Has the ability to manipulate automatons.

TOSU

Member of the Rebedoan Imperial Forces. His brain was implanted into a Regular Frame, making him a Reincarnated. Has the ability to manipulate metal.

Previously

After his home, Irf Nikk, is destroyed, King Kajiwan steals Titania's arm, which has the ability to wield the ancient weapons. Etherow and the others go after Kajiwan, but are intercepted by Jate, who can control automatons at will. Meanwhile, Emperor Nichiko Suou uses his powers to foresee the death of Etherow and his comrades...

APOSIMZ

CHAPTER 18

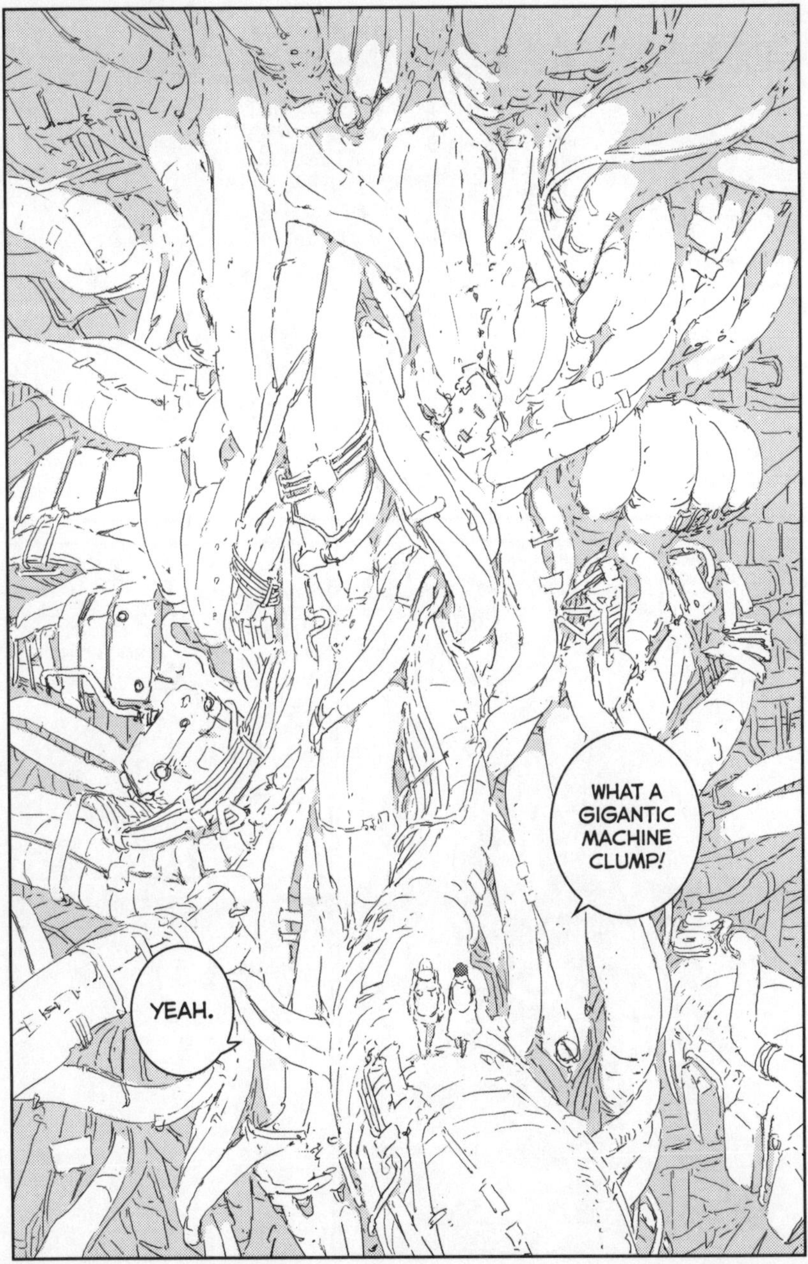
WHAT A GIGANTIC MACHINE CLUMP!
YEAH.

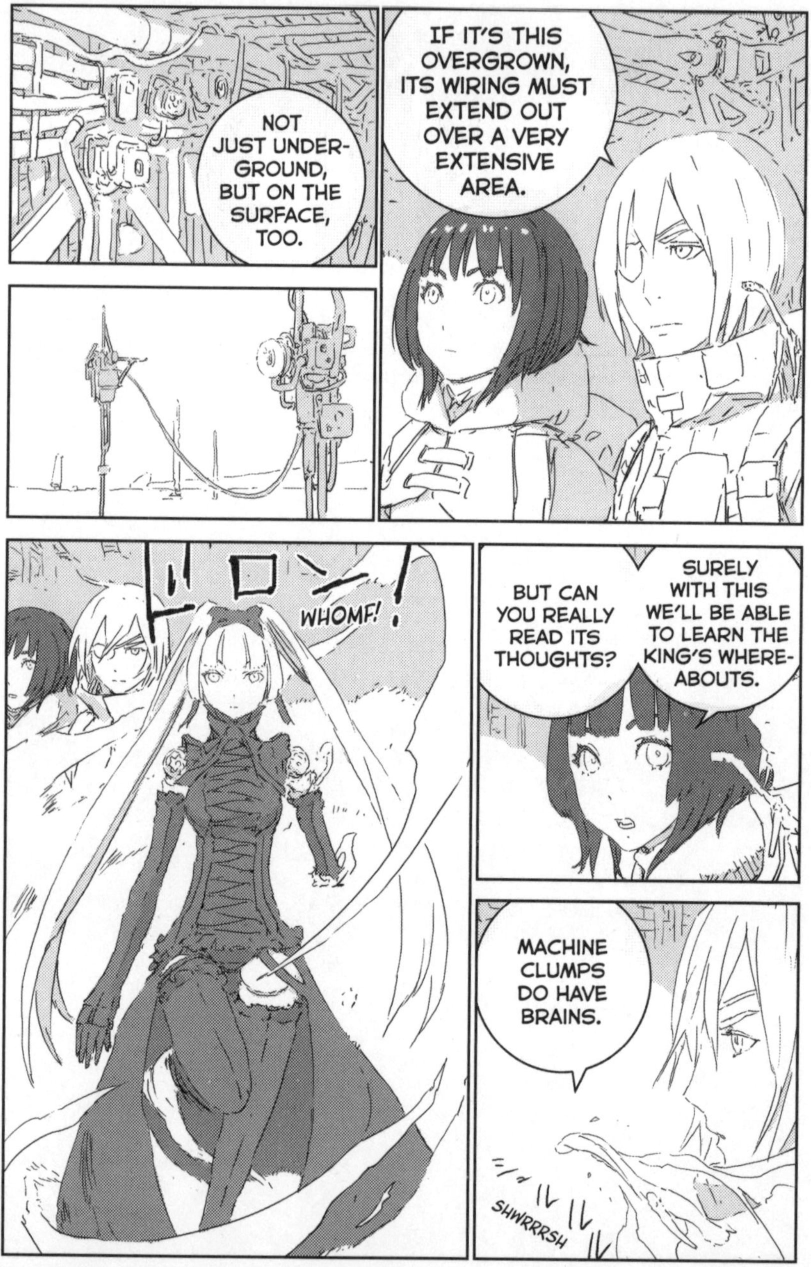
IF IT'S THIS OVERGROWN, ITS WIRING MUST EXTEND OUT OVER A VERY EXTENSIVE AREA.
NOT JUST UNDER-GROUND, BUT ON THE SURFACE, TOO.
SURELY WITH THIS WE'LL BE ABLE TO LEARN THE KING'S WHERE-ABOUTS.
BUT CAN YOU REALLY READ ITS THOUGHTS?
MACHINE CLUMPS DO HAVE BRAINS.
SHWRRRSH
WHOMF!

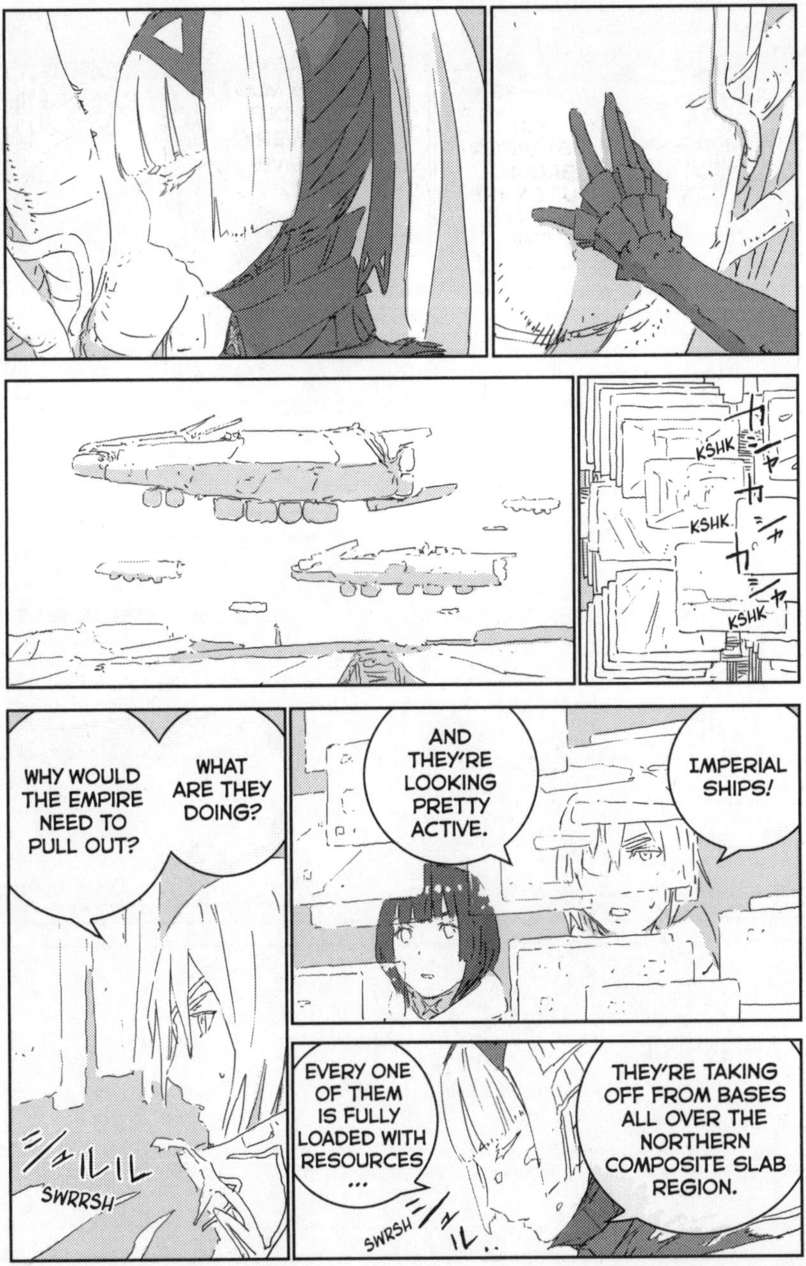

カシャ
KSHK
カシャ
KSHK
カシャ
KSHK
IMPERIAL SHIPS!
AND THEY'RE LOOKING PRETTY ACTIVE.
THEY'RE TAKING OFF FROM BASES ALL OVER THE NORTHERN COMPOSITE SLAB REGION.
EVERY ONE OF THEM IS FULLY LOADED WITH RESOURCES ...
シュル..
SWRSH
WHAT ARE THEY DOING?
WHY WOULD THE EMPIRE NEED TO PULL OUT?
シュルル
SWRRSH

THERE! MY BROTHER !!
WALKING WITHOUT ANY HELP ?!
BUT THE PROGRESS OF THE FRAME DISEASE SHOULD'VE RENDERED HIM ALMOST COMPLETELY IMMOBILE...
HIS ARM!
YES.
HE'S MERGED MY ARM ONTO HIMSELF.
THE THING I WAS MOST AFRAID OF.

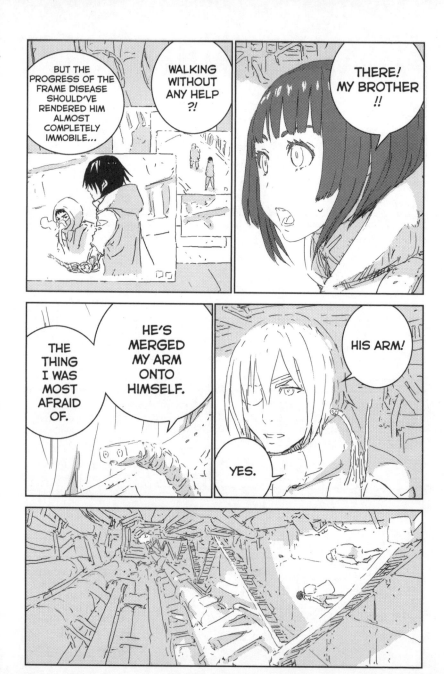

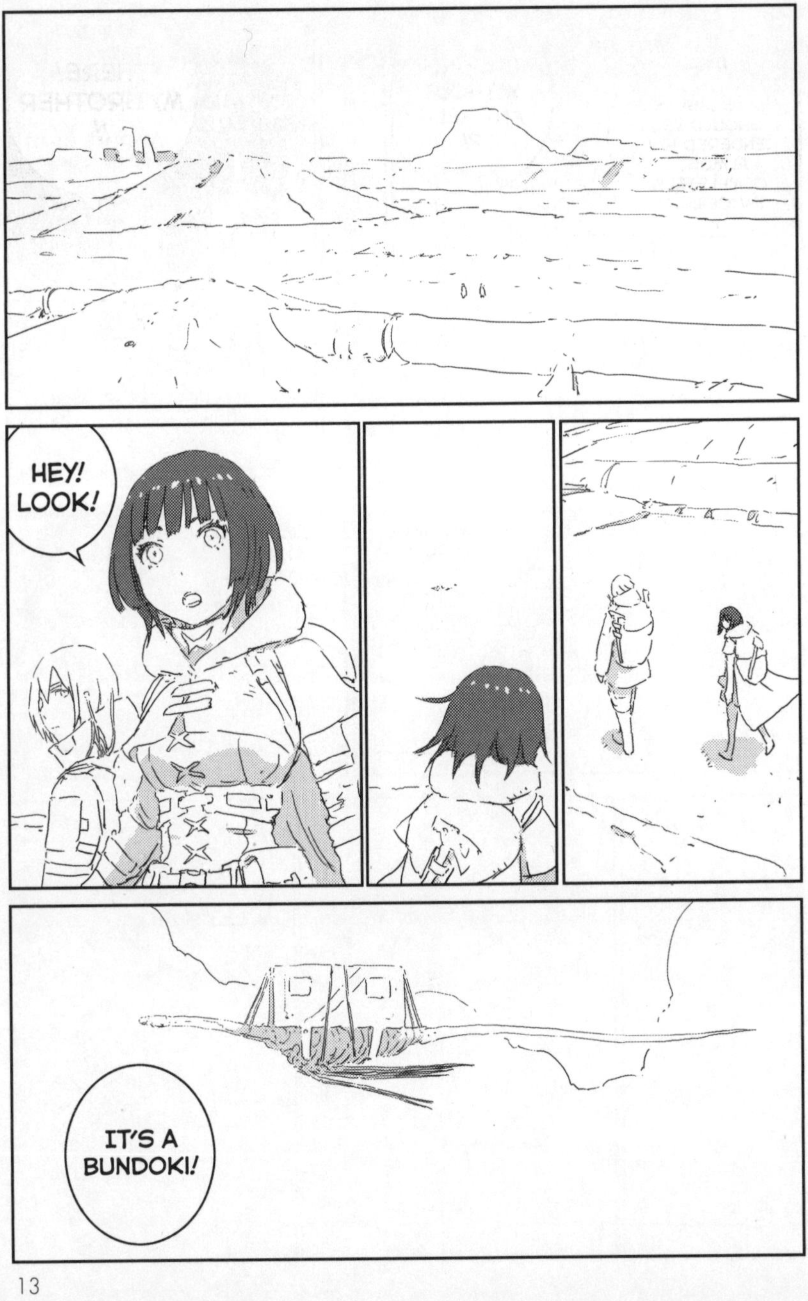
HEY! LOOK!
IT'S A BUNDOKI!

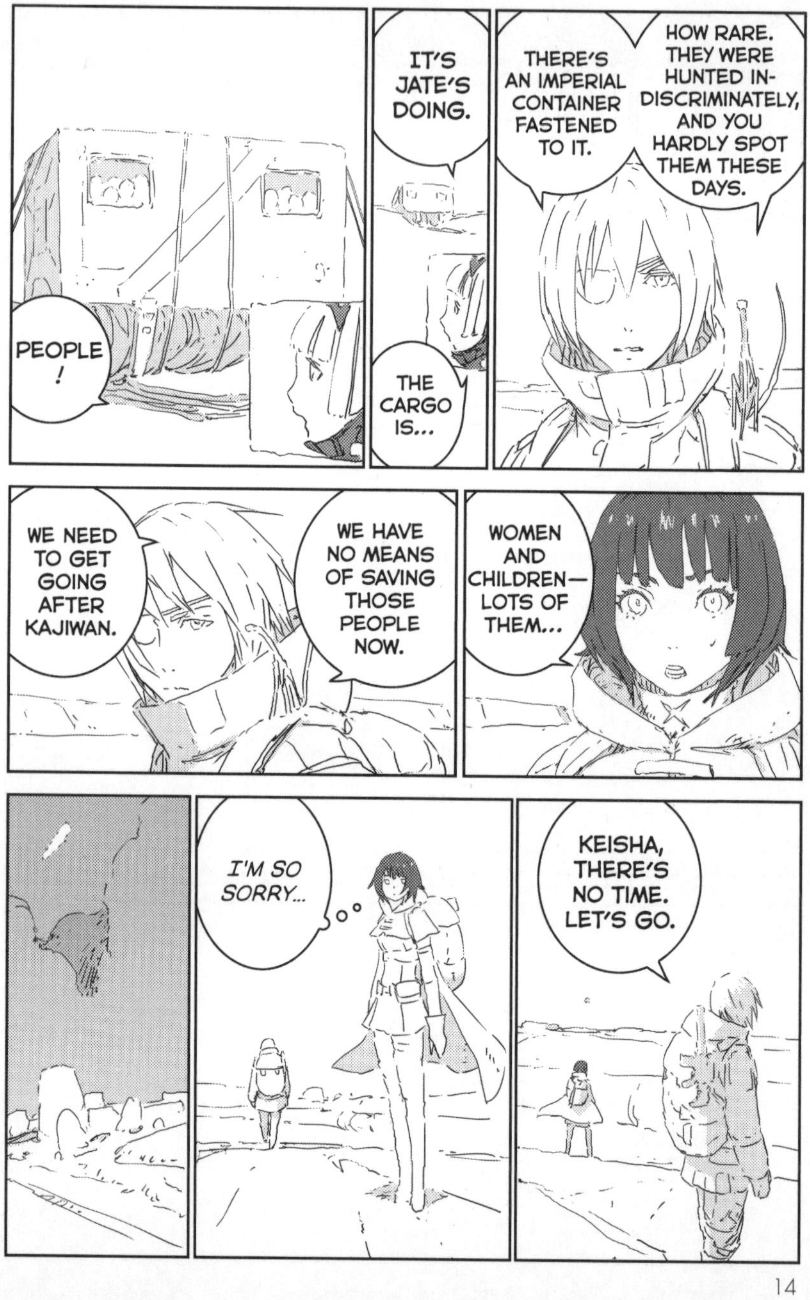
HOW RARE. THEY WERE HUNTED IN-DISCRIMINATELY, AND YOU HARDLY SPOT THEM THESE DAYS.
THERE'S AN IMPERIAL CONTAINER FASTENED TO IT.
IT'S JATE'S DOING.
THE CARGO IS...
PEOPLE!
WOMEN AND CHILDREN—LOTS OF THEM...
WE HAVE NO MEANS OF SAVING THOSE PEOPLE NOW.
WE NEED TO GET GOING AFTER KAJIWAN.
KEISHA, THERE'S NO TIME. LET'S GO.
I'M SO SORRY...

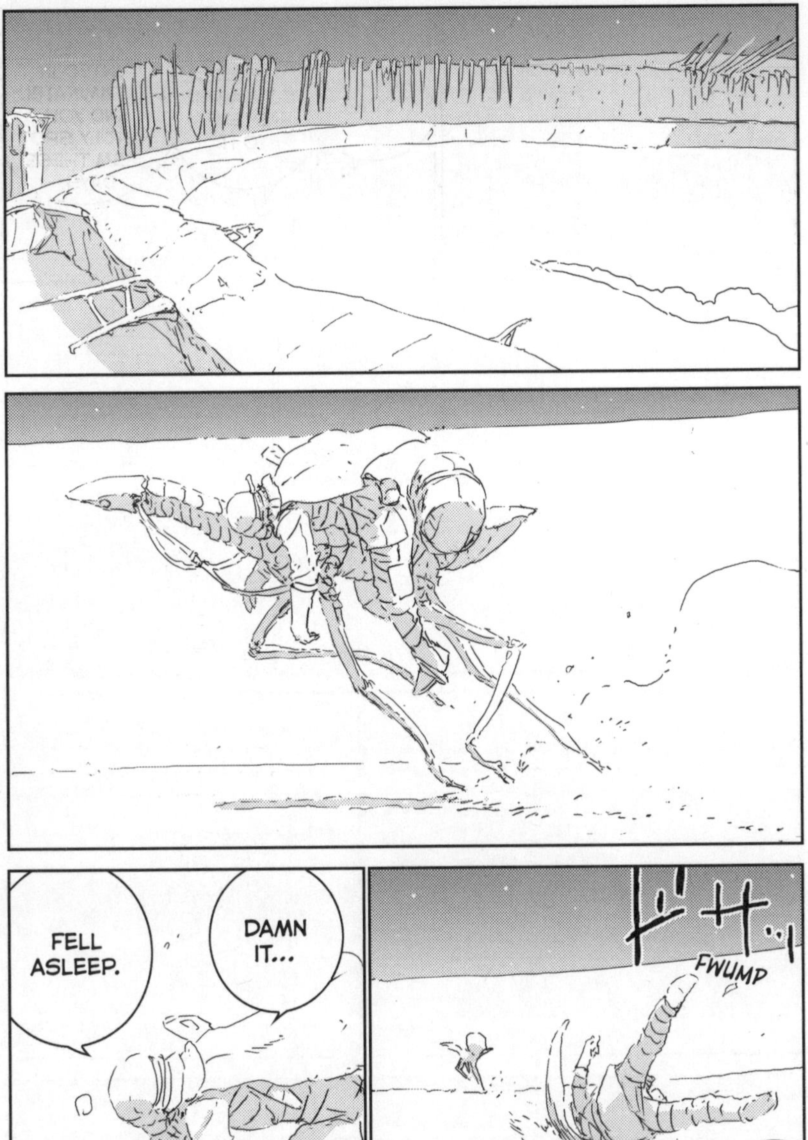
FWUMP
DAMN IT...
FELL ASLEEP.

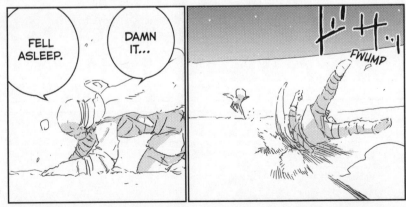

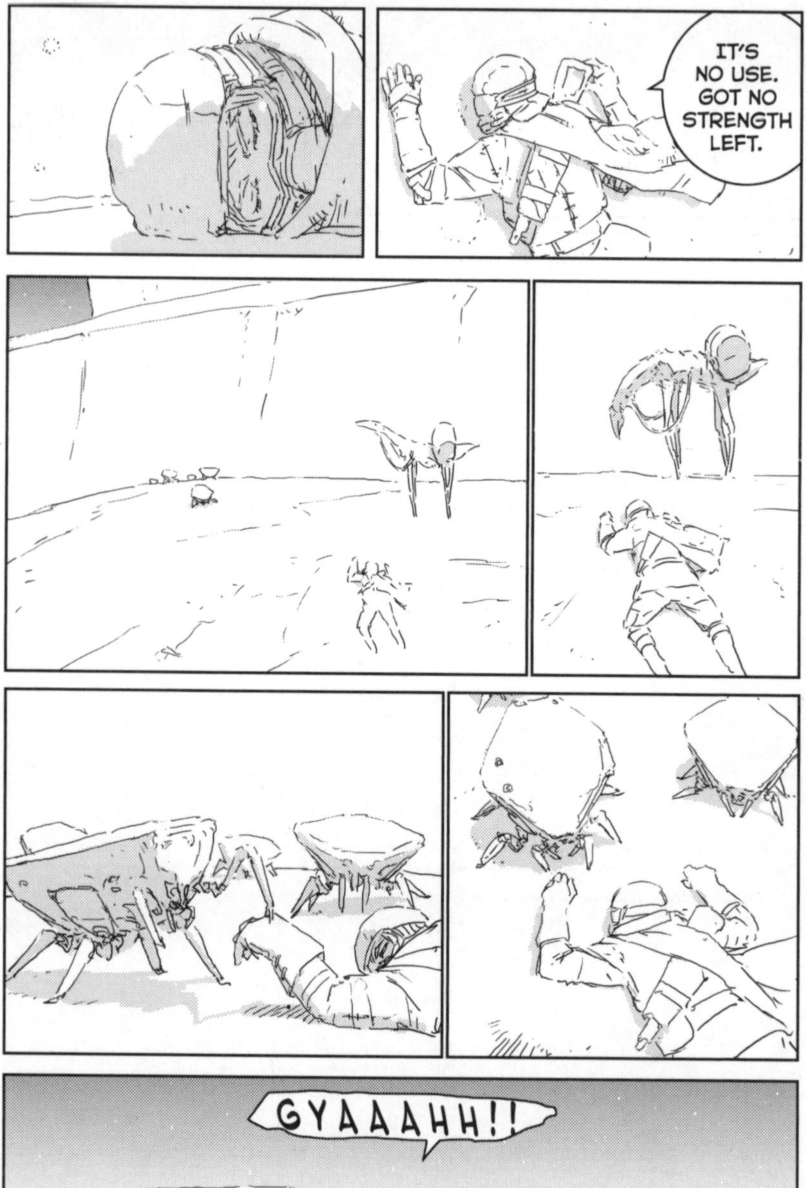
IT'S NO USE. GOT NO STRENGTH LEFT.
GYAAAHH!!

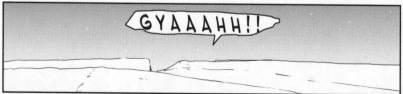

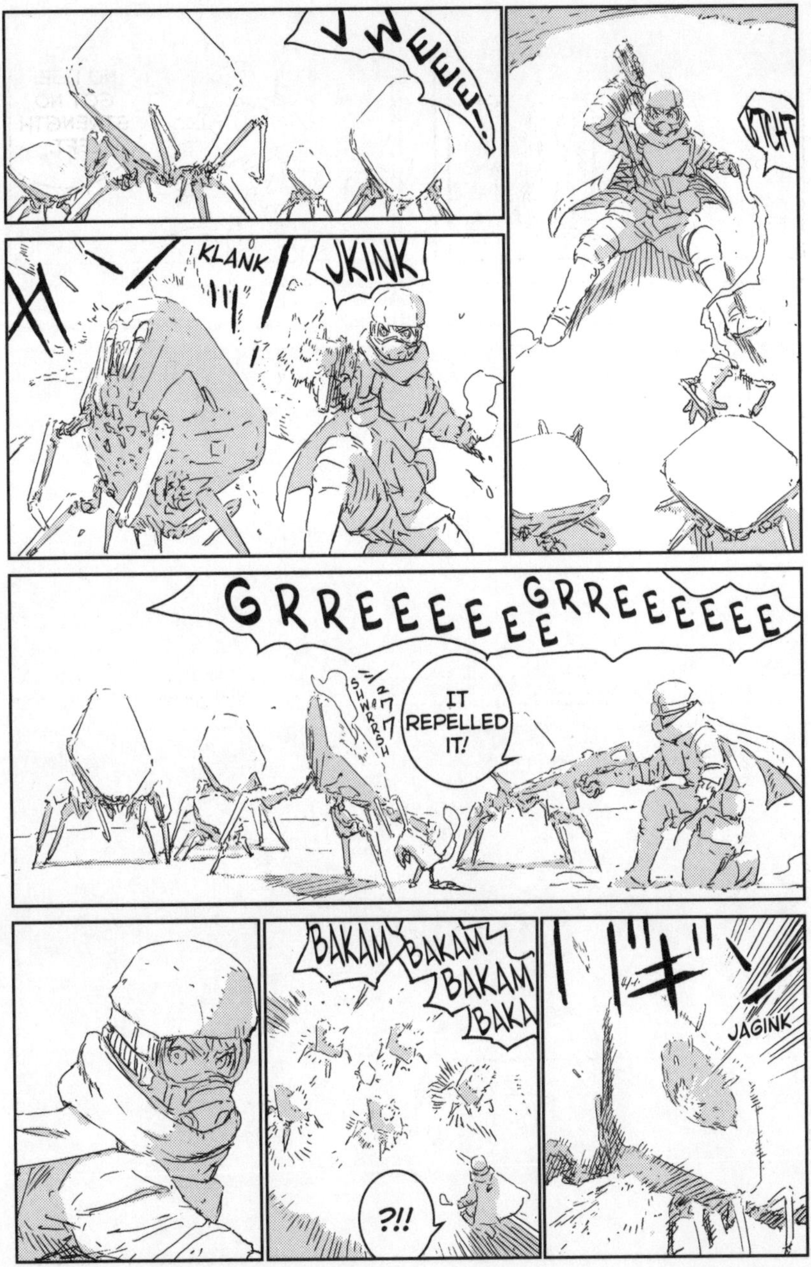
KTCHT
VWEEE!!
JKINK
KLANK
GRREEEEEEGRREEEEEEE
SHWRRSH
IT REPELLED IT!
JAGINK
BAKAM BAKAM BAKAM BAKA
?!!

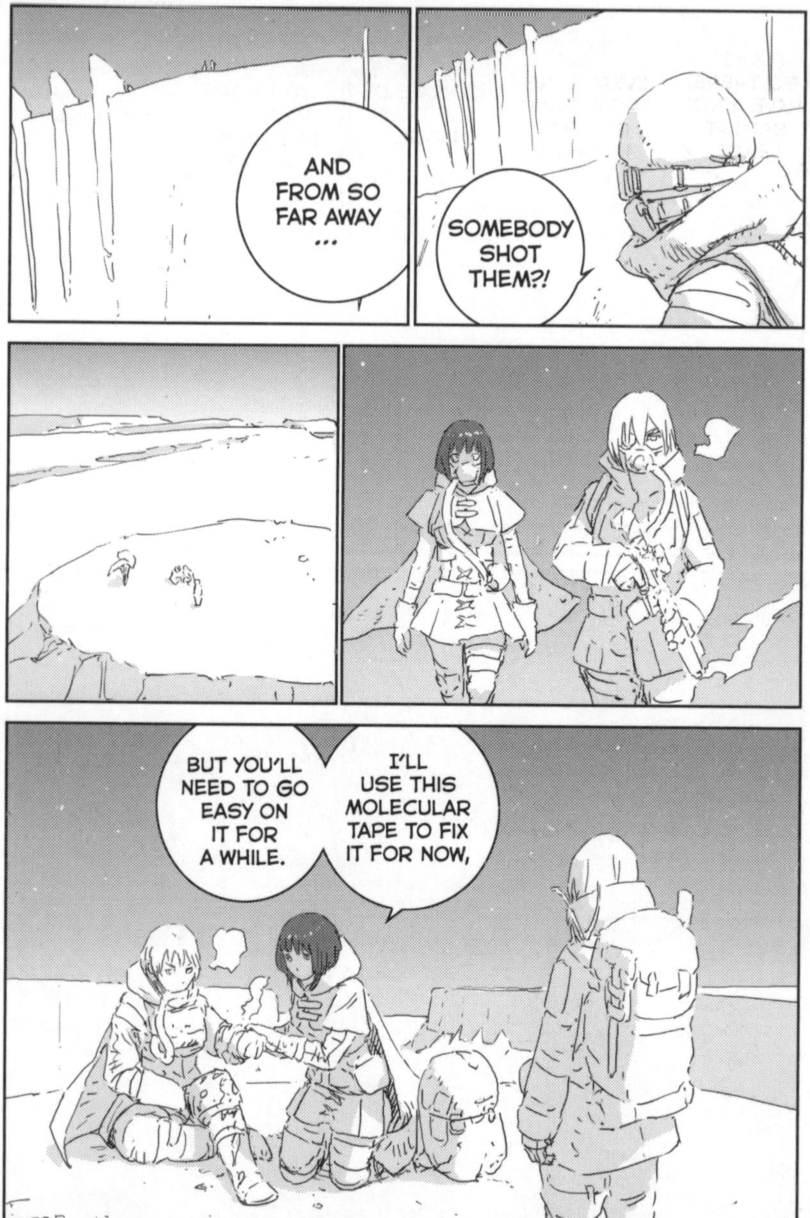
SOMEBODY SHOT THEM?!
AND FROM SO FAR AWAY ...
I'LL USE THIS MOLECULAR TAPE TO FIX IT FOR NOW,
BUT YOU'LL NEED TO GO EASY ON IT FOR A WHILE.

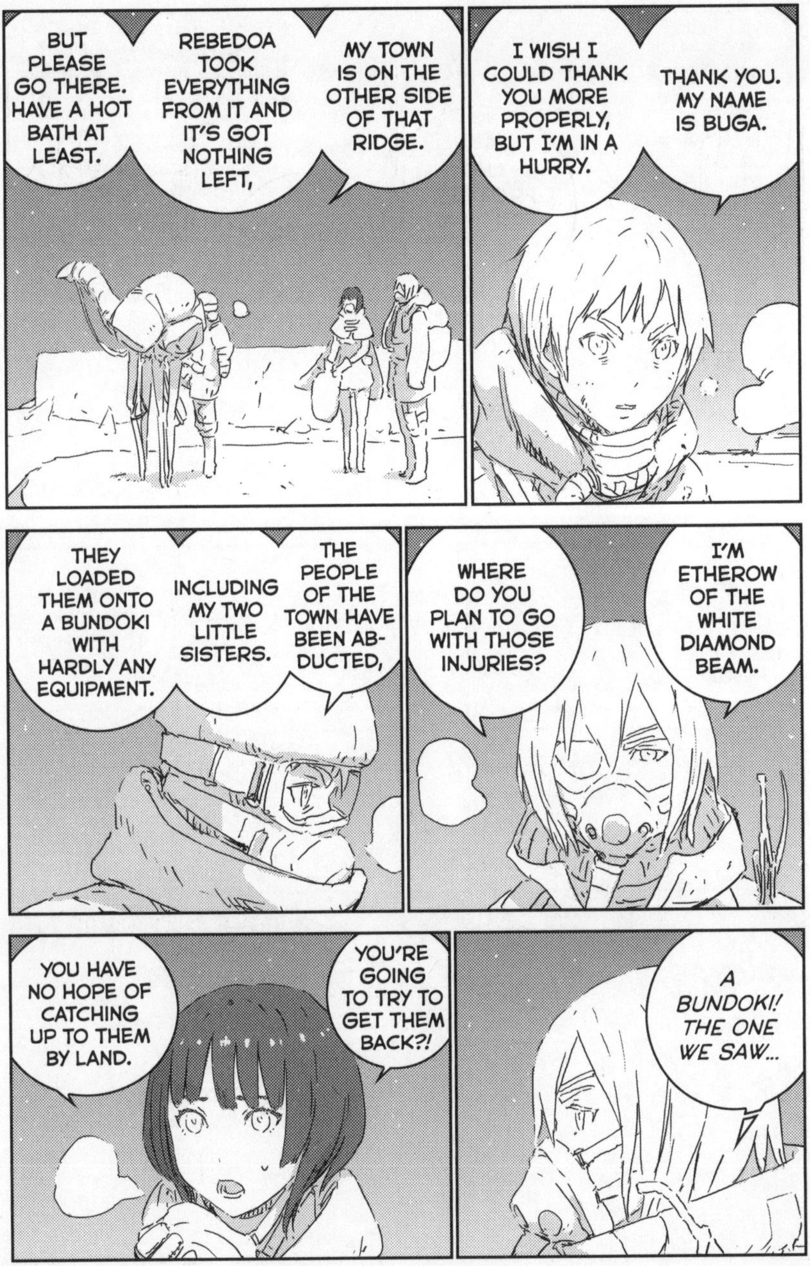
THANK YOU. MY NAME IS BUGA.
I WISH I COULD THANK YOU MORE PROPERLY, BUT I'M IN A HURRY.
MY TOWN IS ON THE OTHER SIDE OF THAT RIDGE.
REBEDOA TOOK EVERYTHING FROM IT AND IT'S GOT NOTHING LEFT,
BUT PLEASE GO THERE. HAVE A HOT BATH AT LEAST.
I'M ETHEROW OF THE WHITE DIAMOND BEAM.
WHERE DO YOU PLAN TO GO WITH THOSE INJURIES?
THE PEOPLE OF THE TOWN HAVE BEEN AB-DUCTED,
INCLUDING MY TWO LITTLE SISTERS.
THEY LOADED THEM ONTO A BUNDOKI WITH HARDLY ANY EQUIPMENT.
A BUNDOKI! THE ONE WE SAW...
YOU'RE GOING TO TRY TO GET THEM BACK?!
YOU HAVE NO HOPE OF CATCHING UP TO THEM BY LAND.

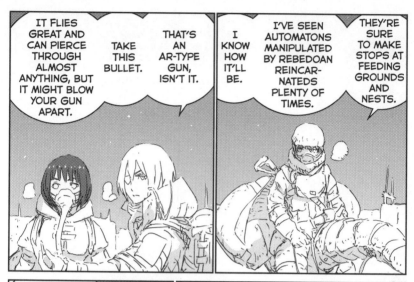

THEY'RE SURE TO MAKE STOPS AT FEEDING GROUNDS AND NESTS.
I'VE SEEN AUTOMATONS MANIPULATED BY REBEDOAN REINCAR-NATEDS PLENTY OF TIMES.
I KNOW HOW IT'LL BE.
THAT'S AN AR-TYPE GUN, ISN'T IT.
TAKE THIS BULLET.
IT FLIES GREAT AND CAN PIERCE THROUGH ALMOST ANYTHING, BUT IT MIGHT BLOW YOUR GUN APART.
YOU CAN TAKE IT DOWN IN ONE SHOT.
WHOA ...
WE'RE SORRY WE CAN'T HELP YOU, BUT WE'RE IN A HURRY TOO.
WELL, SEE YA!
YOU GUYS TAKE CARE, TOO!

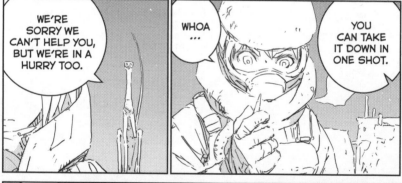

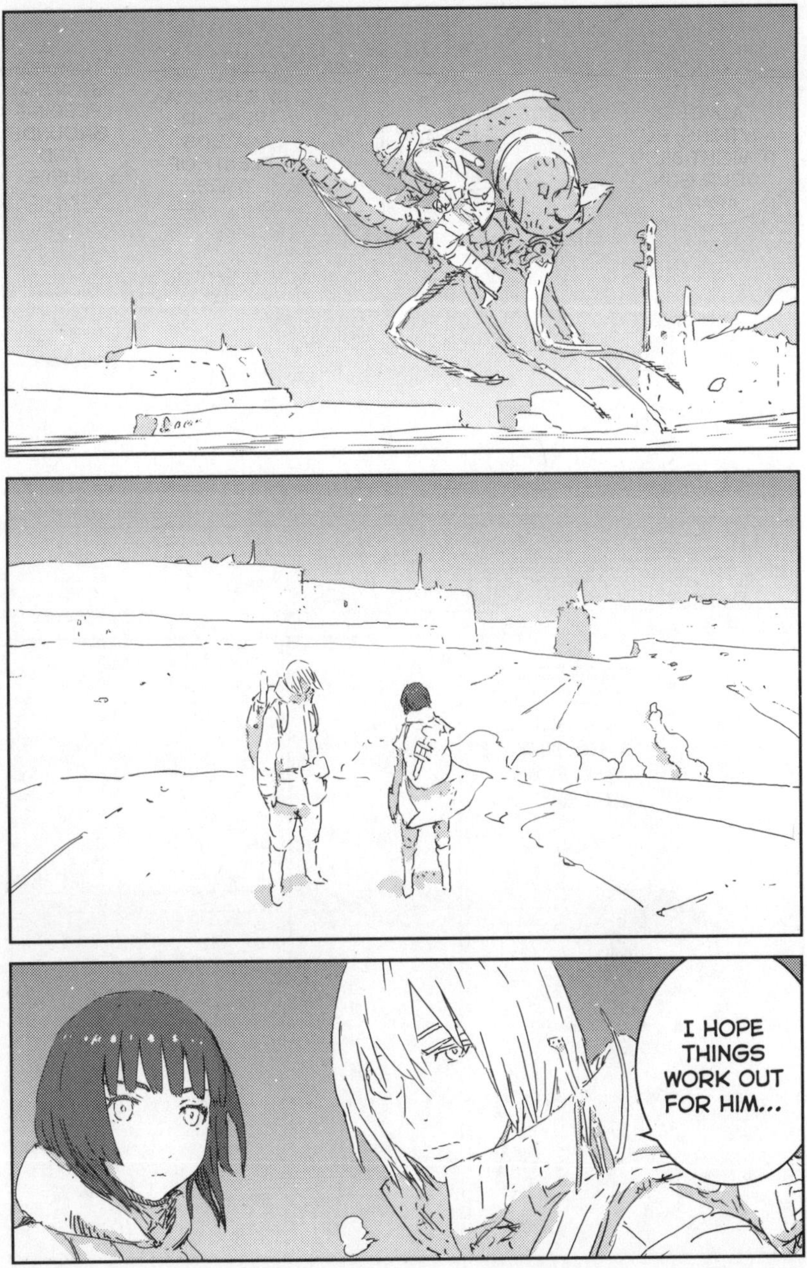
I HOPE THINGS WORK OUT FOR HIM...

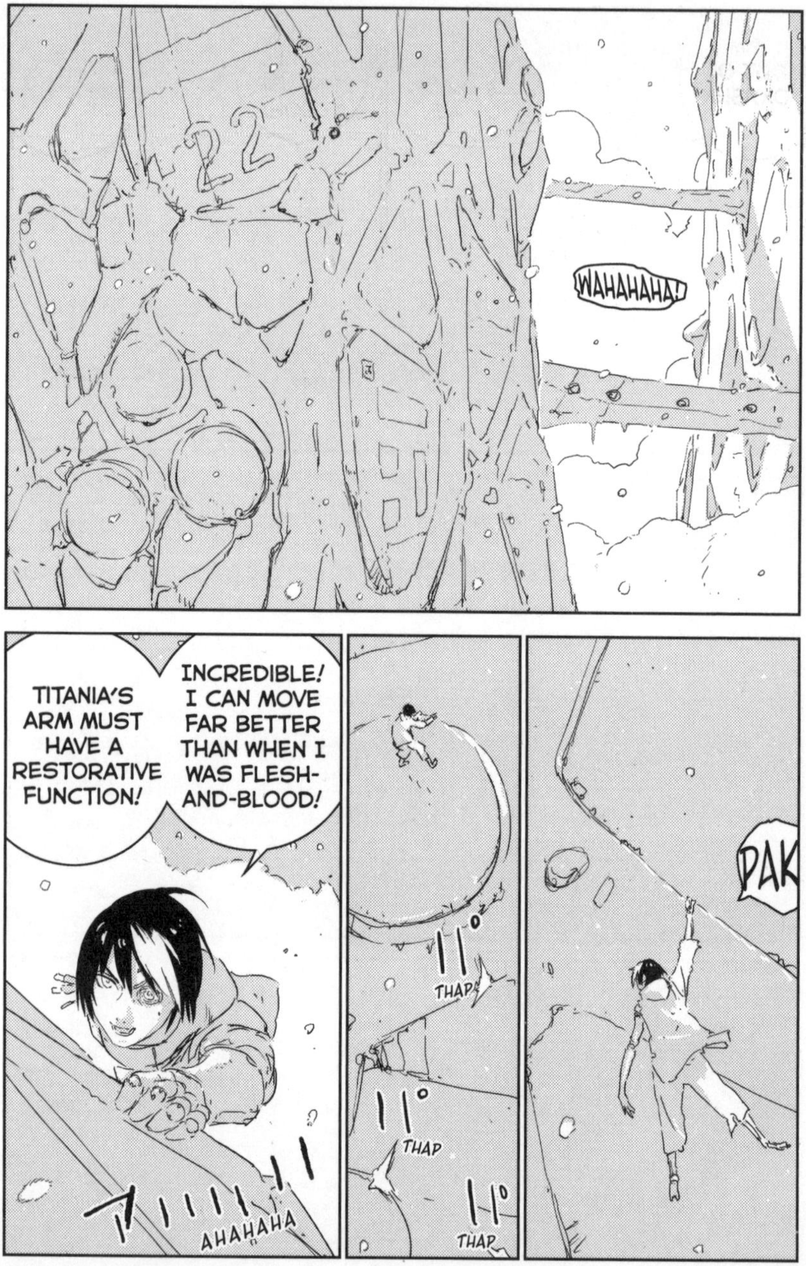
WAHAHAHA!
PAK
THAP
THAP
THAP
INCREDIBLE! I CAN MOVE FAR BETTER THAN WHEN I WAS FLESH-AND-BLOOD!
TITANIA'S ARM MUST HAVE A RESTORATIVE FUNCTION!
AHAHAHA

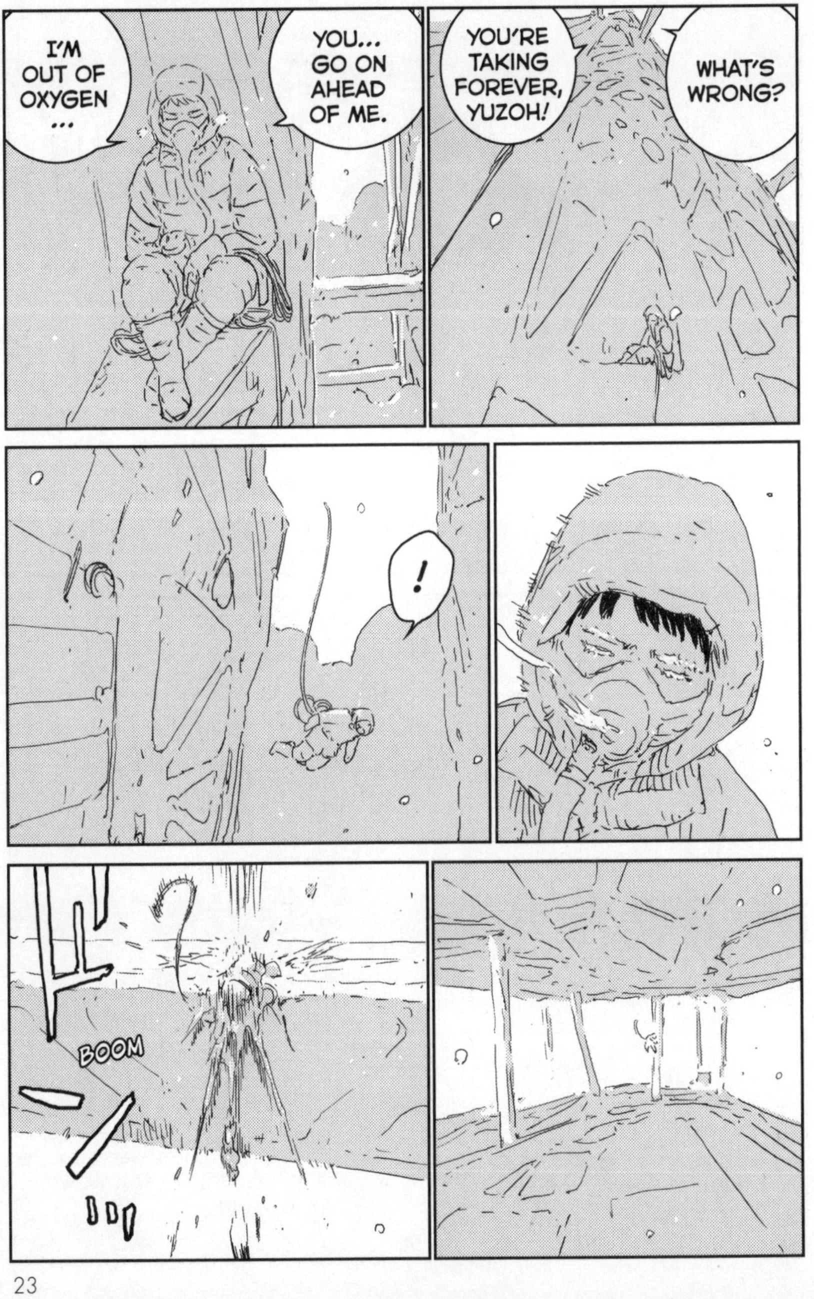
WHAT'S WRONG?
YOU'RE TAKING FOREVER, YUZOH!
YOU... GO ON AHEAD OF ME.
I'M OUT OF OXYGEN ...
!
BOOM

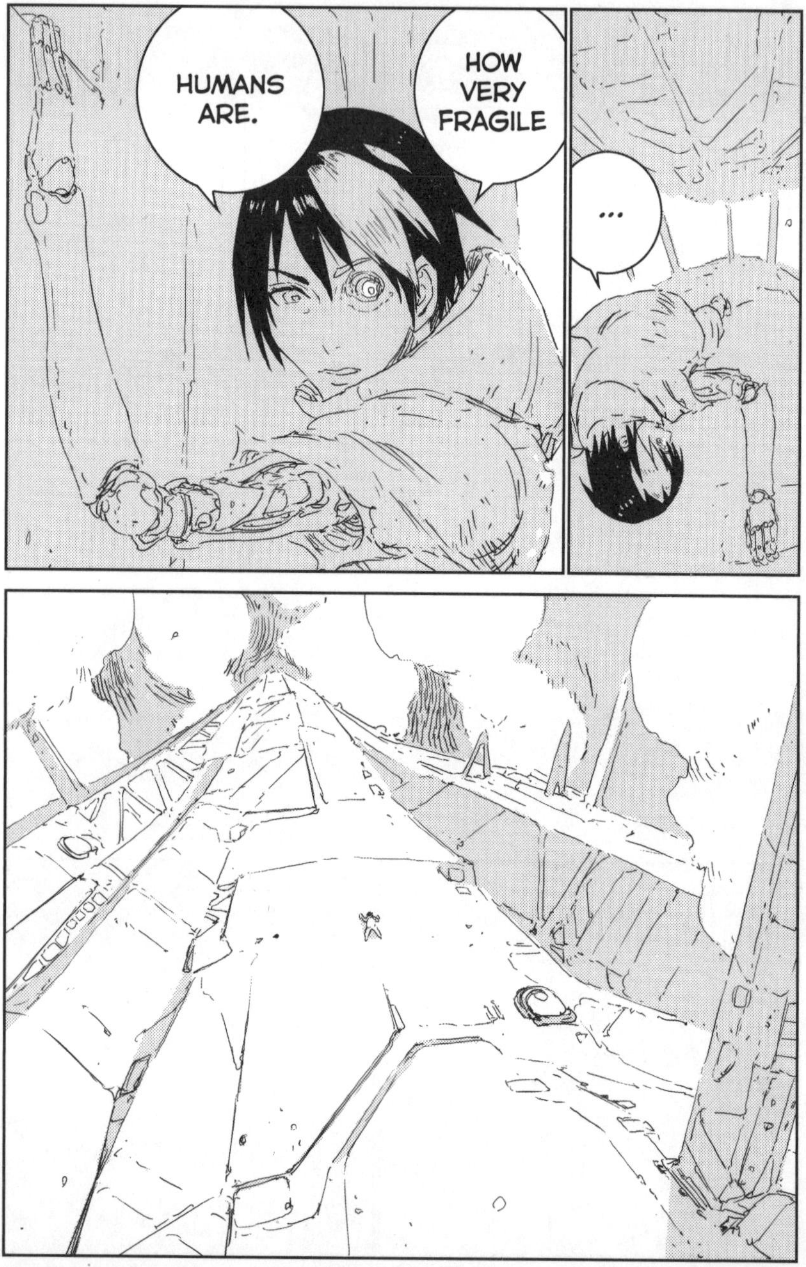
...
HOW VERY FRAGILE
HUMANS ARE.

MUNCH
MUNCH
VWEEN

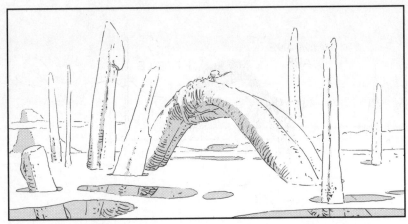

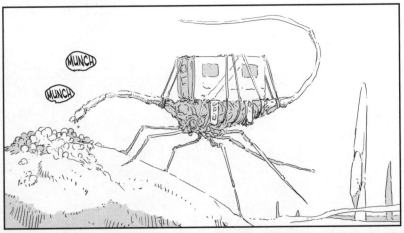

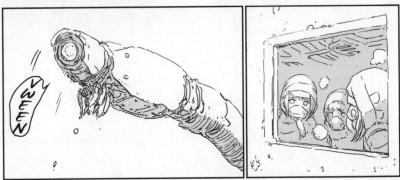

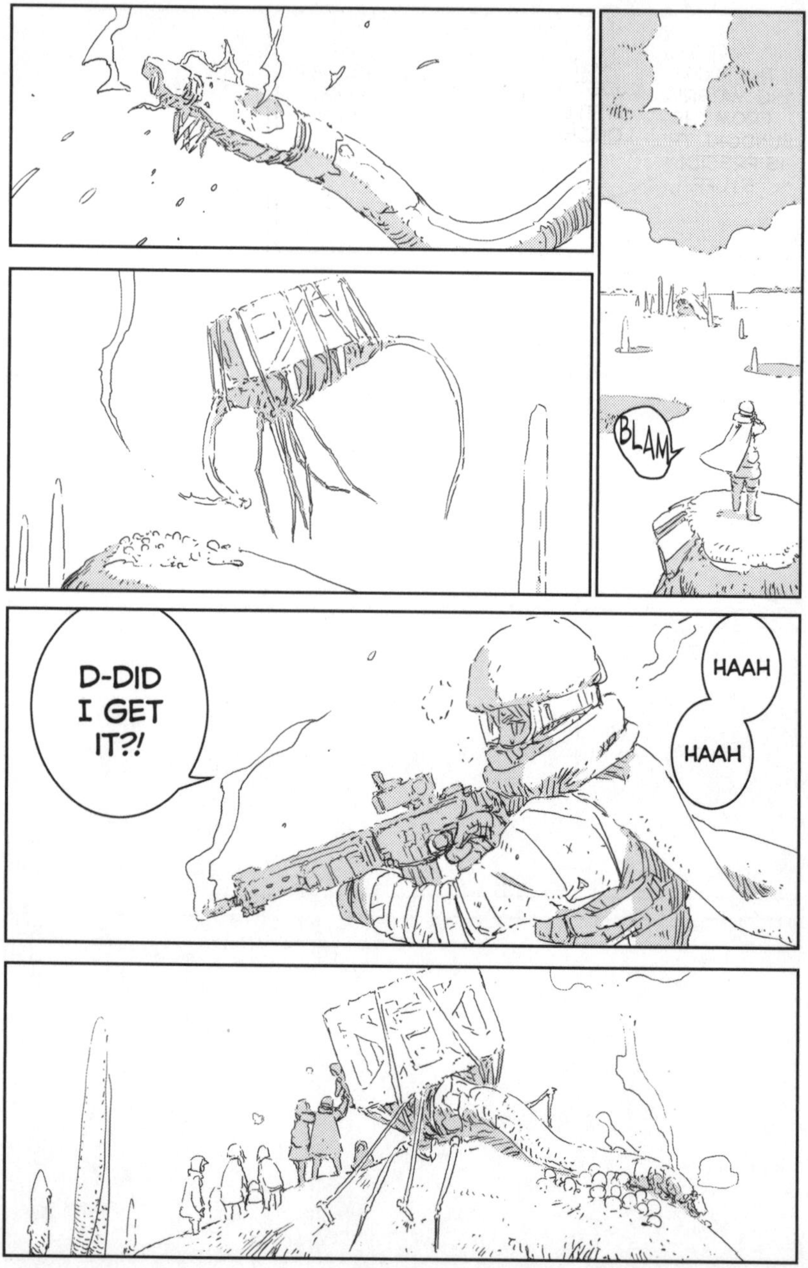
BLAM
HAAH
HAAH
D-DID I GET IT?!

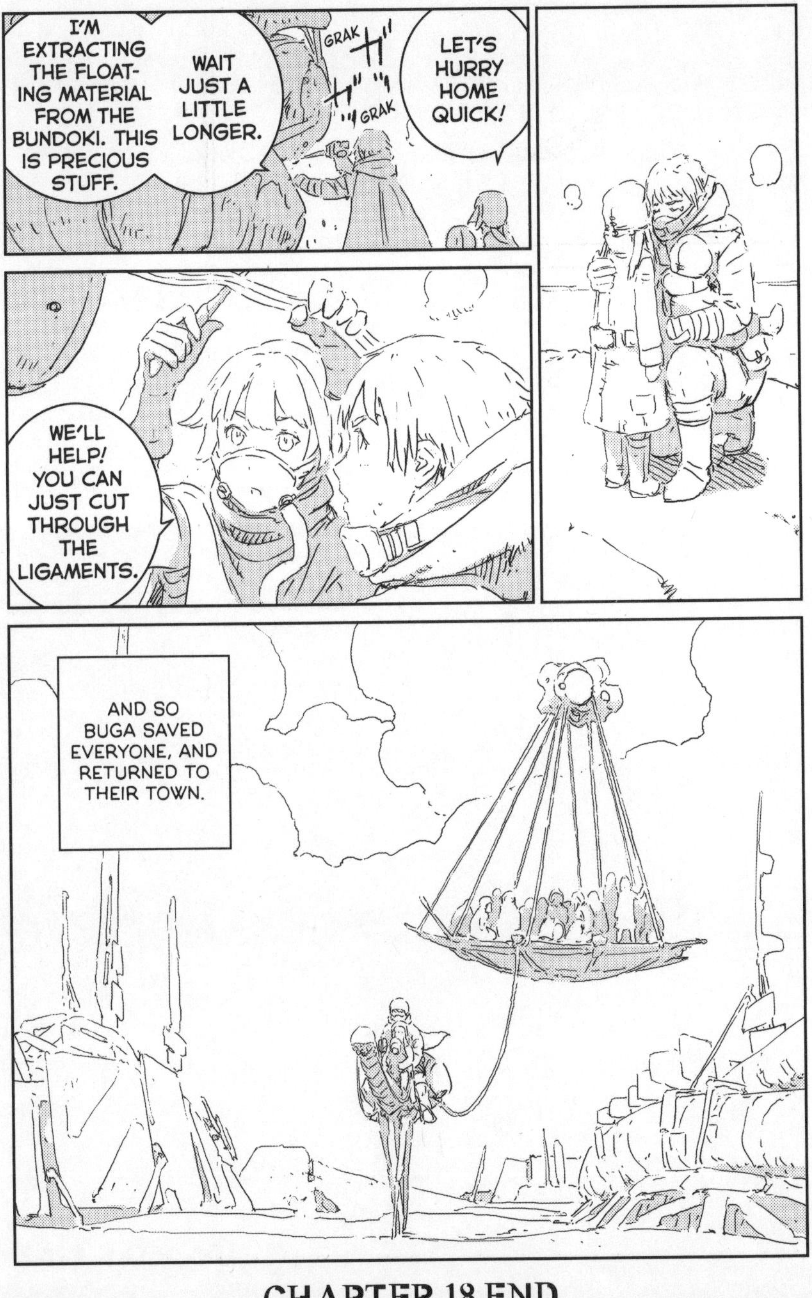
LET'S HURRY HOME QUICK!
GRAK
GRAK
WAIT JUST A LITTLE LONGER.
I'M EXTRACTING THE FLOATING MATERIAL FROM THE BUNDOKI. THIS IS PRECIOUS STUFF.
WE'LL HELP! YOU CAN JUST CUT THROUGH THE LIGAMENTS.
AND SO BUGA SAVED EVERYONE, AND RETURNED TO THEIR TOWN.

CHAPTER 18 END

APOSIMZ

CHAPTER 19

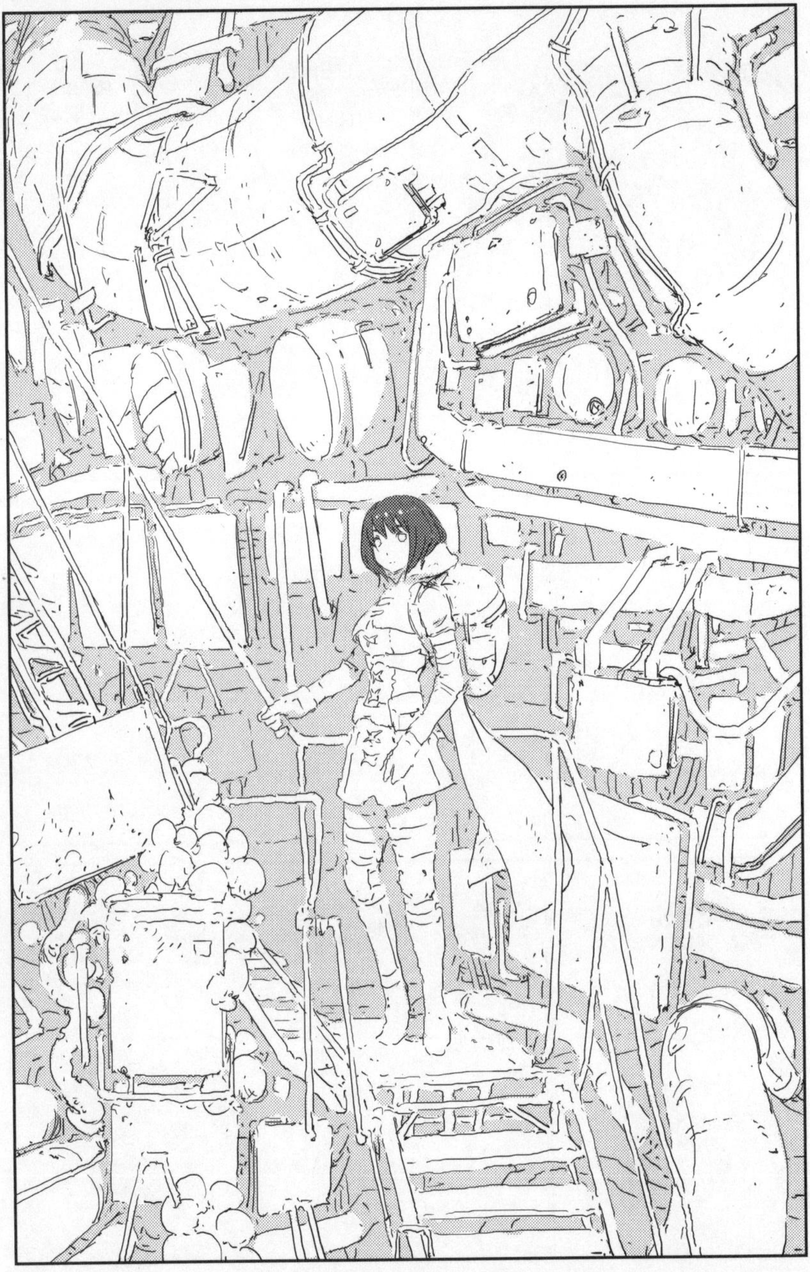

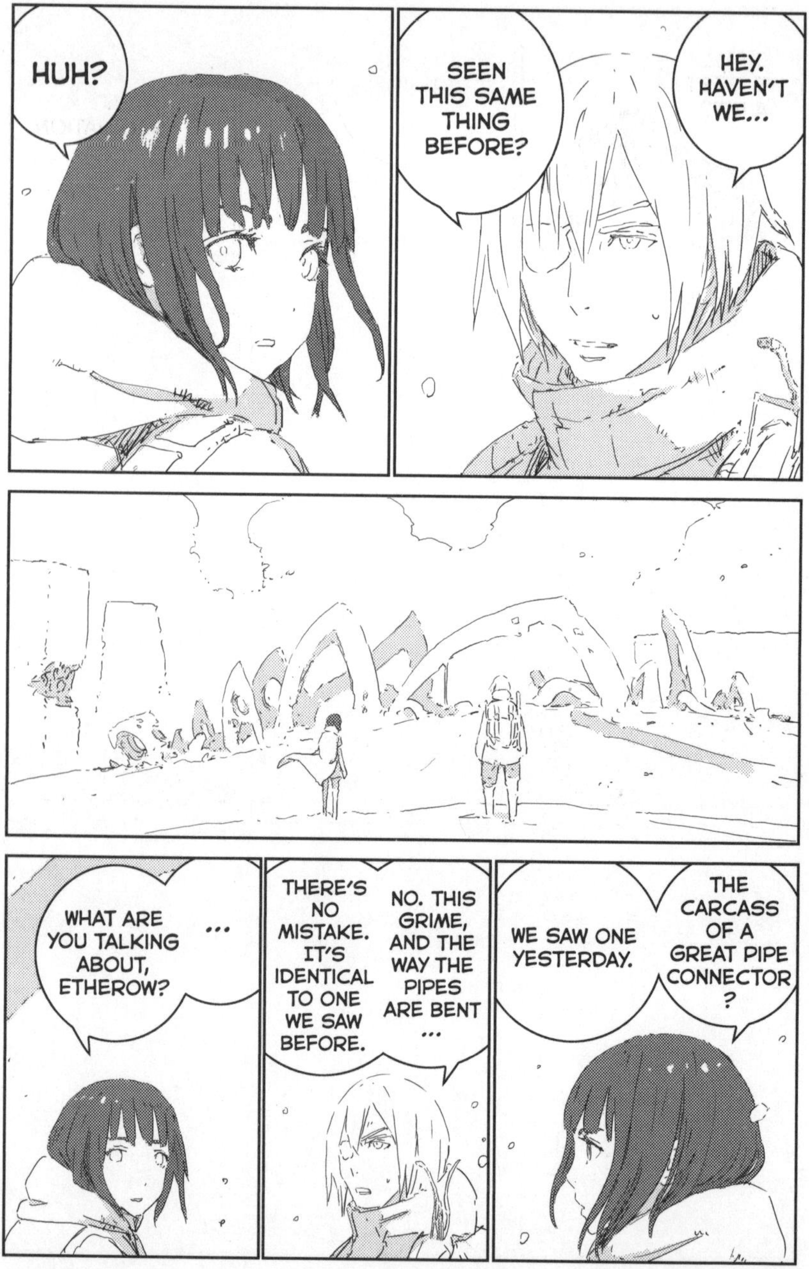
HEY. HAVEN'T WE...
SEEN THIS SAME THING BEFORE?
HUH?
THE CARCASS OF A GREAT PIPE CONNECTOR ?
WE SAW ONE YESTERDAY.
NO. THIS GRIME, AND THE WAY THE PIPES ARE BENT ...
THERE'S NO MISTAKE. IT'S IDENTICAL TO ONE WE SAW BEFORE.
...
WHAT ARE YOU TALKING ABOUT, ETHEROW?

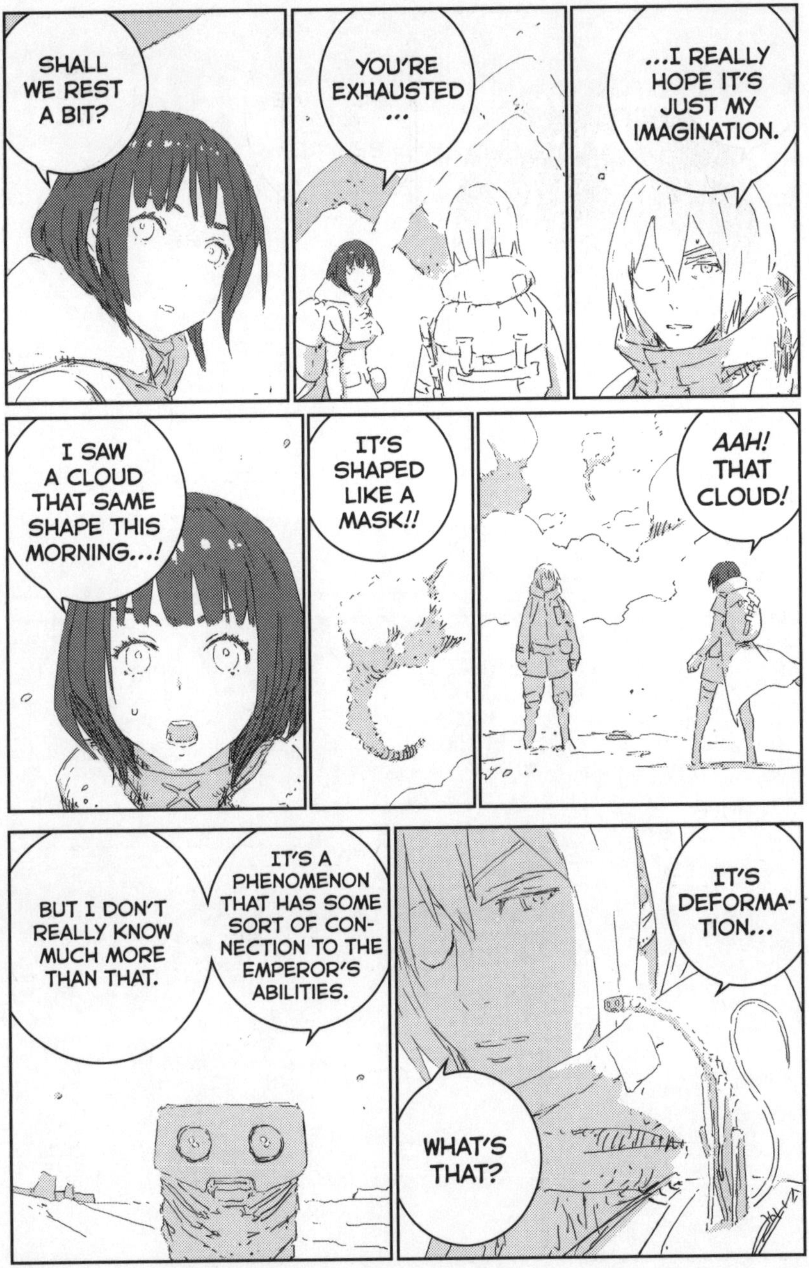
...I REALLY HOPE IT'S JUST MY IMAGINATION.
YOU'RE EXHAUSTED ...
SHALL WE REST A BIT?
AAH! THAT CLOUD!
IT'S SHAPED LIKE A MASK!!
I SAW A CLOUD THAT SAME SHAPE THIS MORNING...!
IT'S DEFORMA-TION...
WHAT'S THAT?
IT'S A PHENOMENON THAT HAS SOME SORT OF CON-NECTION TO THE EMPEROR'S ABILITIES.
BUT I DON'T REALLY KNOW MUCH MORE THAN THAT.

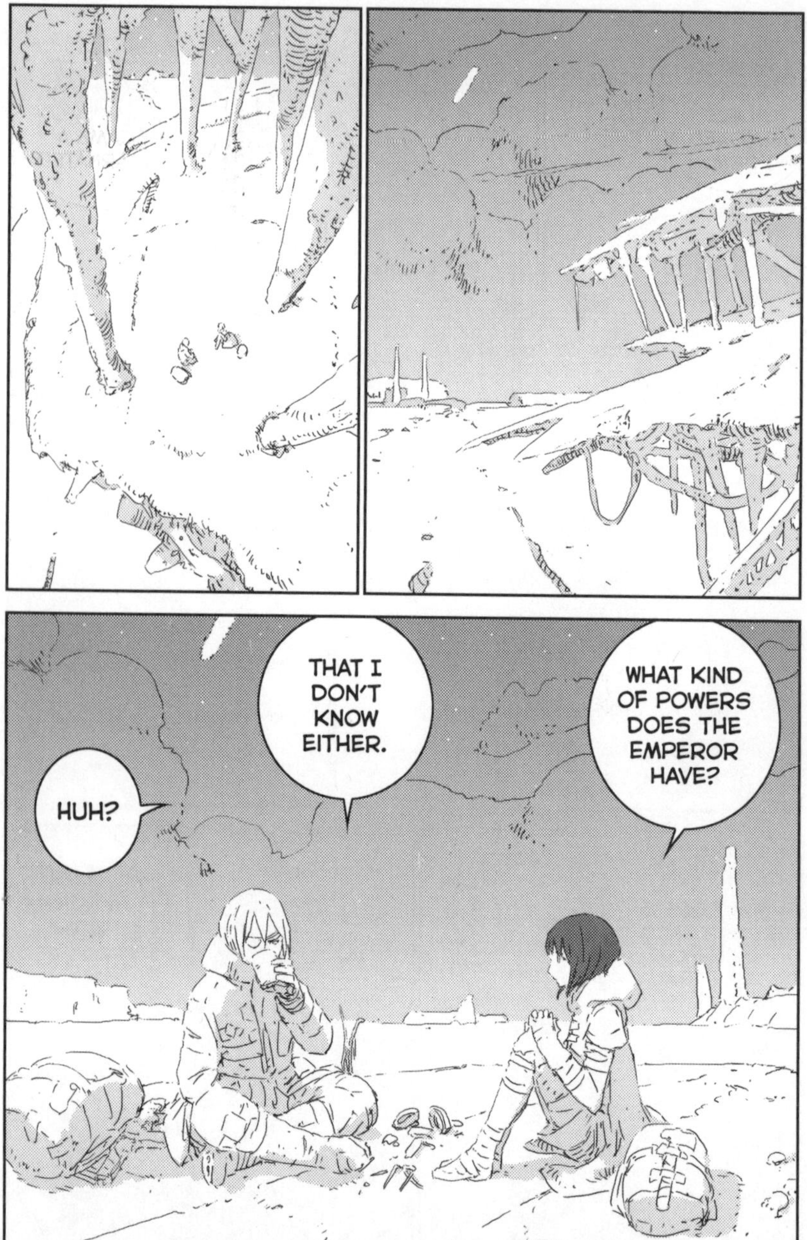
WHAT KIND OF POWERS DOES THE EMPEROR HAVE?
THAT I DON'T KNOW EITHER.
HUH?

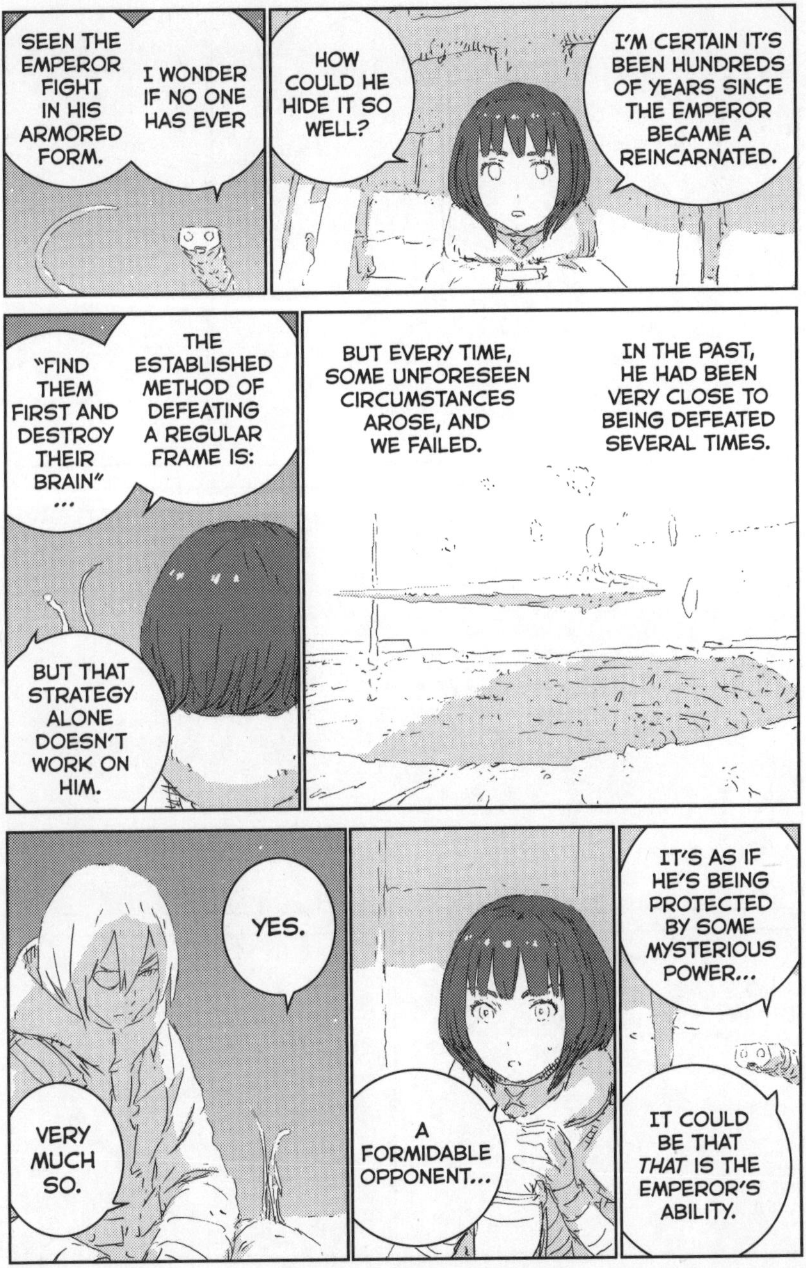
I'M CERTAIN IT'S BEEN HUNDREDS OF YEARS SINCE THE EMPEROR BECAME A REINCARNATED.
HOW COULD HE HIDE IT SO WELL?
I WONDER IF NO ONE HAS EVER
SEEN THE EMPEROR FIGHT IN HIS ARMORED FORM.
IN THE PAST, HE HAD BEEN VERY CLOSE TO BEING DEFEATED SEVERAL TIMES.
BUT EVERY TIME, SOME UNFORESEEN CIRCUMSTANCES AROSE, AND WE FAILED.
THE ESTABLISHED METHOD OF DEFEATING A REGULAR FRAME IS:
"FIND THEM FIRST AND DESTROY THEIR BRAIN"...
BUT THAT STRATEGY ALONE DOESN'T WORK ON HIM.
IT'S AS IF HE'S BEING PROTECTED BY SOME MYSTERIOUS POWER...
IT COULD BE THAT *THAT* IS THE EMPEROR'S ABILITY.
A FORMIDABLE OPPONENT...
YES.
VERY MUCH SO.

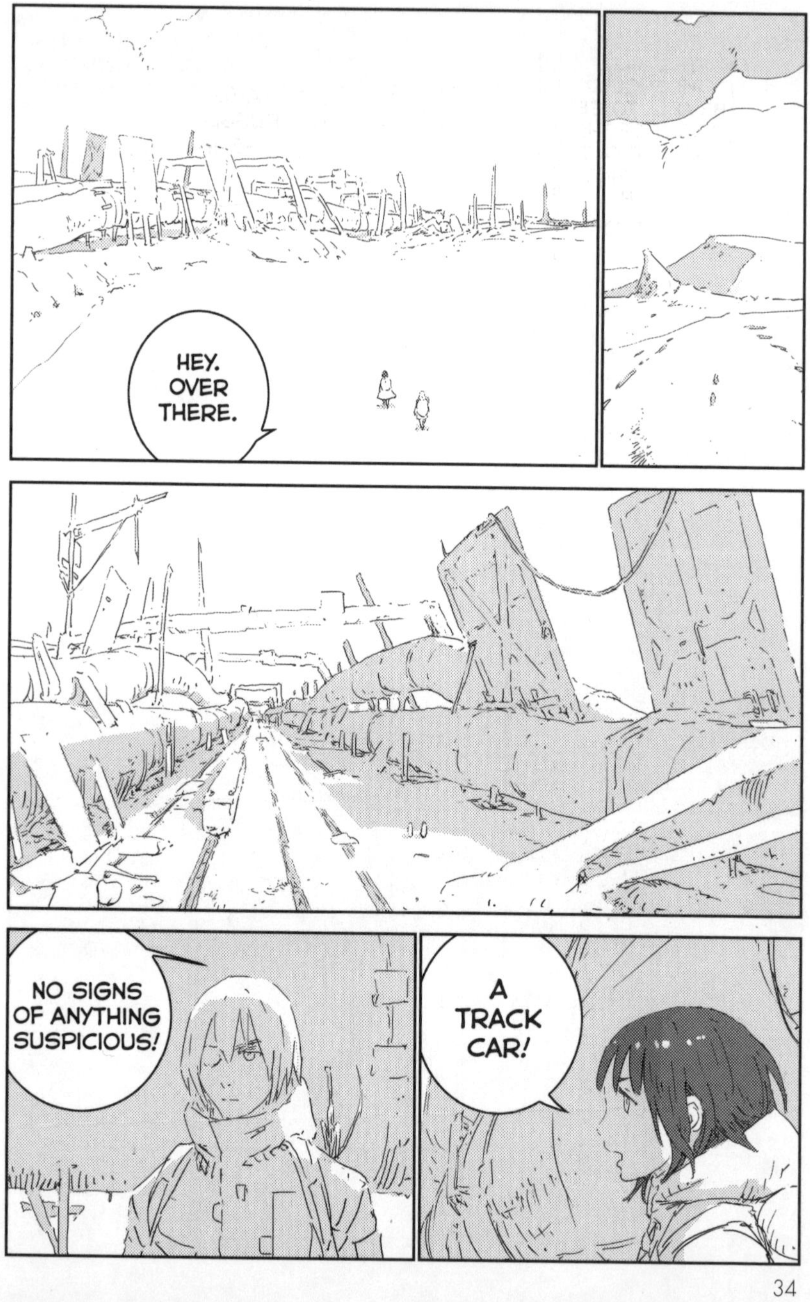
HEY. OVER THERE.
A TRACK CAR!
NO SIGNS OF ANYTHING SUSPICIOUS!

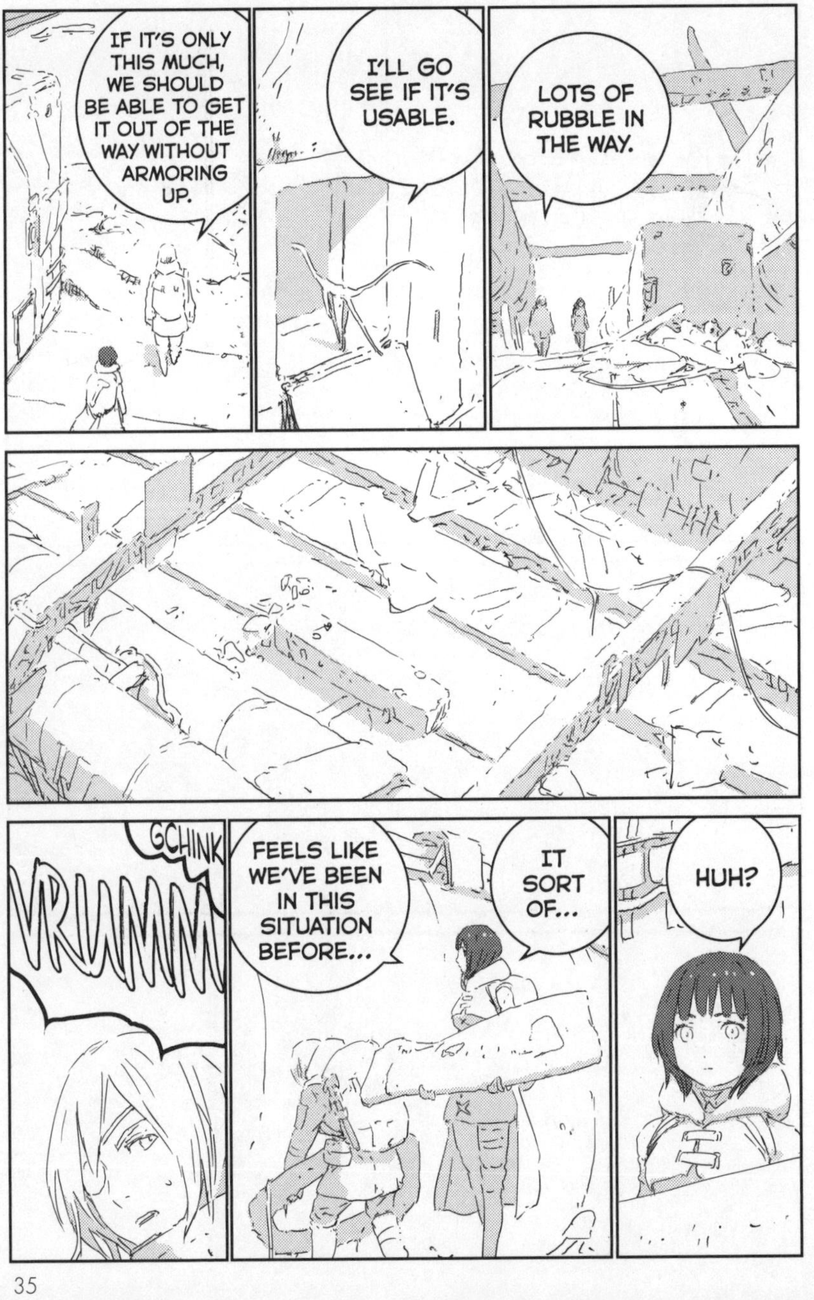
LOTS OF RUBBLE IN THE WAY.
I'LL GO SEE IF IT'S USABLE.
IF IT'S ONLY THIS MUCH, WE SHOULD BE ABLE TO GET IT OUT OF THE WAY WITHOUT ARMORING UP.
HUH?
IT SORT OF...
FEELS LIKE WE'VE BEEN IN THIS SITUATION BEFORE...
GCHINK
VRUMMM

DOOOM
GWOOM
OOO
...

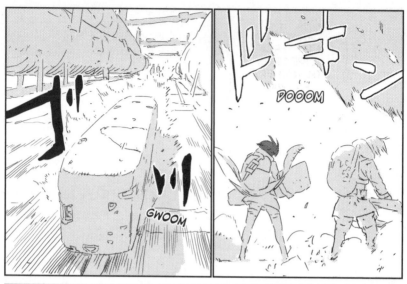

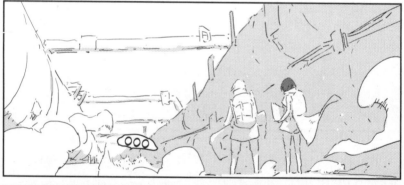

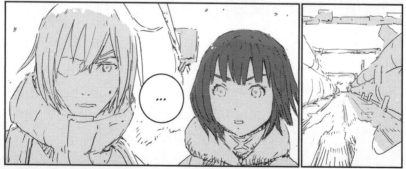

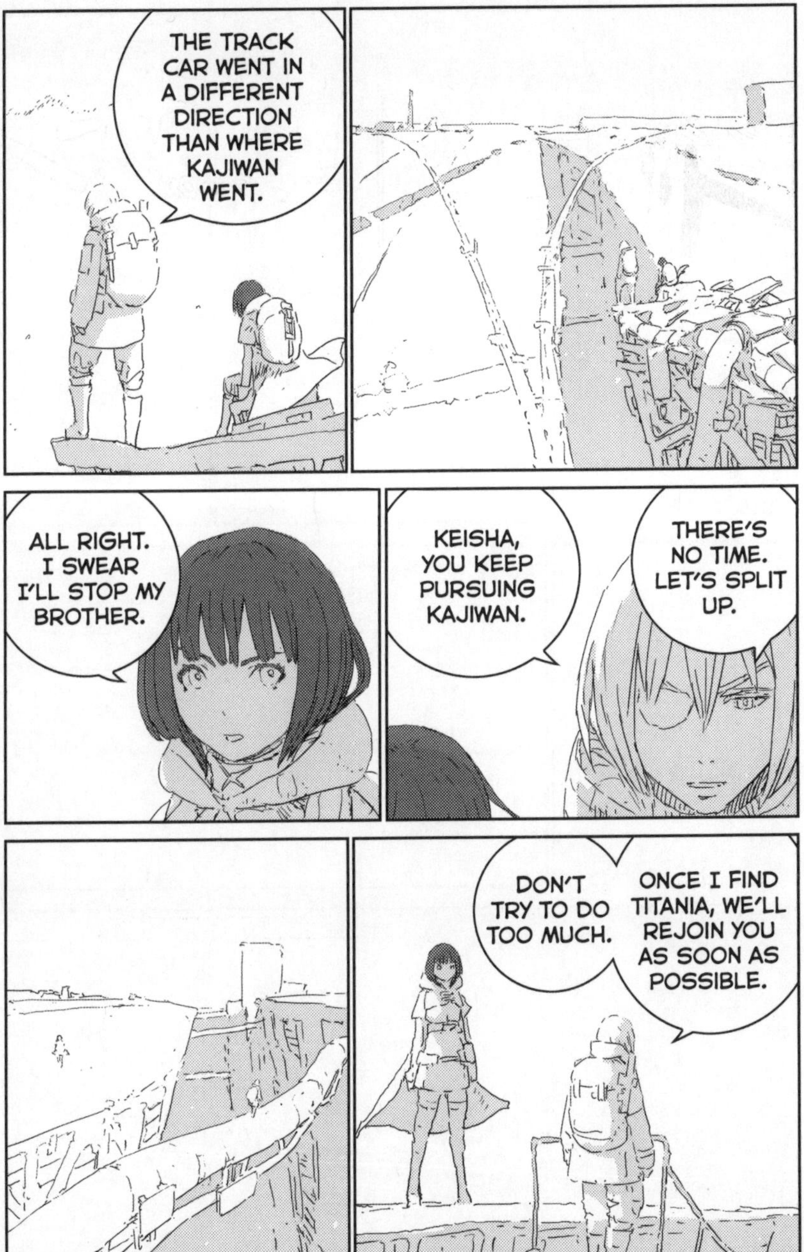
THE TRACK CAR WENT IN A DIFFERENT DIRECTION THAN WHERE KAJIWAN WENT.
THERE'S NO TIME. LET'S SPLIT UP.
KEISHA, YOU KEEP PURSUING KAJIWAN.
ALL RIGHT. I SWEAR I'LL STOP MY BROTHER.
ONCE I FIND TITANIA, WE'LL REJOIN YOU AS SOON AS POSSIBLE.
DON'T TRY TO DO TOO MUCH.

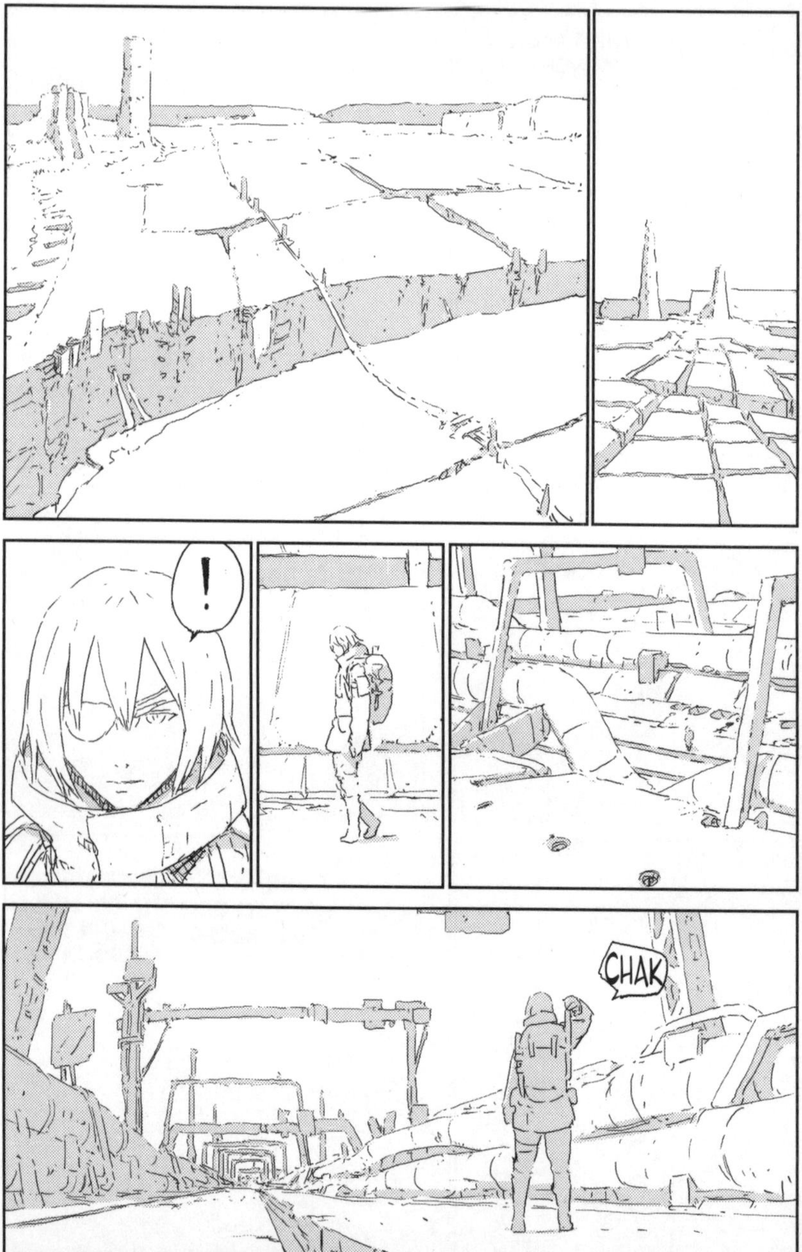
!
CHAK

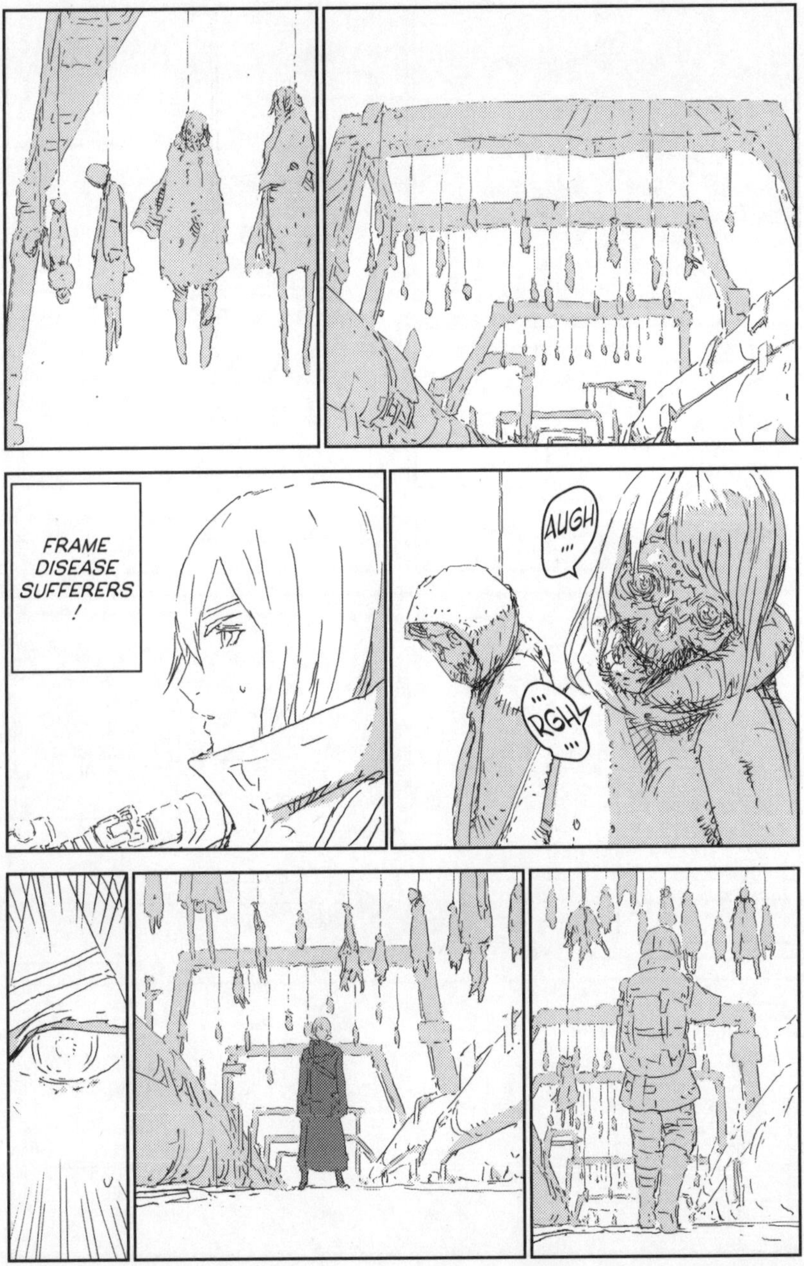
AUGH ...
... RGH ...
FRAME DISEASE SUFFERERS !

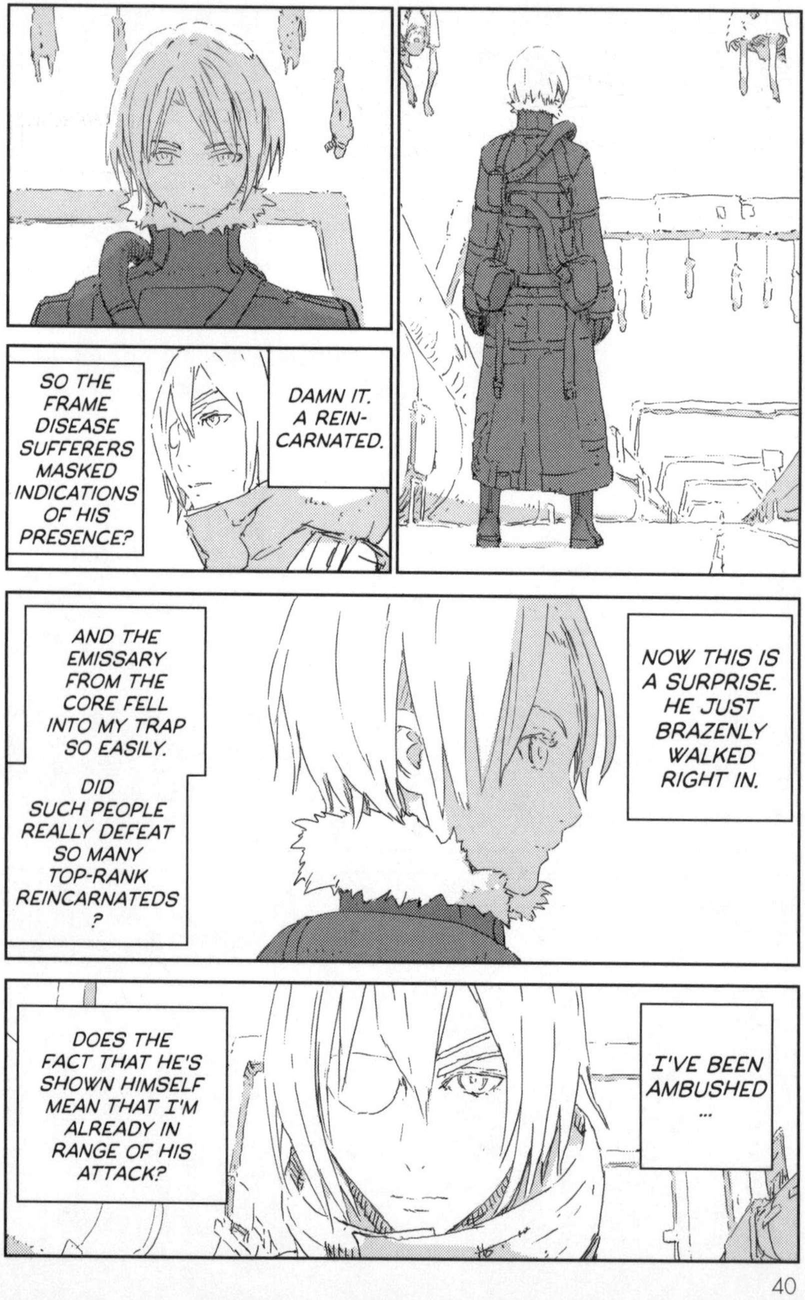
DAMN IT. A REIN-CARNATED.
SO THE FRAME DISEASE SUFFERERS MASKED INDICATIONS OF HIS PRESENCE?
NOW THIS IS A SURPRISE. HE JUST BRAZENLY WALKED RIGHT IN.
AND THE EMISSARY FROM THE CORE FELL INTO MY TRAP SO EASILY.
DID SUCH PEOPLE REALLY DEFEAT SO MANY TOP-RANK REINCARNATEDS?
I'VE BEEN AMBUSHED...
DOES THE FACT THAT HE'S SHOWN HIMSELF MEAN THAT I'M ALREADY IN RANGE OF HIS ATTACK?

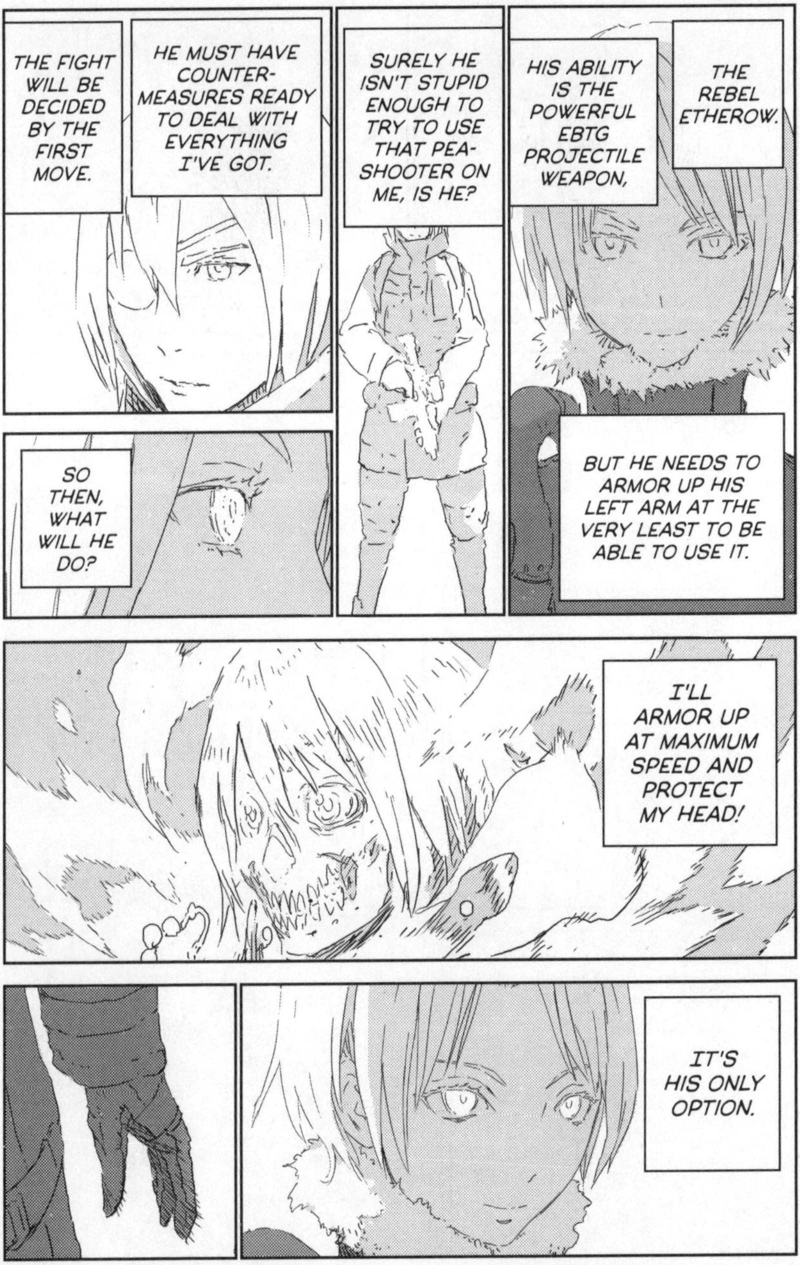
THE REBEL ETHEROW.
HIS ABILITY IS THE POWERFUL EBTG PROJECTILE WEAPON,
BUT HE NEEDS TO ARMOR UP HIS LEFT ARM AT THE VERY LEAST TO BE ABLE TO USE IT.
SURELY HE ISN'T STUPID ENOUGH TO TRY TO USE THAT PEA-SHOOTER ON ME, IS HE?
HE MUST HAVE COUNTER-MEASURES READY TO DEAL WITH EVERYTHING I'VE GOT.
THE FIGHT WILL BE DECIDED BY THE FIRST MOVE.
SO THEN, WHAT WILL HE DO?
I'LL ARMOR UP AT MAXIMUM SPEED AND PROTECT MY HEAD!
IT'S HIS ONLY OPTION.

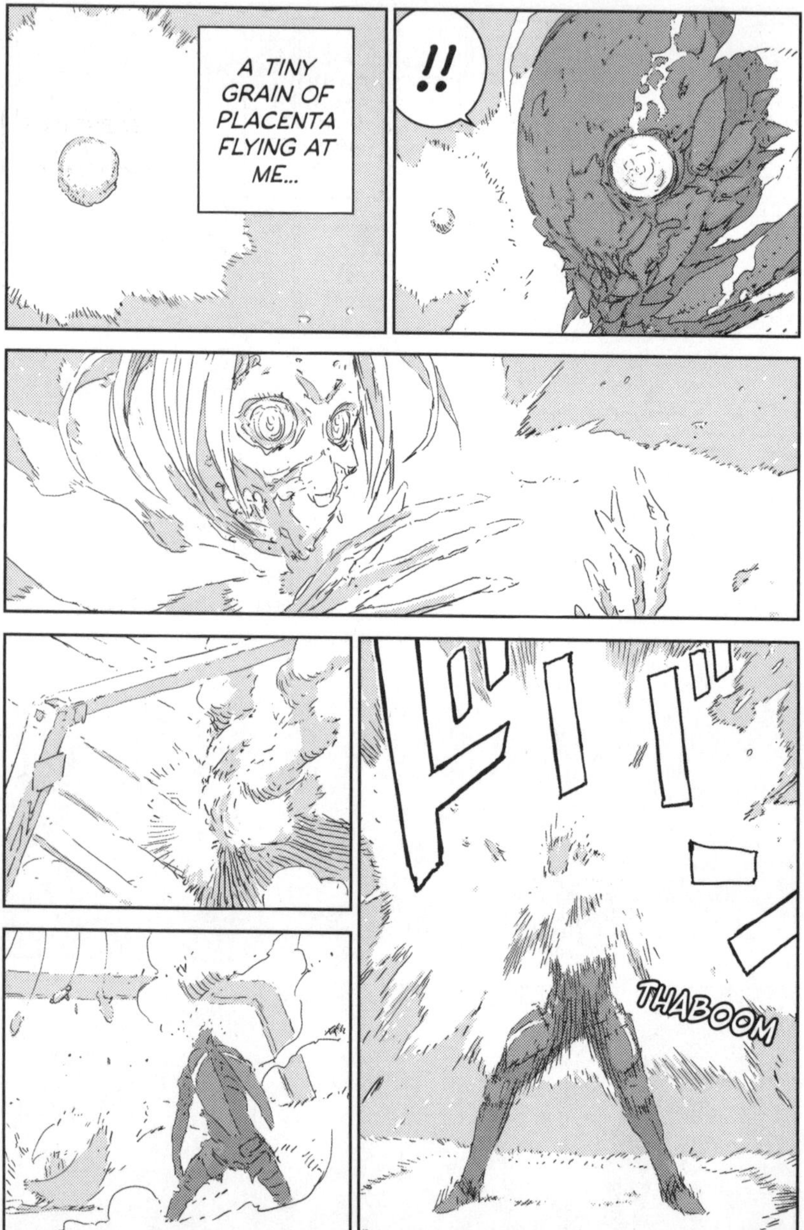
!!
A TINY GRAIN OF PLACENTA FLYING AT ME...
THABOOM

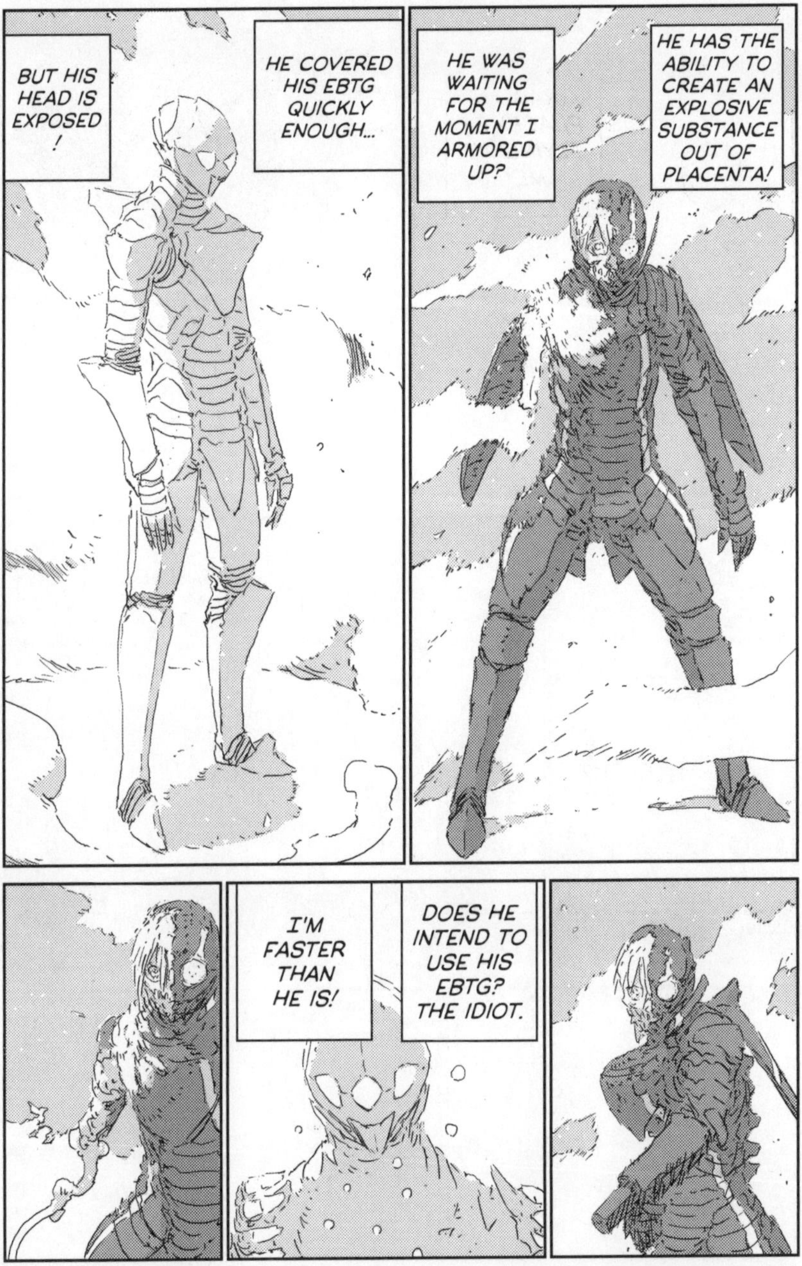
HE HAS THE ABILITY TO CREATE AN EXPLOSIVE SUBSTANCE OUT OF PLACENTA!
HE WAS WAITING FOR THE MOMENT I ARMORED UP?
HE COVERED HIS EBTG QUICKLY ENOUGH...
BUT HIS HEAD IS EXPOSED!
DOES HE INTEND TO USE HIS EBTG? THE IDIOT.
I'M FASTER THAN HE IS!

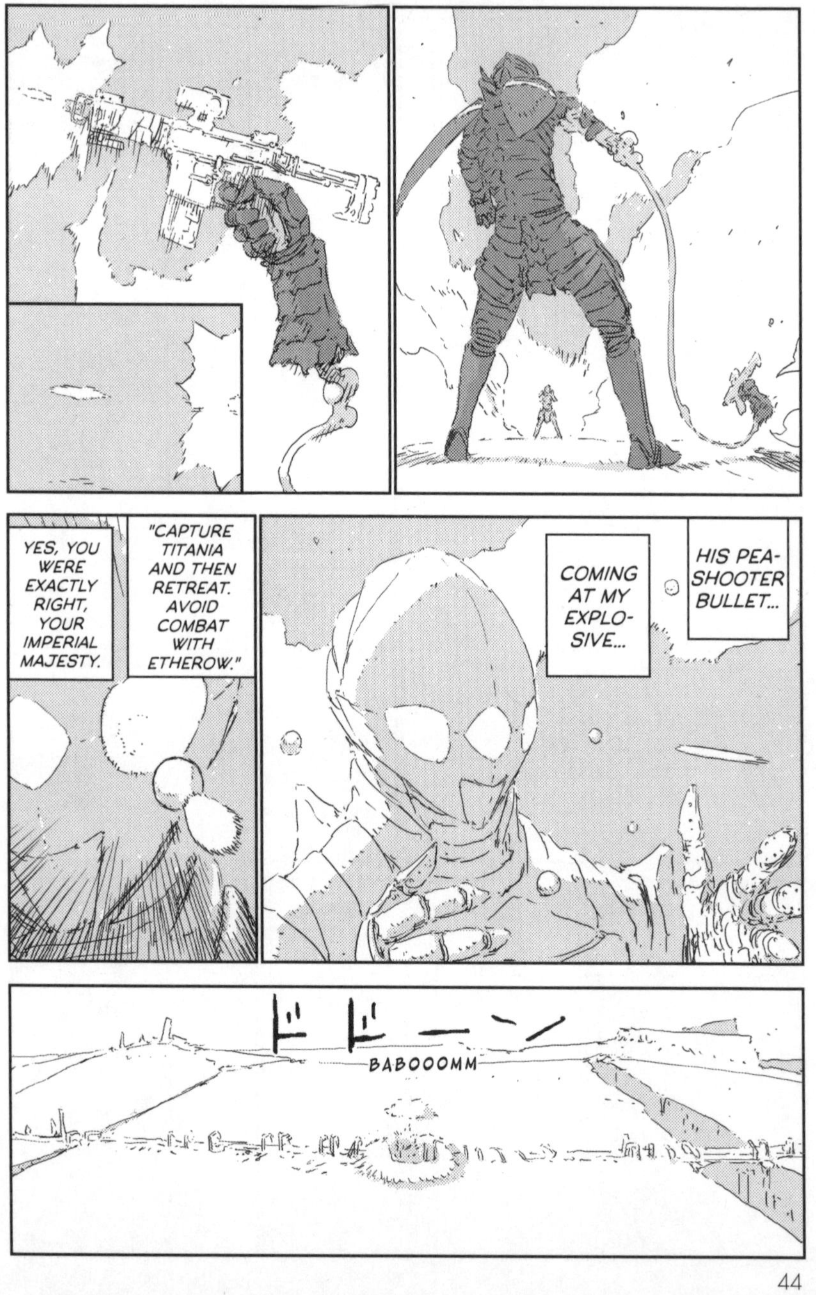
HIS PEA-SHOOTER BULLET...
COMING AT MY EXPLOSIVE...
"CAPTURE TITANIA AND THEN RETREAT. AVOID COMBAT WITH ETHEROW."
YES, YOU WERE EXACTLY RIGHT, YOUR IMPERIAL MAJESTY.
ドドーン
BABOOOMM

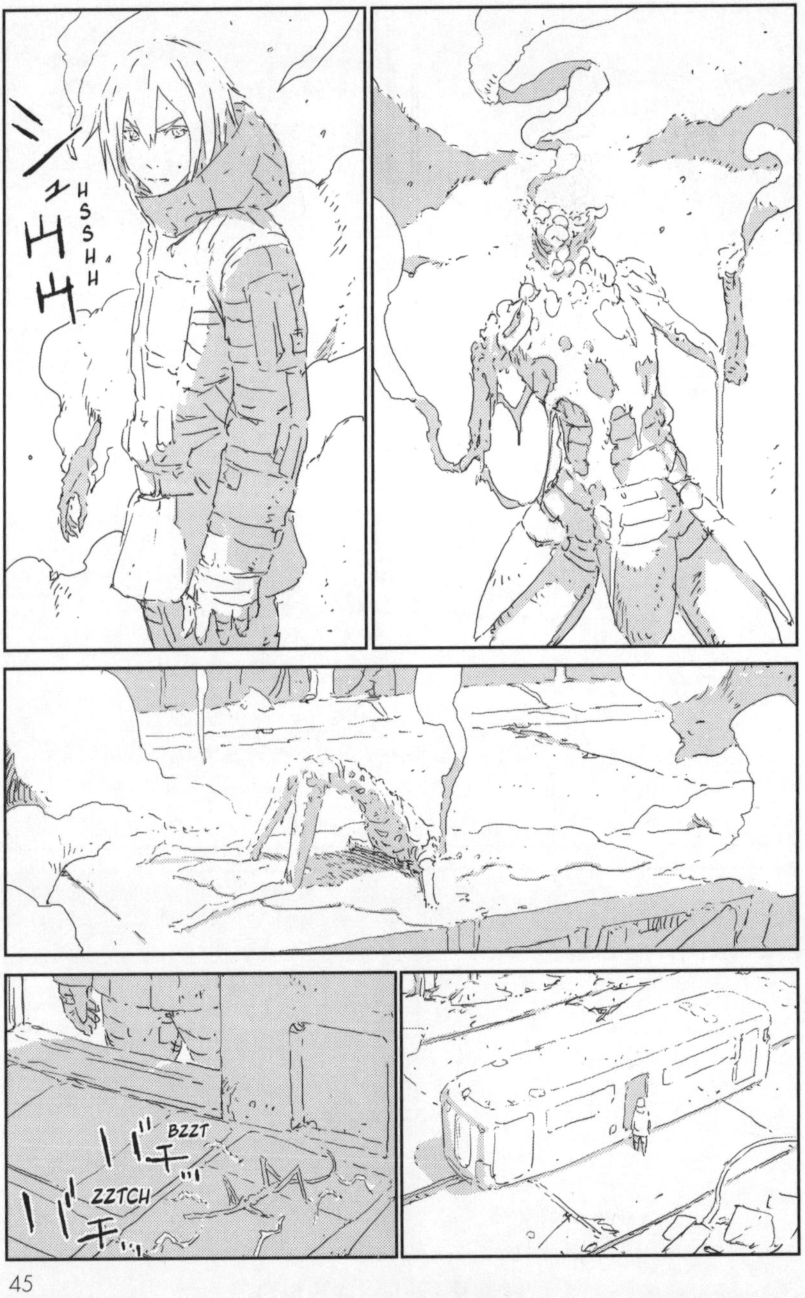
HSSHH
BZZT
ZZTCH

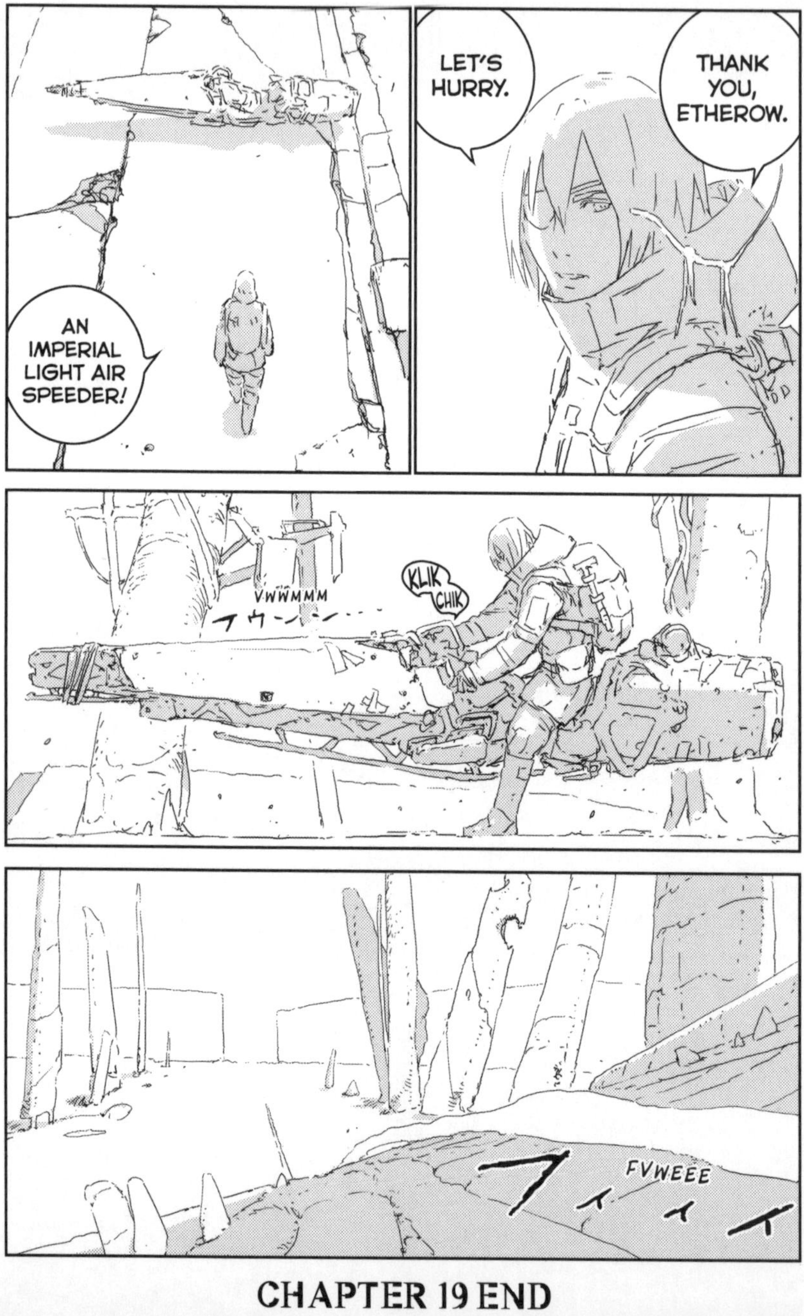
THANK YOU, ETHEROW.
LET'S HURRY.
AN IMPERIAL LIGHT AIR SPEEDER!
KLIK CHIK
VWWMMM
FVWEEE

CHAPTER 19 END

APOSIMZ

X

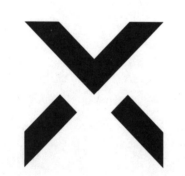

CHAPTER 20

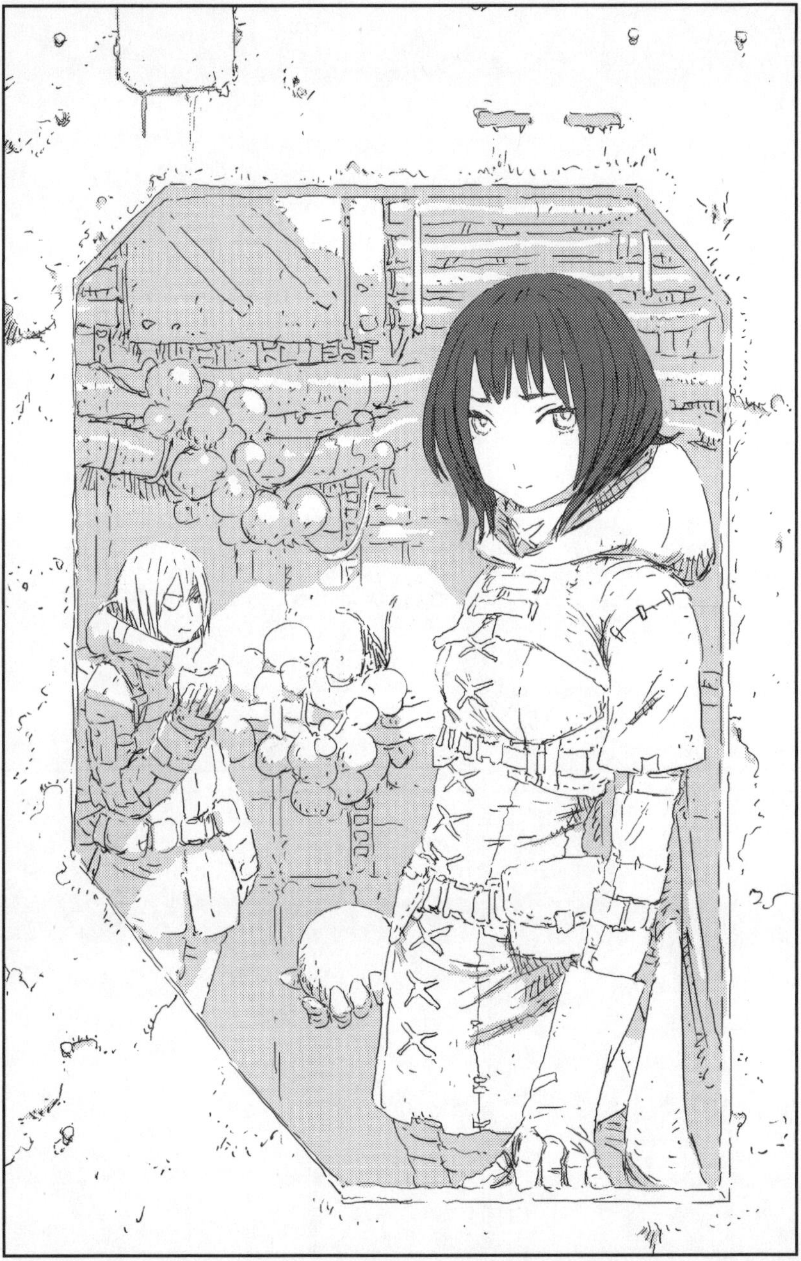

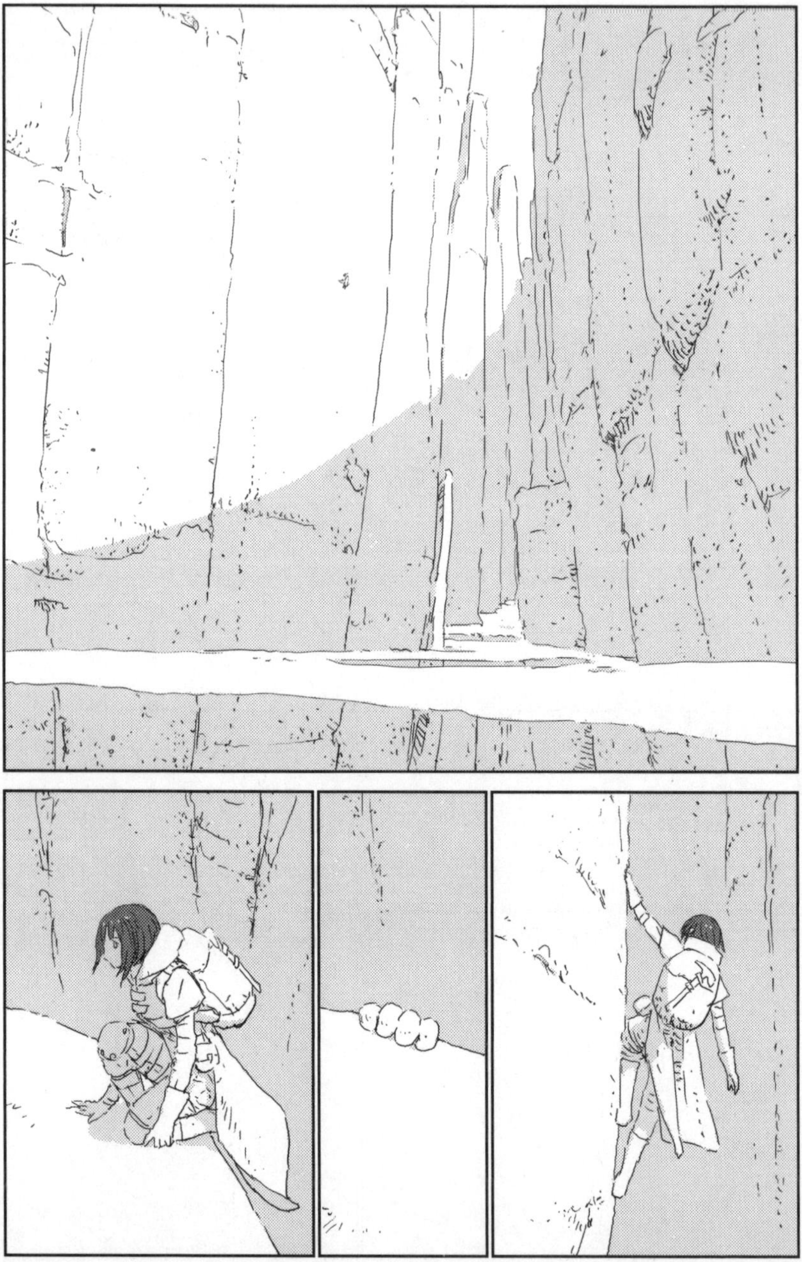

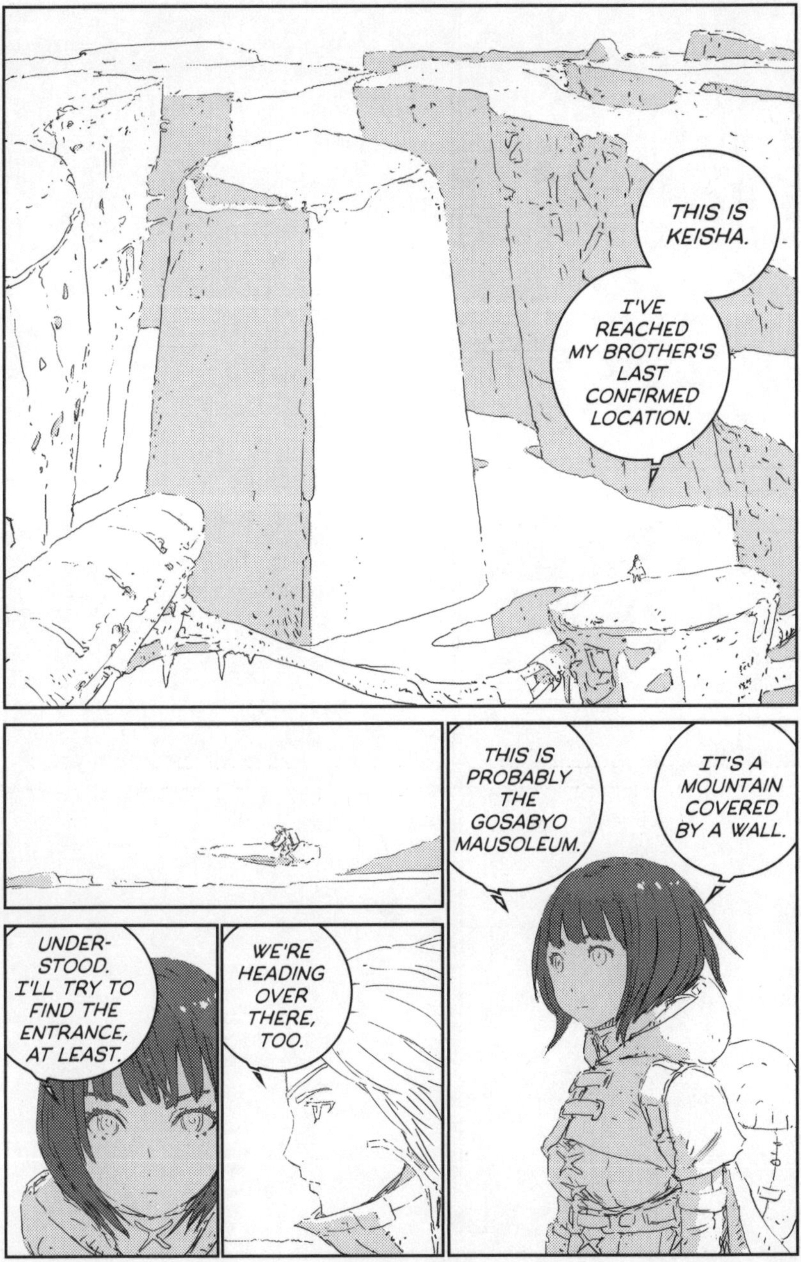
THIS IS KEISHA.
I'VE REACHED MY BROTHER'S LAST CONFIRMED LOCATION.
IT'S A MOUNTAIN COVERED BY A WALL.
THIS IS PROBABLY THE GOSABYO MAUSOLEUM.
WE'RE HEADING OVER THERE, TOO.
UNDER-STOOD. I'LL TRY TO FIND THE ENTRANCE, AT LEAST.

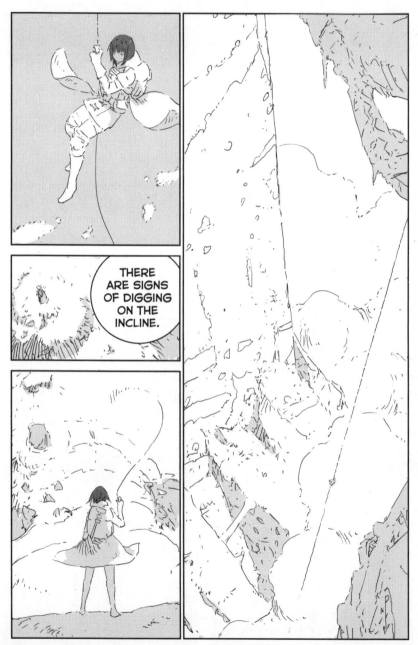

THERE
ARE SIGNS
OF DIGGING
ON THE
INCLINE.

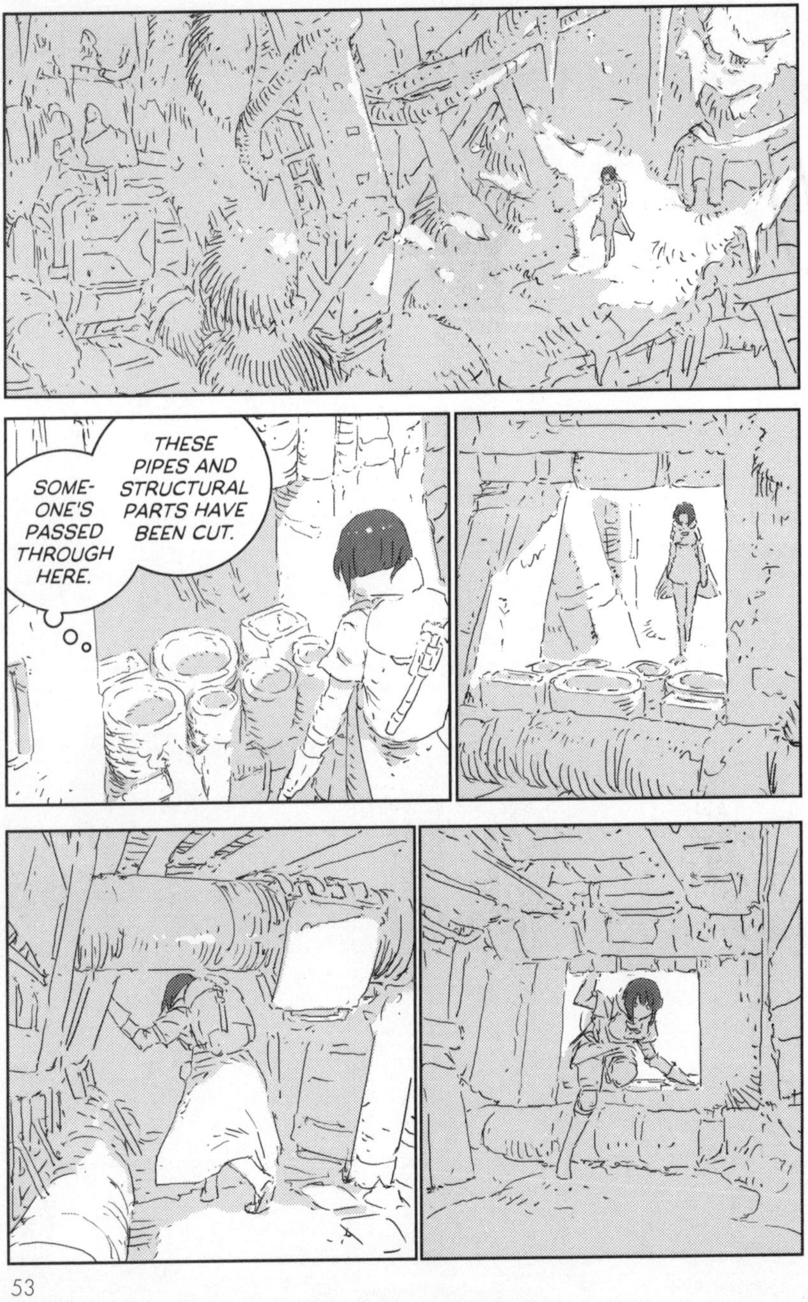
THESE PIPES AND STRUCTURAL PARTS HAVE BEEN CUT.
SOME-ONE'S PASSED THROUGH HERE.

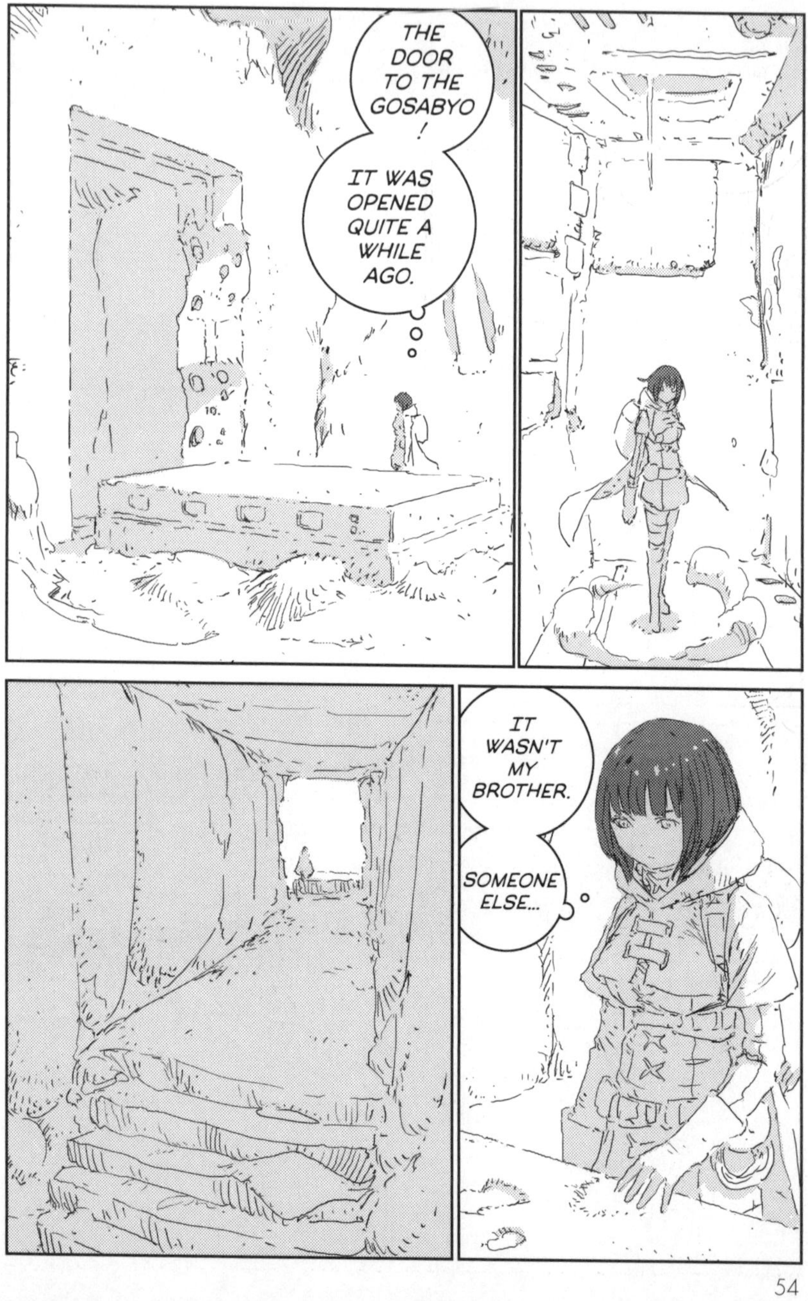
THE DOOR TO THE GOSABYO!
IT WAS OPENED QUITE A WHILE AGO.
IT WASN'T MY BROTHER.
SOMEONE ELSE...

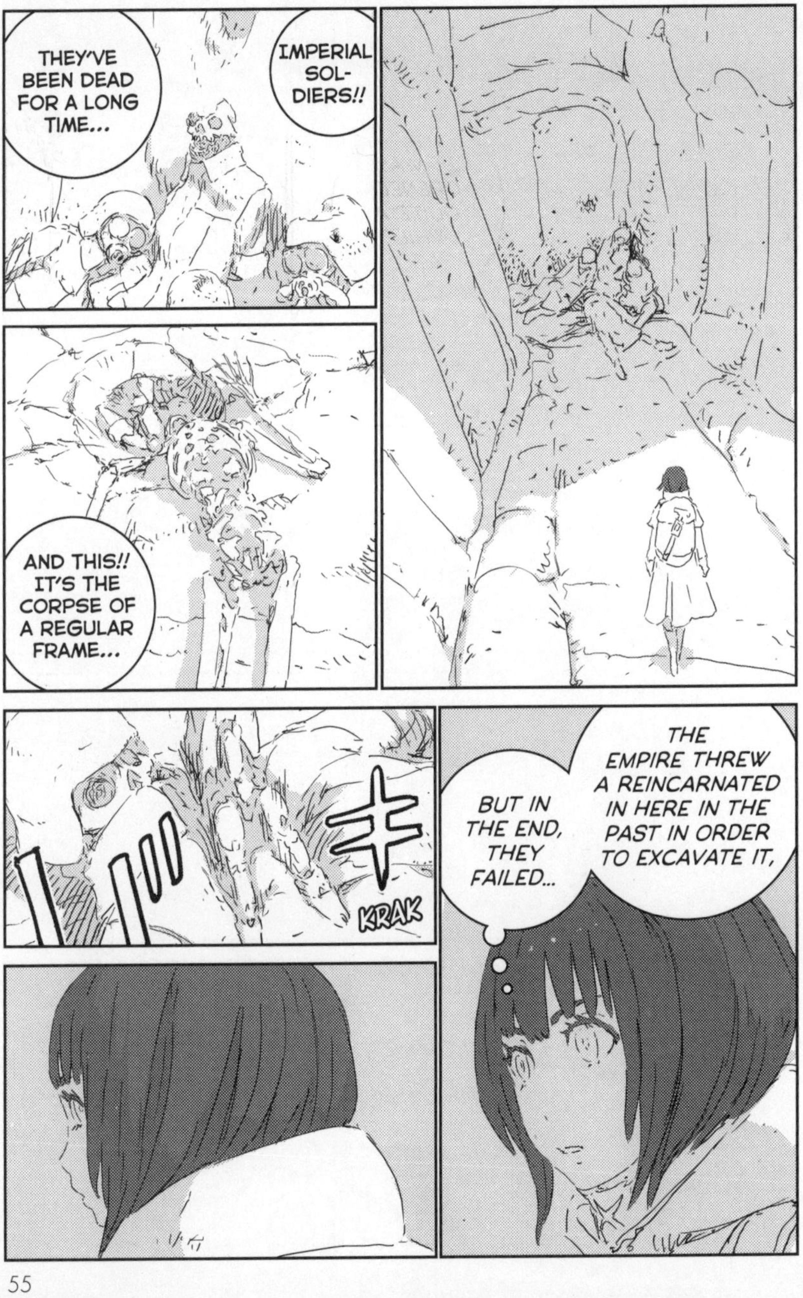
IMPERIAL SOL-DIERS!!
THEY'VE BEEN DEAD FOR A LONG TIME...
AND THIS!! IT'S THE CORPSE OF A REGULAR FRAME...
THE EMPIRE THREW A REINCARNATED IN HERE IN THE PAST IN ORDER TO EXCAVATE IT,
BUT IN THE END, THEY FAILED...
KRAK

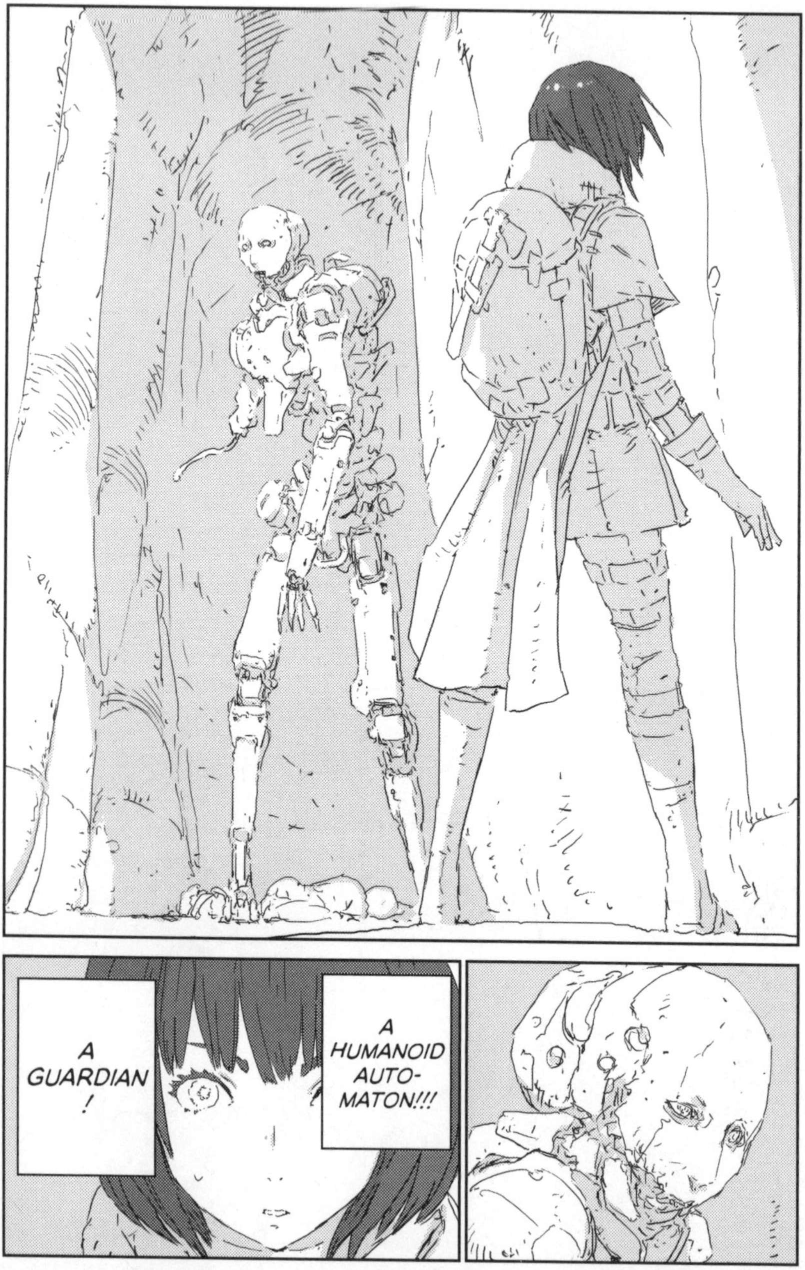
A HUMANOID AUTO-MATON!!!
A GUARDIAN!

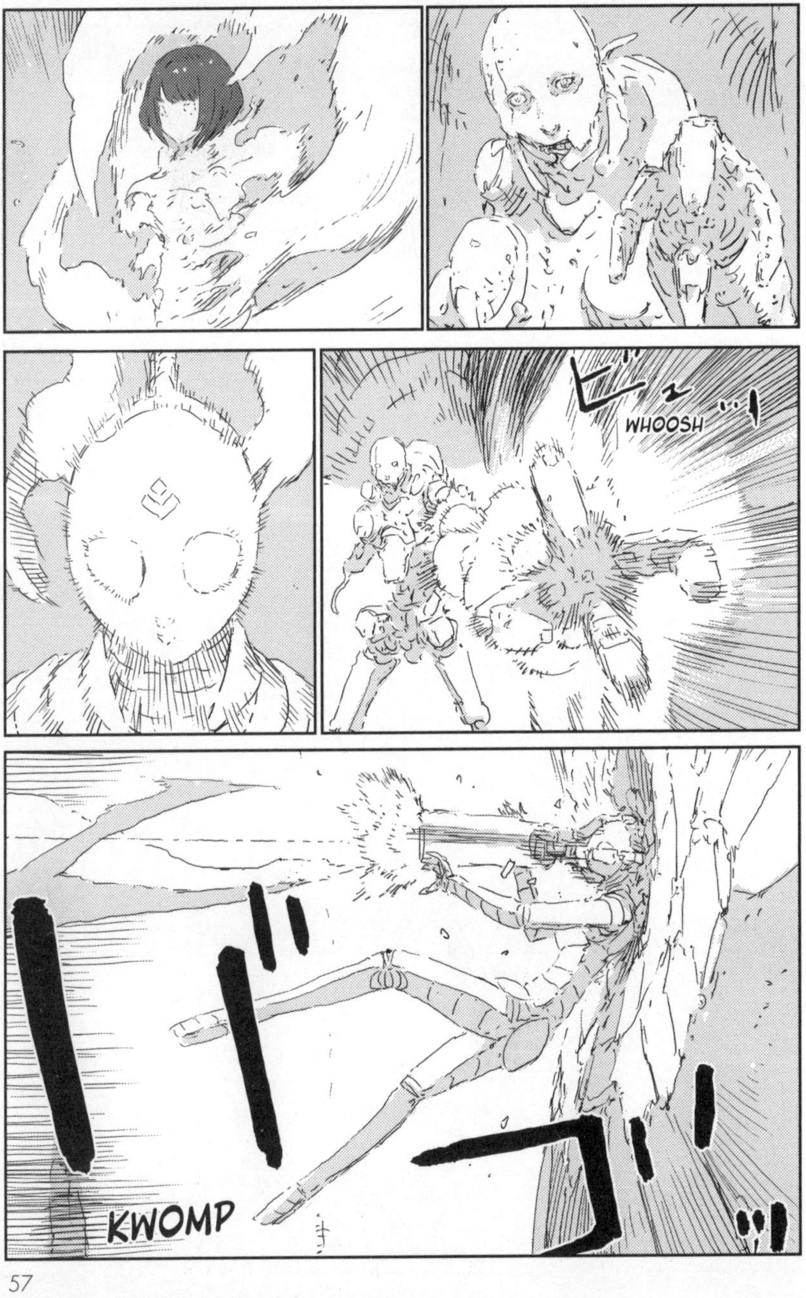
WHOOSH
KWOMP

VWMP
GCHINK

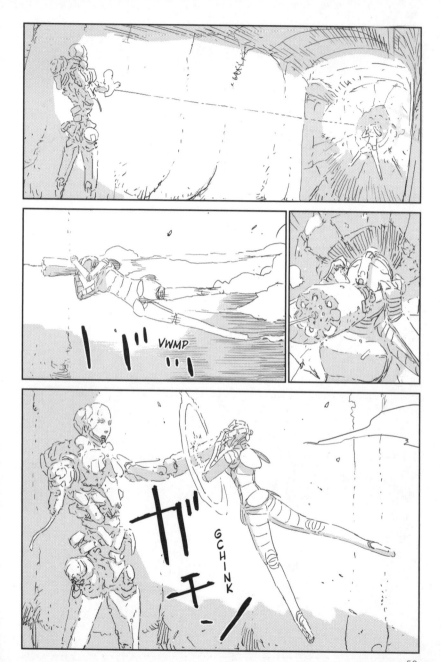

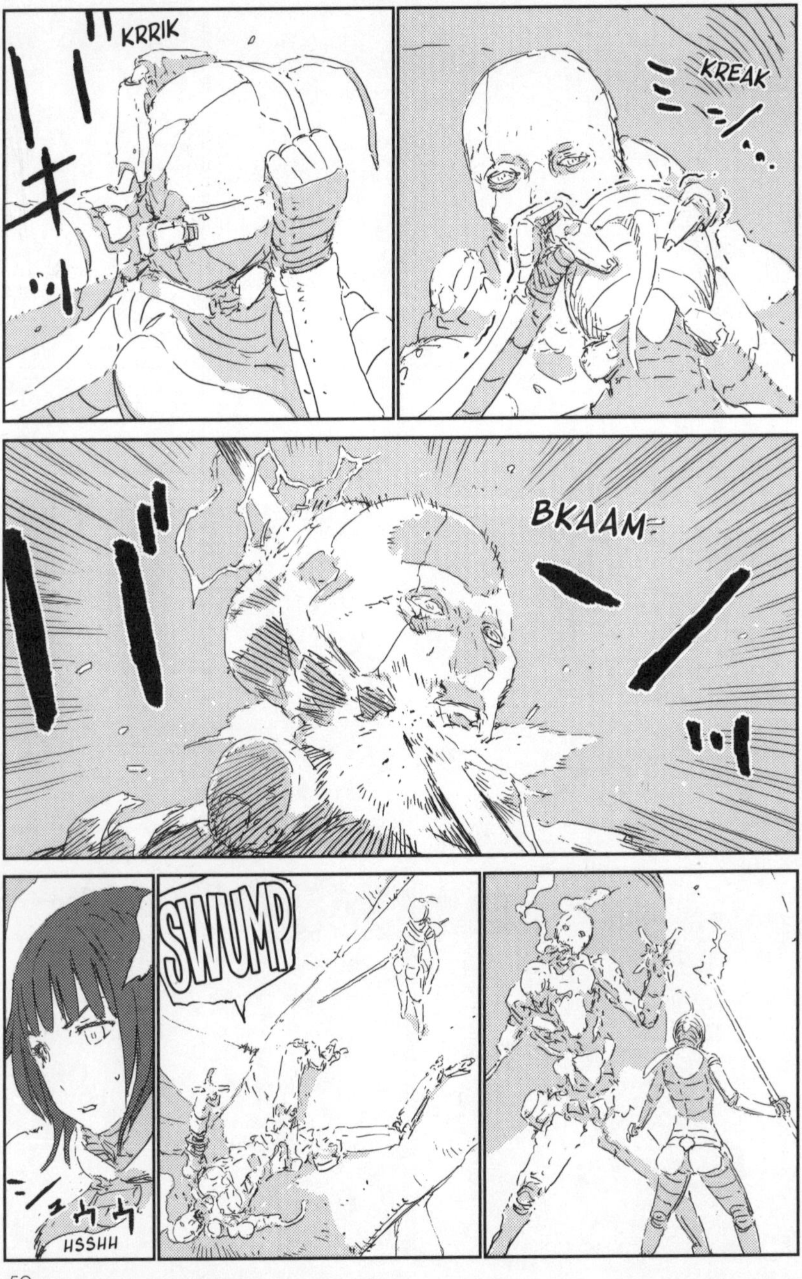

KREAK
KRRIK
BKAAM
SWUMP
HSSHH

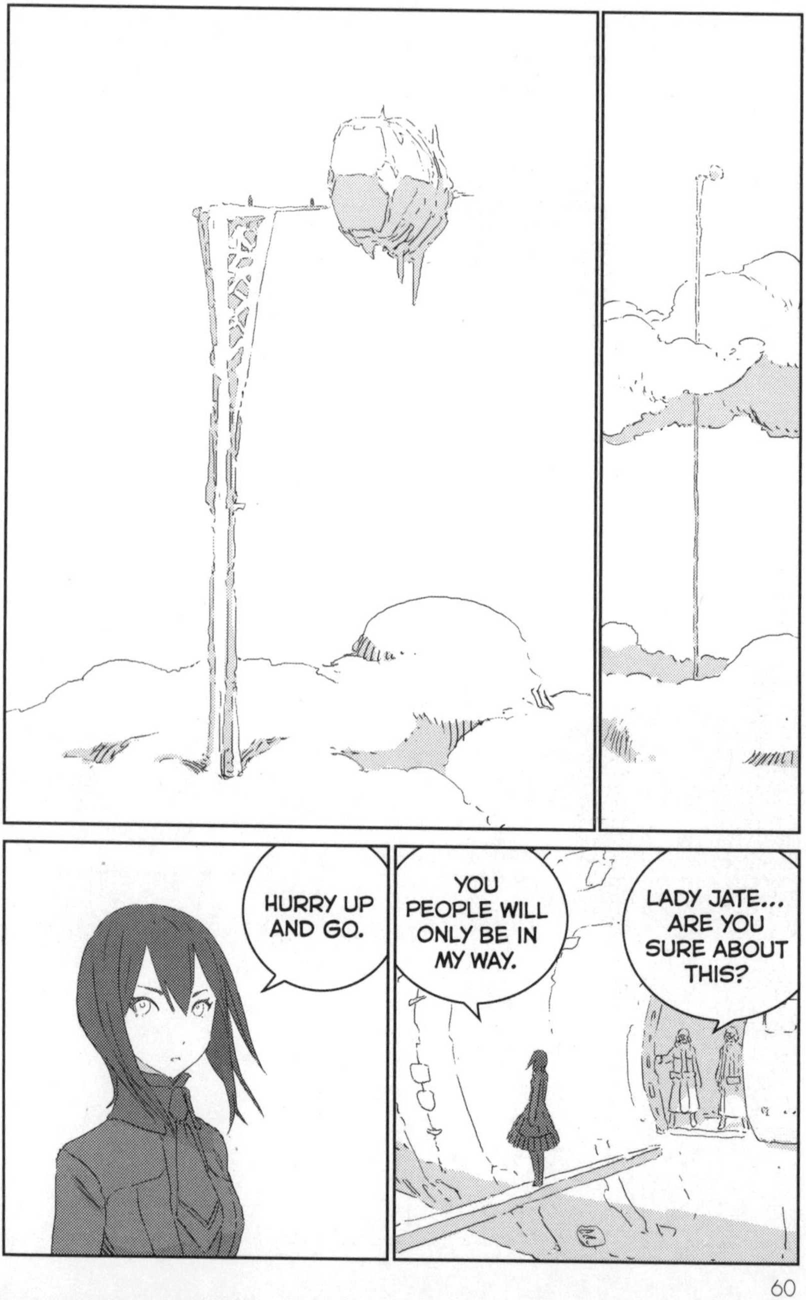

LADY JATE... ARE YOU SURE ABOUT THIS?
YOU PEOPLE WILL ONLY BE IN MY WAY.
HURRY UP AND GO.

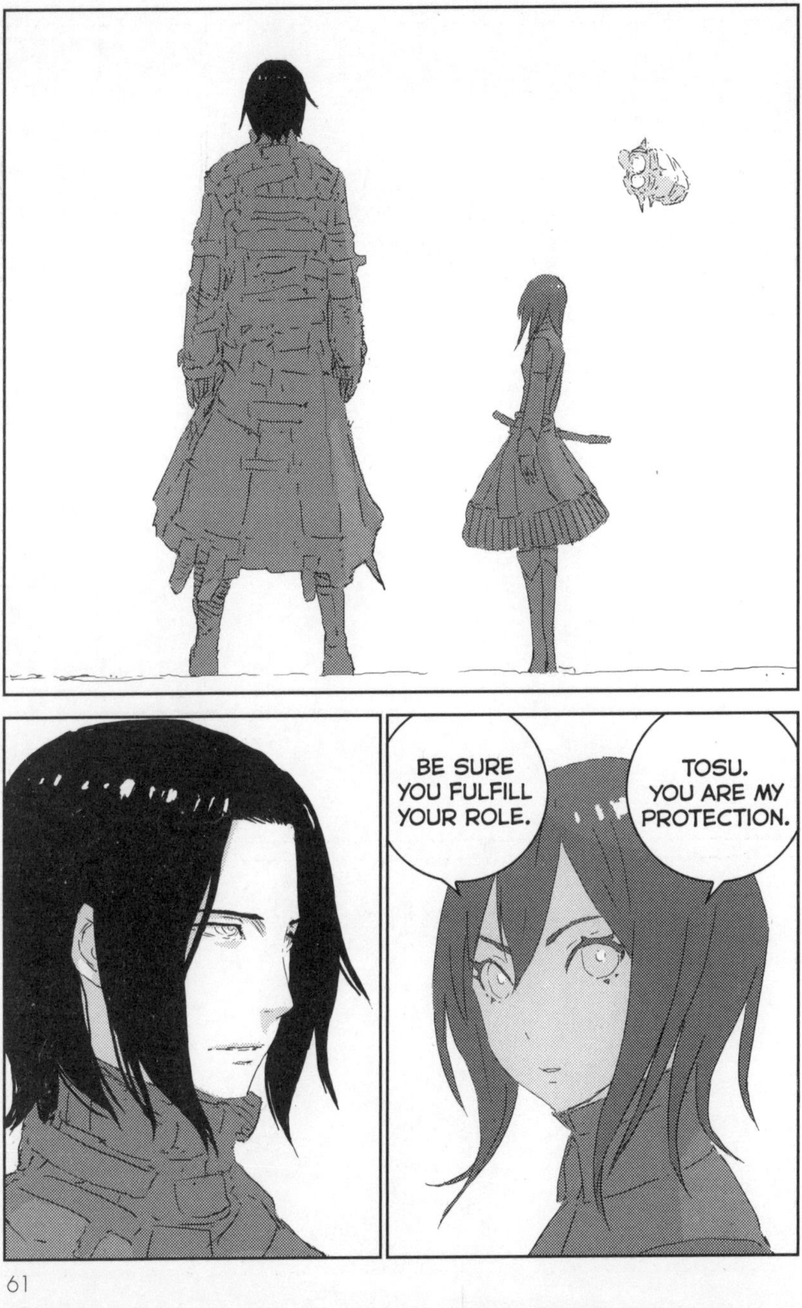
TOSU. YOU ARE MY PROTECTION.
BE SURE YOU FULFILL YOUR ROLE.

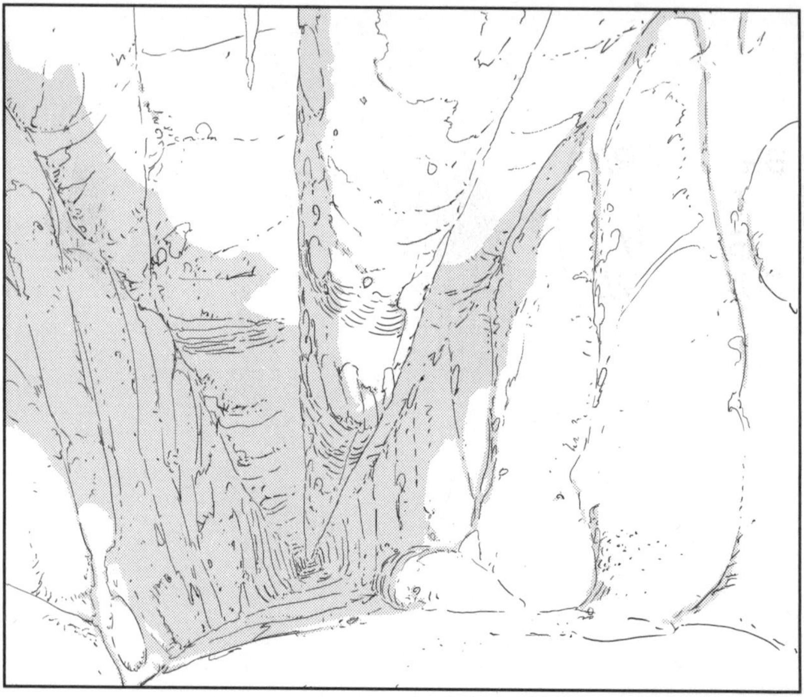
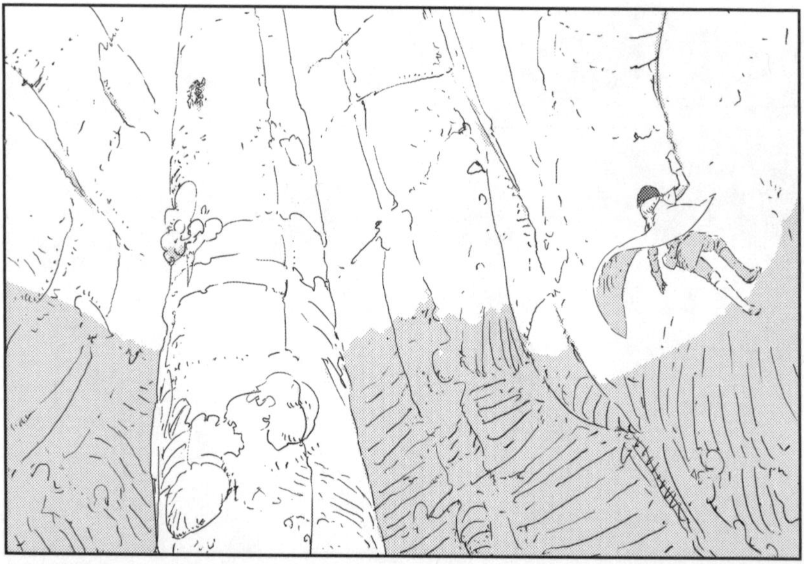

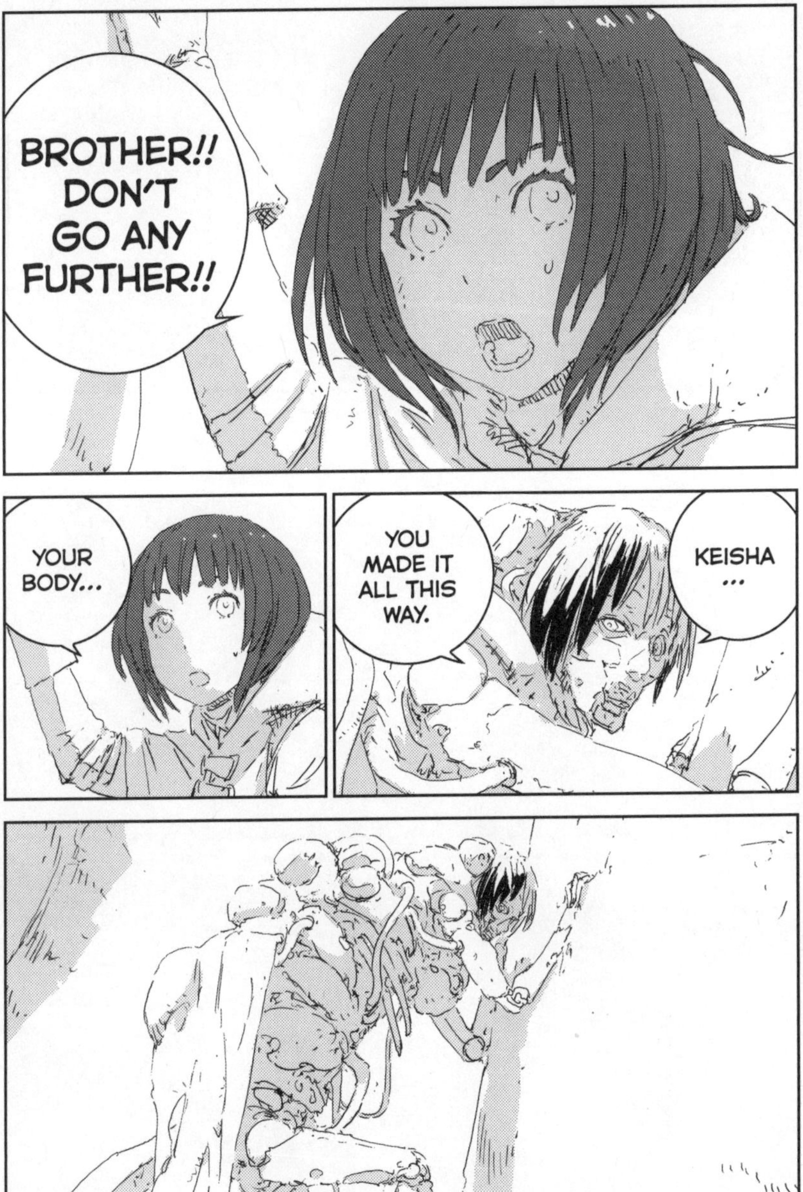
BROTHER!! DON'T GO ANY FURTHER!!
KEISHA ...
YOU MADE IT ALL THIS WAY.
YOUR BODY...

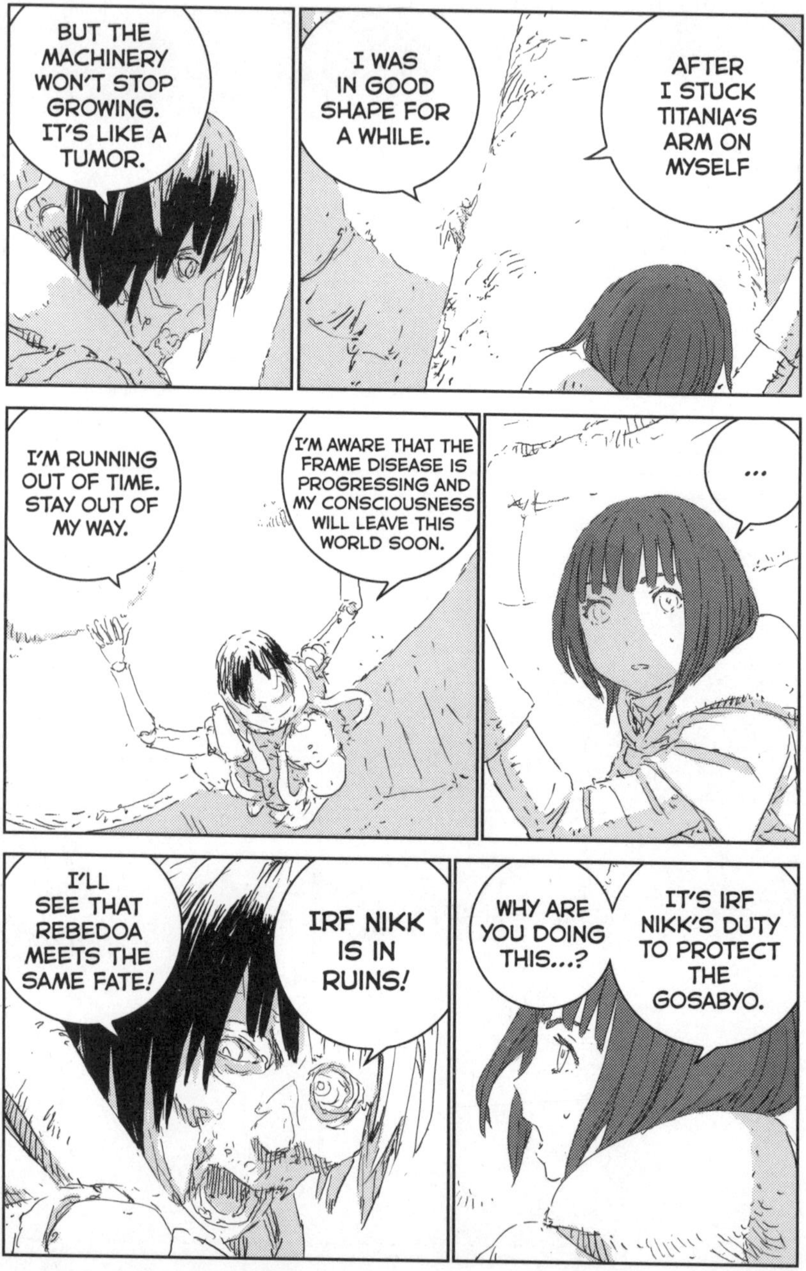
AFTER I STUCK TITANIA'S ARM ON MYSELF
I WAS IN GOOD SHAPE FOR A WHILE.
BUT THE MACHINERY WON'T STOP GROWING. IT'S LIKE A TUMOR.
...
I'M AWARE THAT THE FRAME DISEASE IS PROGRESSING AND MY CONSCIOUSNESS WILL LEAVE THIS WORLD SOON.
I'M RUNNING OUT OF TIME. STAY OUT OF MY WAY.
IT'S IRF NIKK'S DUTY TO PROTECT THE GOSABYO.
WHY ARE YOU DOING THIS...?
IRF NIKK IS IN RUINS!
I'LL SEE THAT REBEDOA MEETS THE SAME FATE!

JUST WHAT IS THIS PLACE?!
WHAT DO YOU INTEND TO DO?!!
THE GOSABYO'S PURPOSE IS TO COMMUNICATE WITH UME.
HUH ?!
I WILL TAKE CONTROL OF UME'S ORBIT, AND DROP IT ON THE EMPIRE'S CAPITAL CITY.
!!
BUT IF YOU DO THAT—!!
THE HUMANS, OF COURSE, AND EVEN THE REINCARNATEDS OF THE CAPITAL WILL BE ANNIHILATED.
BUT YOU'LL BE FINE. YOU'RE A REGULAR FRAME,
AND WE'RE QUITE FAR FROM THE CAPITAL.

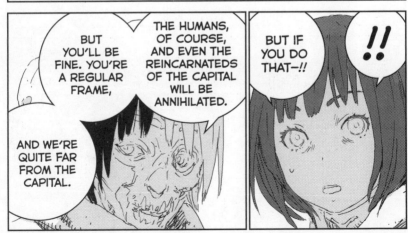

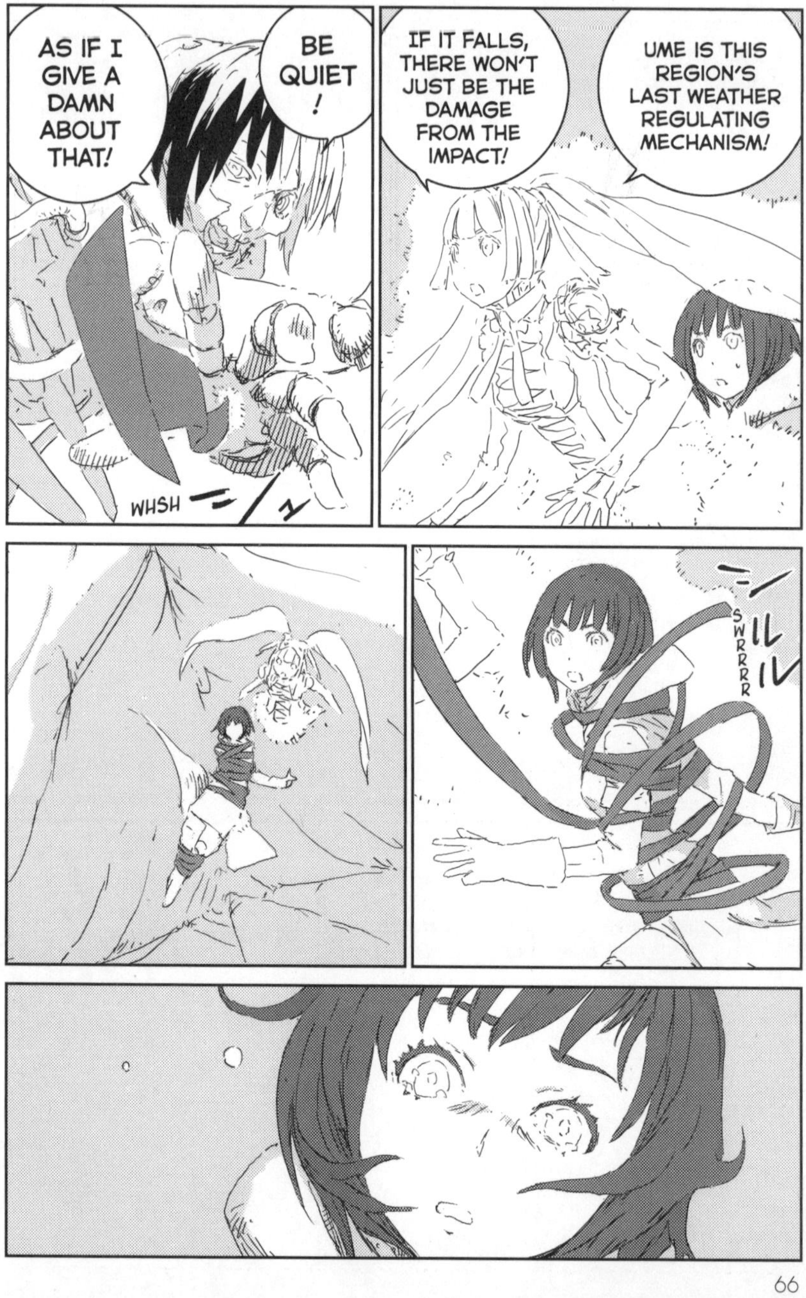
UME IS THIS REGION'S LAST WEATHER REGULATING MECHANISM!
IF IT FALLS, THERE WON'T JUST BE THE DAMAGE FROM THE IMPACT!
BE QUIET!
AS IF I GIVE A DAMN ABOUT THAT!
WHSH
SWRRRR

THUMP
HMF...
SWF
ス

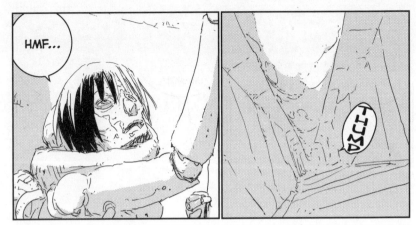

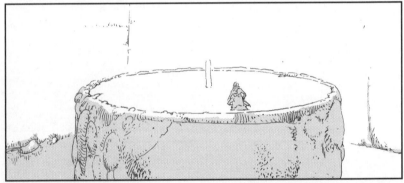

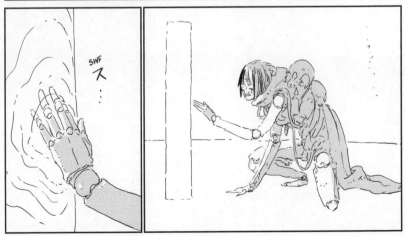

GSSHT
VWWMM
OOH ...!
I'VE SUCCESS-FULLY CONNECTED!

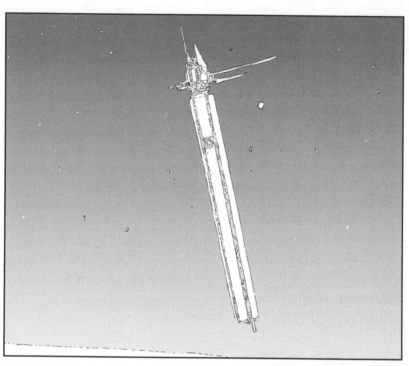

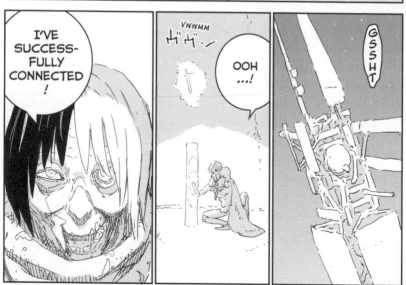

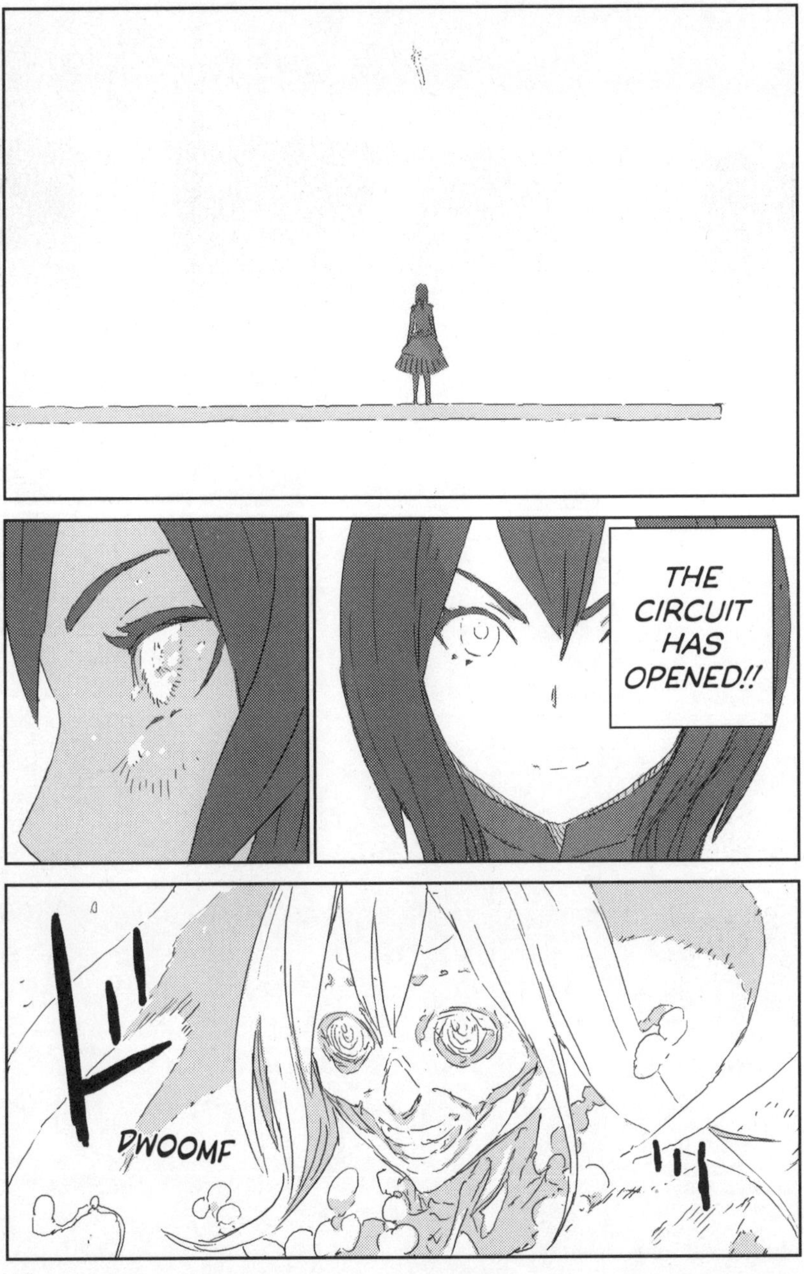
THE CIRCUIT HAS OPENED!!
DWOOMF

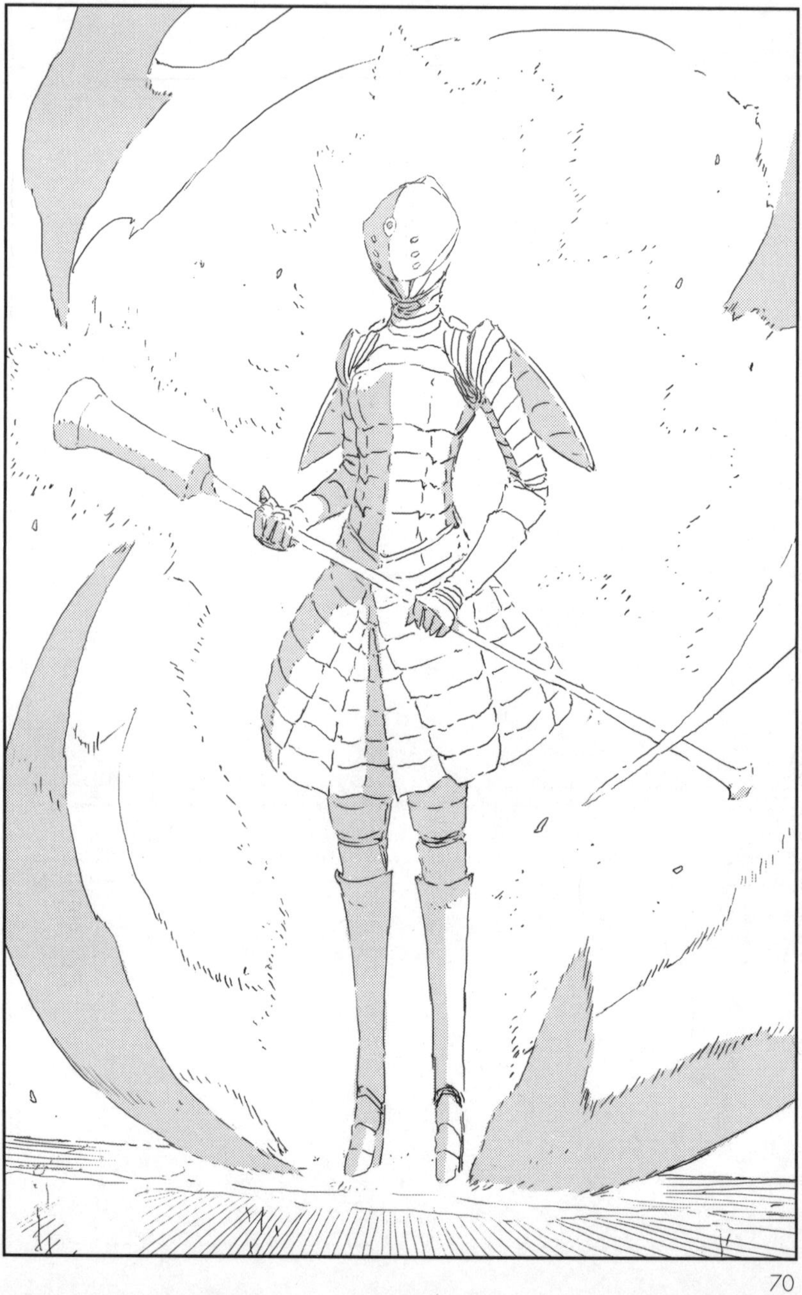

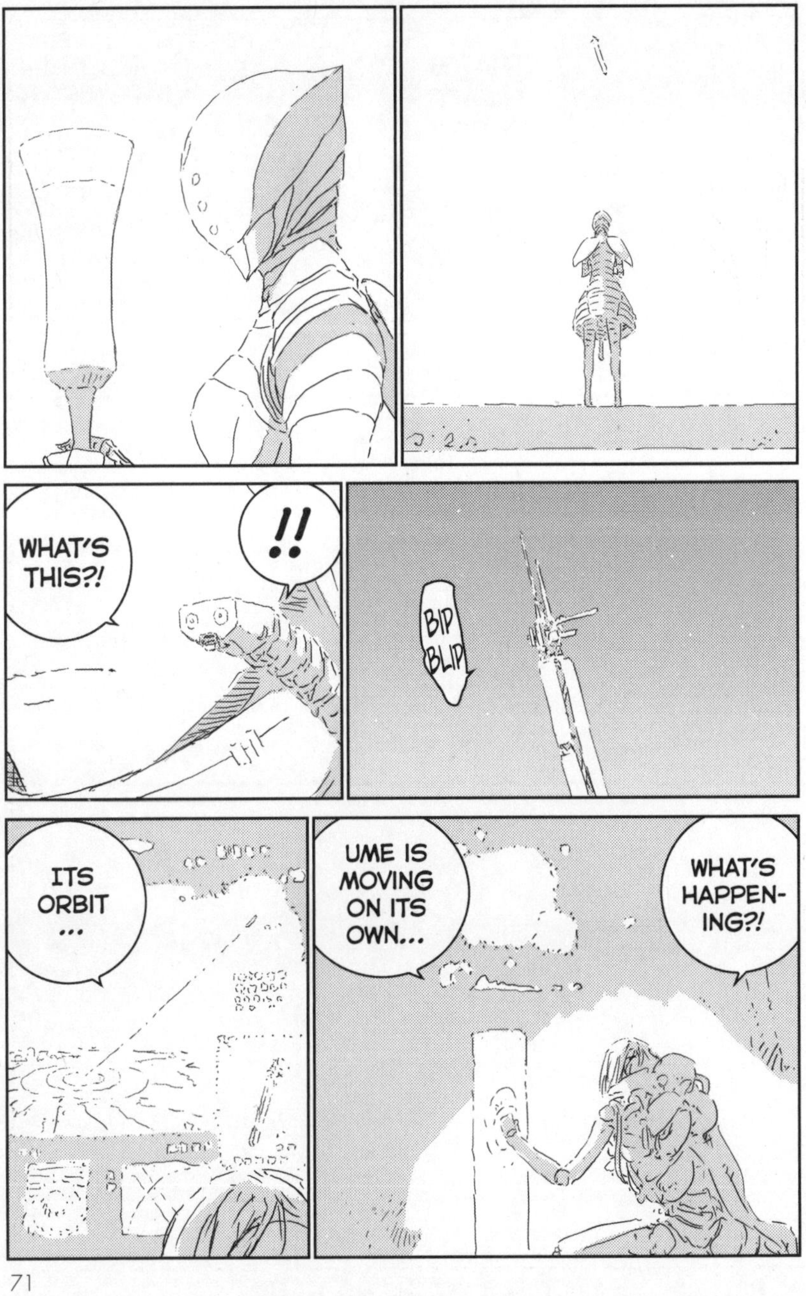
BIP BLIP
!!
WHAT'S THIS?!
WHAT'S HAPPEN-ING?!
UME IS MOVING ON ITS OWN...
ITS ORBIT ...

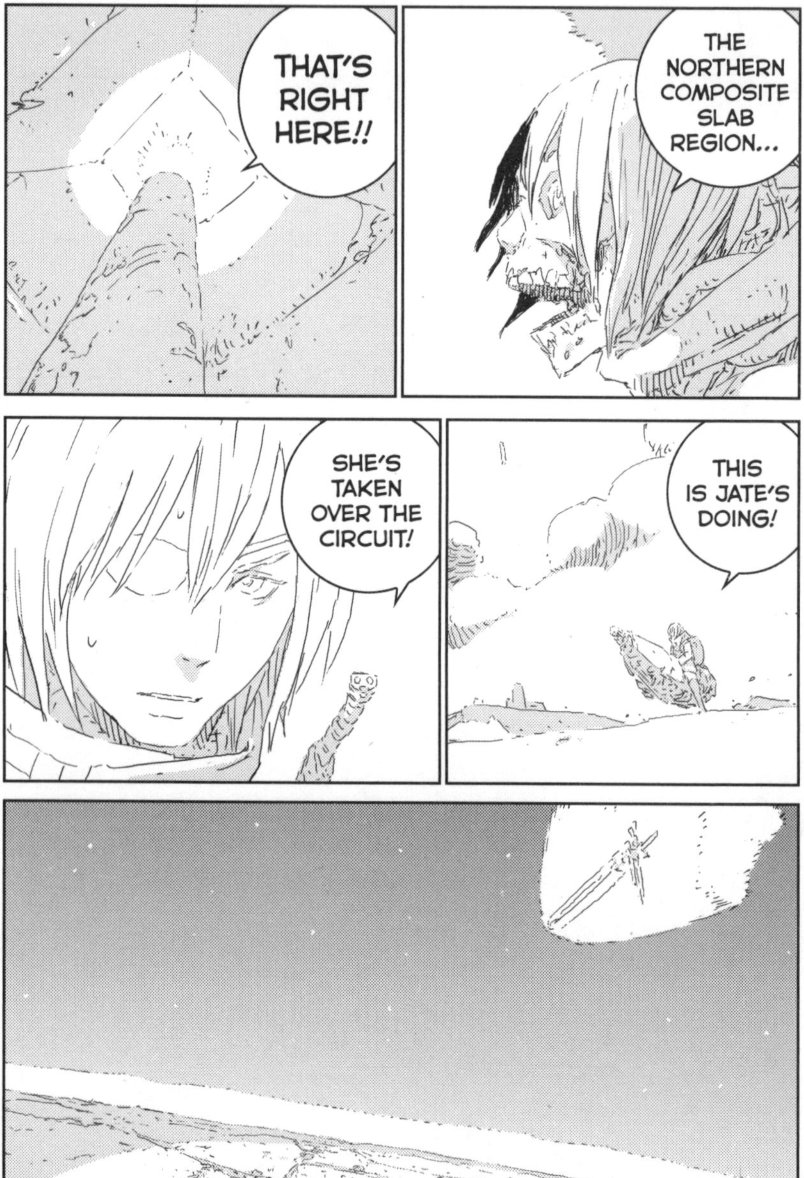
THE NORTHERN COMPOSITE SLAB REGION...
THAT'S RIGHT HERE!!
THIS IS JATE'S DOING!
SHE'S TAKEN OVER THE CIRCUIT!

CHAPTER 20 END

APOSIMZ

CHAPTER 21

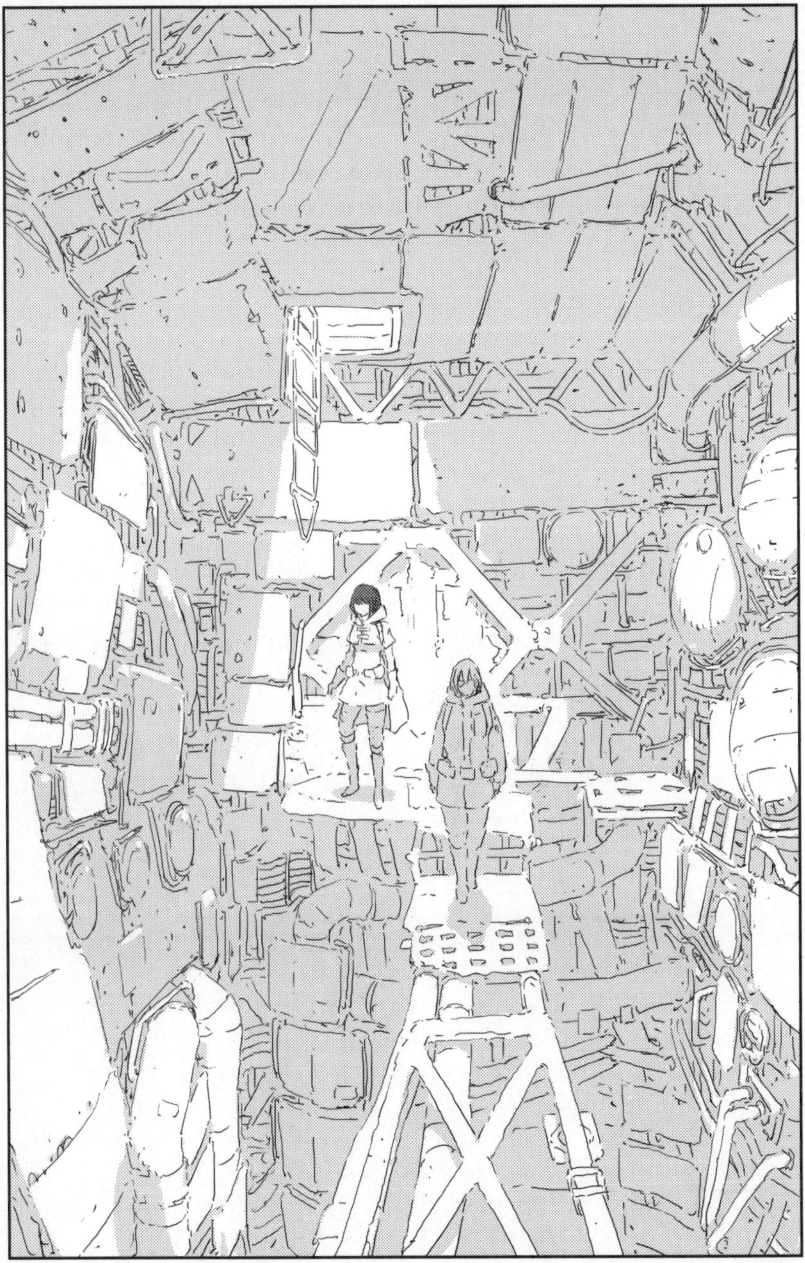

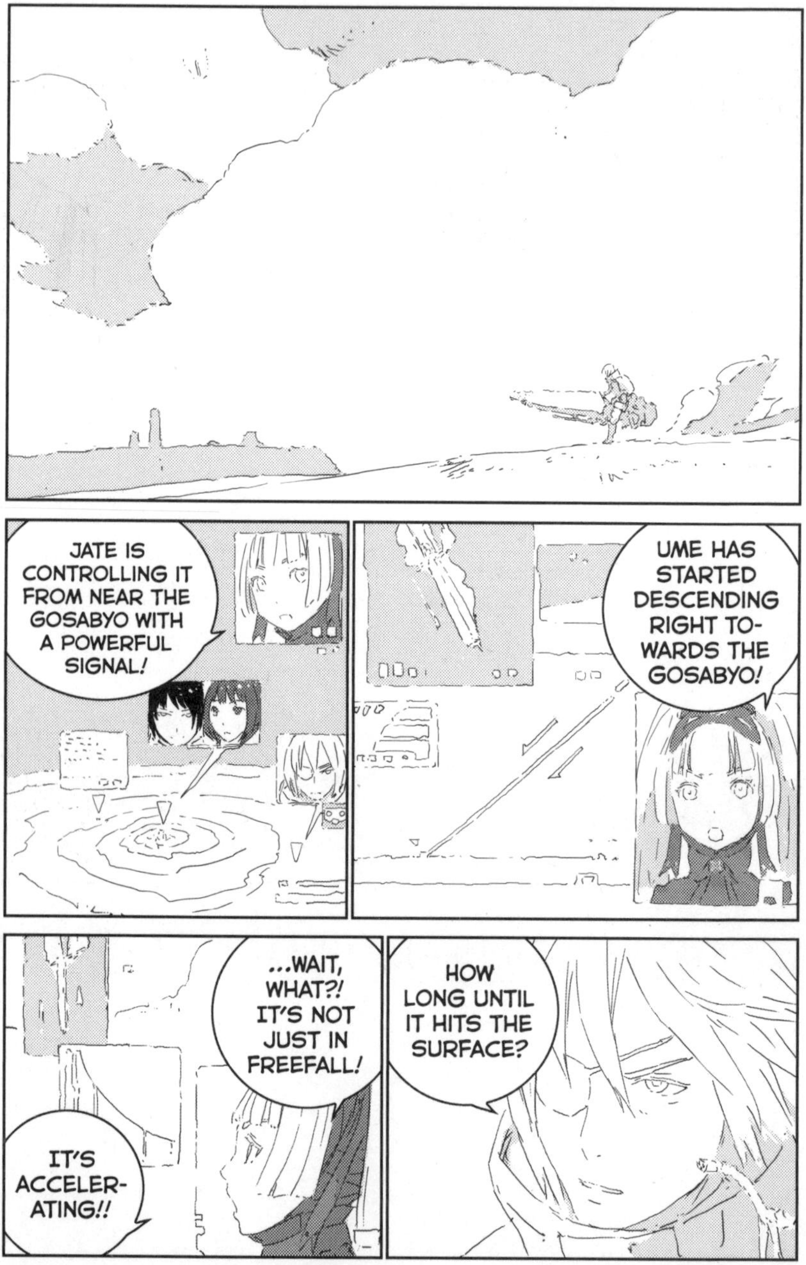
UME HAS STARTED DESCENDING RIGHT TOWARDS THE GOSABYO!
JATE IS CONTROLLING IT FROM NEAR THE GOSABYO WITH A POWERFUL SIGNAL!
HOW LONG UNTIL IT HITS THE SURFACE?
...WAIT, WHAT?! IT'S NOT JUST IN FREEFALL!
IT'S ACCELERATING!!

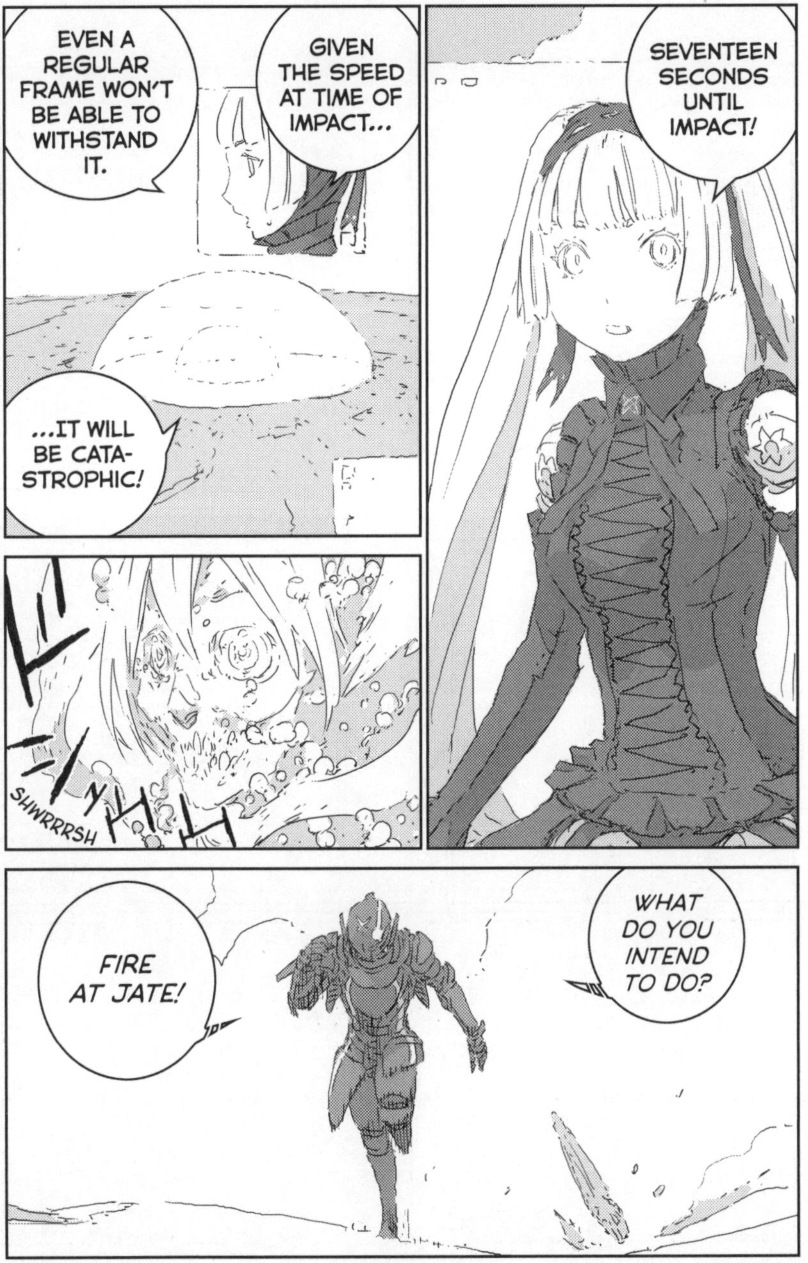
SEVENTEEN SECONDS UNTIL IMPACT!
GIVEN THE SPEED AT TIME OF IMPACT...
EVEN A REGULAR FRAME WON'T BE ABLE TO WITHSTAND IT.
...IT WILL BE CATA-STROPHIC!
SHWRRRSH
WHAT DO YOU INTEND TO DO?
FIRE AT JATE!

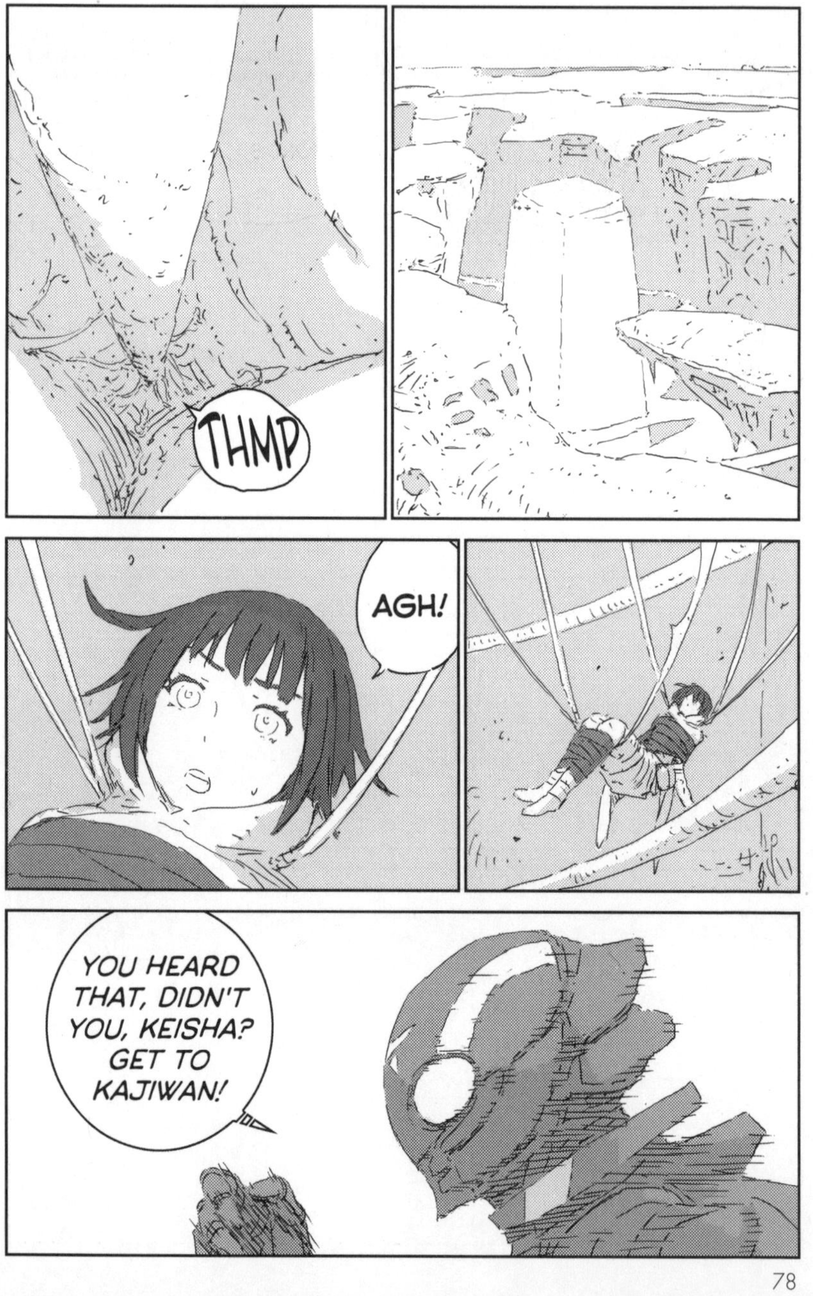
THMP
AGH!
YOU HEARD THAT, DIDN'T YOU, KEISHA? GET TO KAJIWAN!

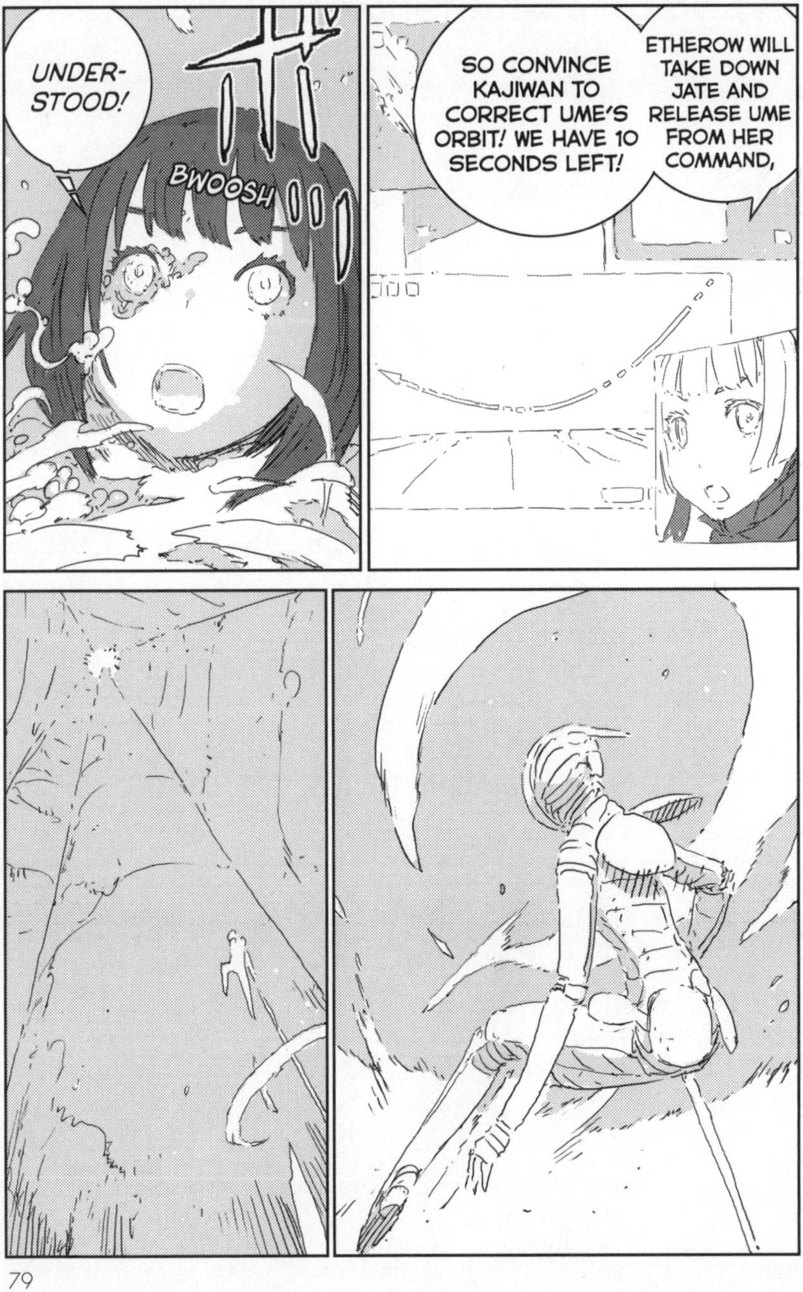
ETHEROW WILL TAKE DOWN JATE AND RELEASE UME FROM HER COMMAND,
SO CONVINCE KAJIWAN TO CORRECT UME'S ORBIT! WE HAVE 10 SECONDS LEFT!
UNDER-STOOD!
BWOOSH

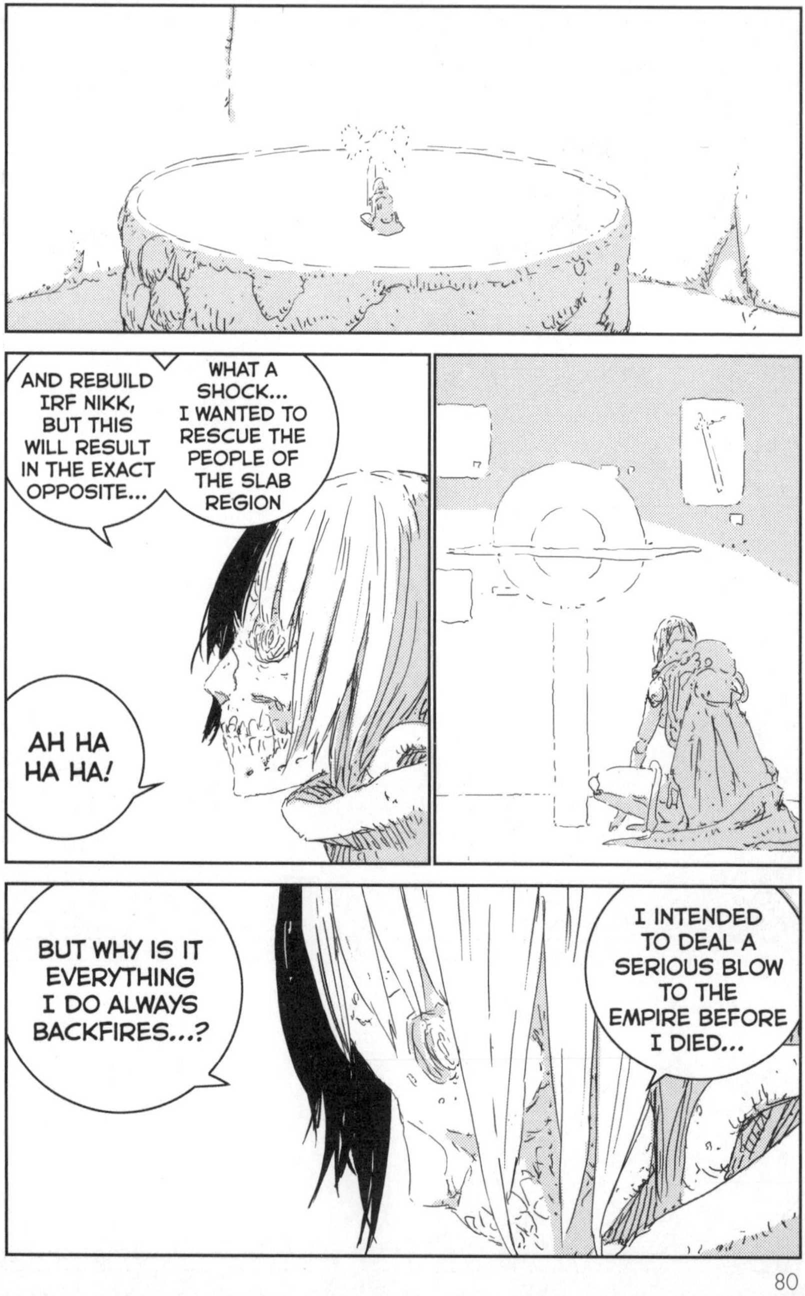
WHAT A SHOCK... I WANTED TO RESCUE THE PEOPLE OF THE SLAB REGION
AND REBUILD IRF NIKK, BUT THIS WILL RESULT IN THE EXACT OPPOSITE...
AH HA HA HA!
I INTENDED TO DEAL A SERIOUS BLOW TO THE EMPIRE BEFORE I DIED...
BUT WHY IS IT EVERYTHING I DO ALWAYS BACKFIRES...?

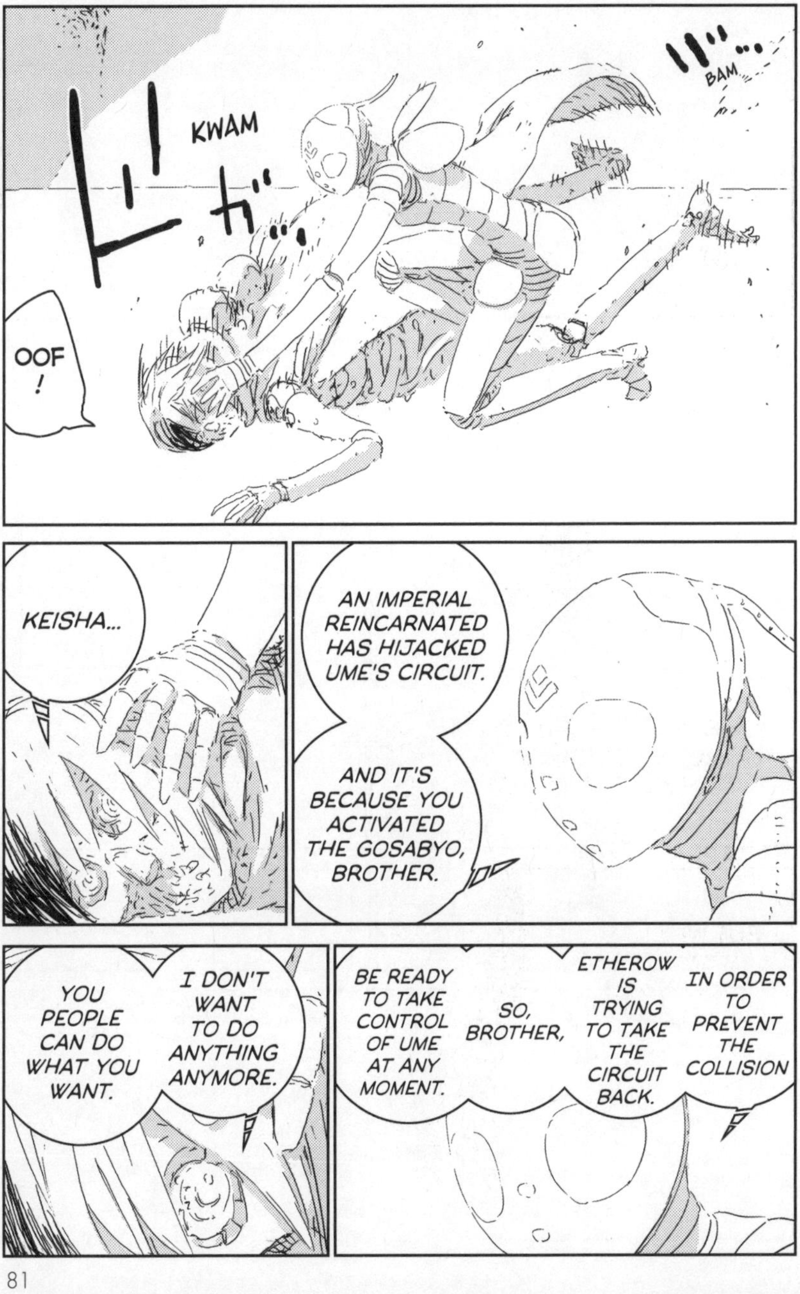
BAM
KWAM
OOF!
AN IMPERIAL REINCARNATED HAS HIJACKED UME'S CIRCUIT.
AND IT'S BECAUSE YOU ACTIVATED THE GOSABYO, BROTHER.
KEISHA...
IN ORDER TO PREVENT THE COLLISION
ETHEROW IS TRYING TO TAKE THE CIRCUIT BACK.
SO, BROTHER,
BE READY TO TAKE CONTROL OF UME AT ANY MOMENT.
I DON'T WANT TO DO ANYTHING ANYMORE.
YOU PEOPLE CAN DO WHAT YOU WANT.

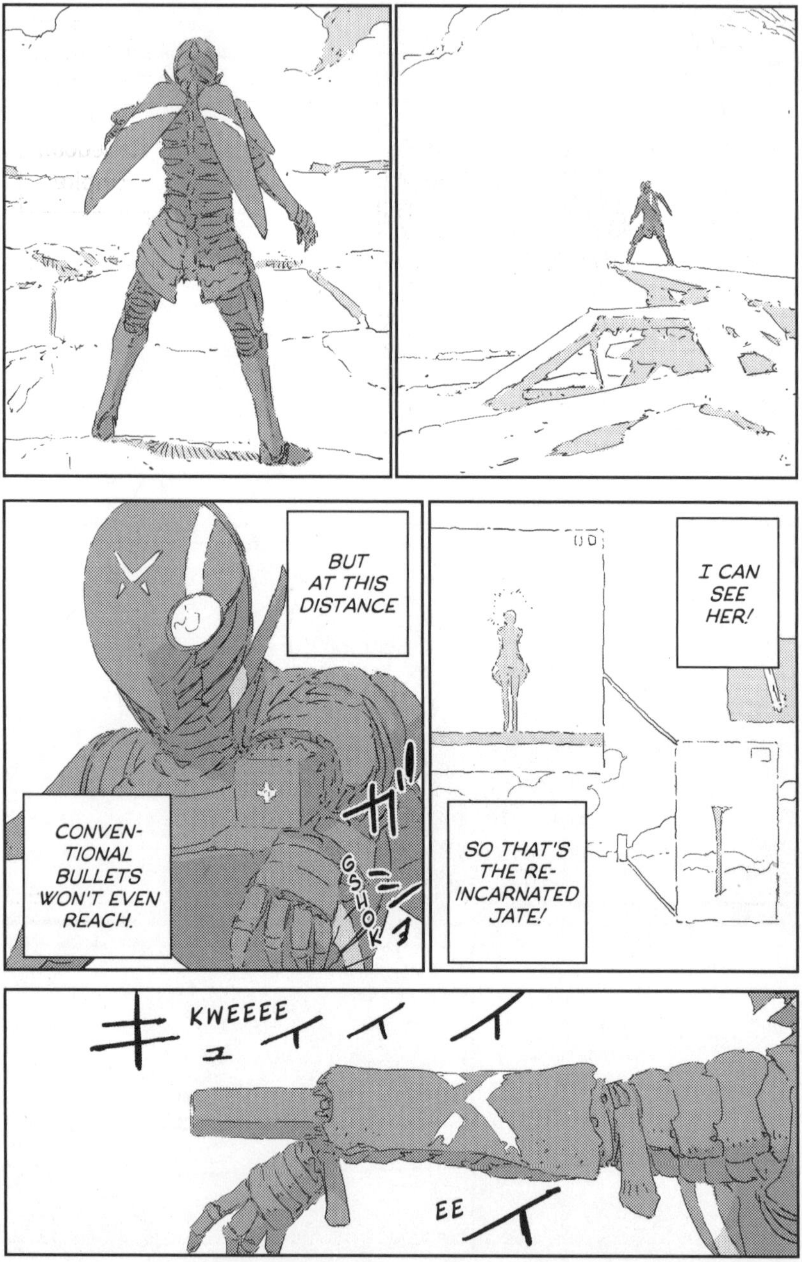
I CAN SEE HER!
SO THAT'S THE RE-INCARNATED JATE!
BUT AT THIS DISTANCE
CONVEN-TIONAL BULLETS WON'T EVEN REACH.
GSHOK
KWEEEE
EE

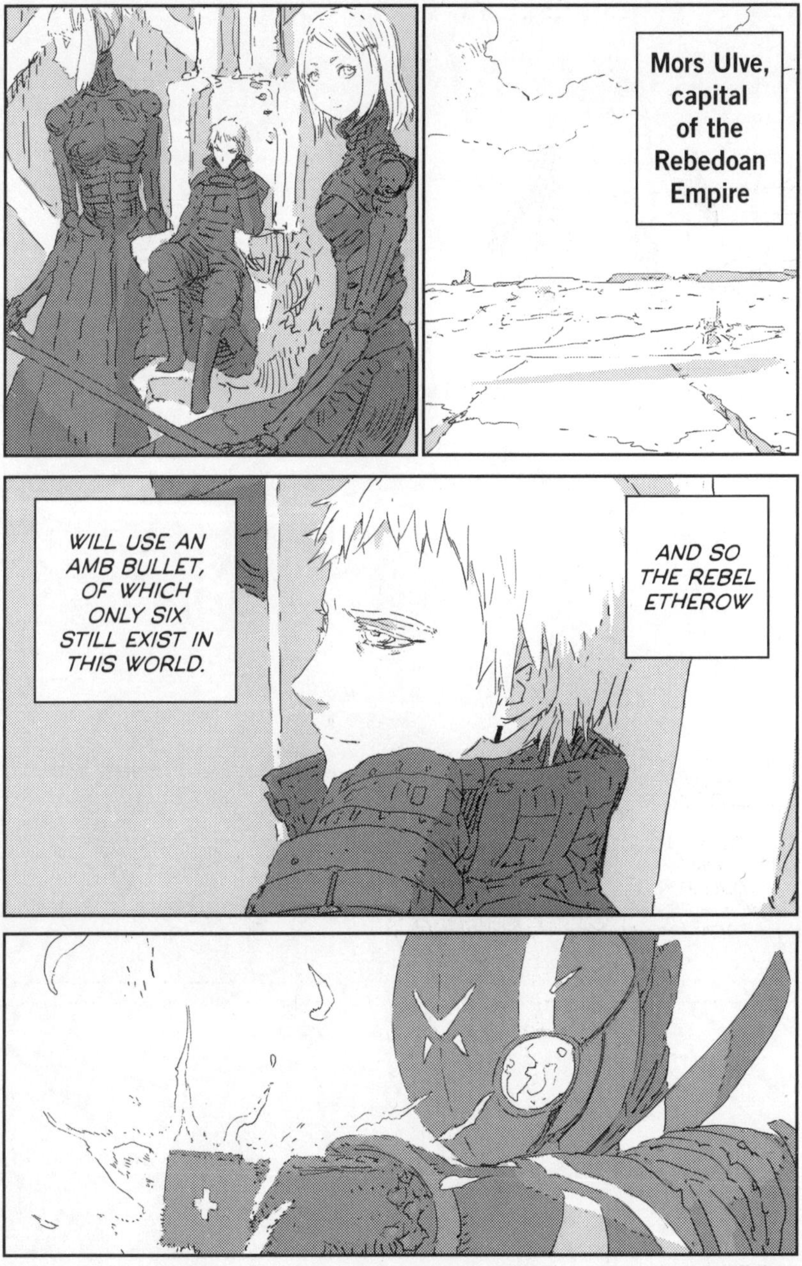
Mors Ulve, capital of the Rebedoan Empire
AND SO THE REBEL ETHEROW
WILL USE AN AMB BULLET, OF WHICH ONLY SIX STILL EXIST IN THIS WORLD.

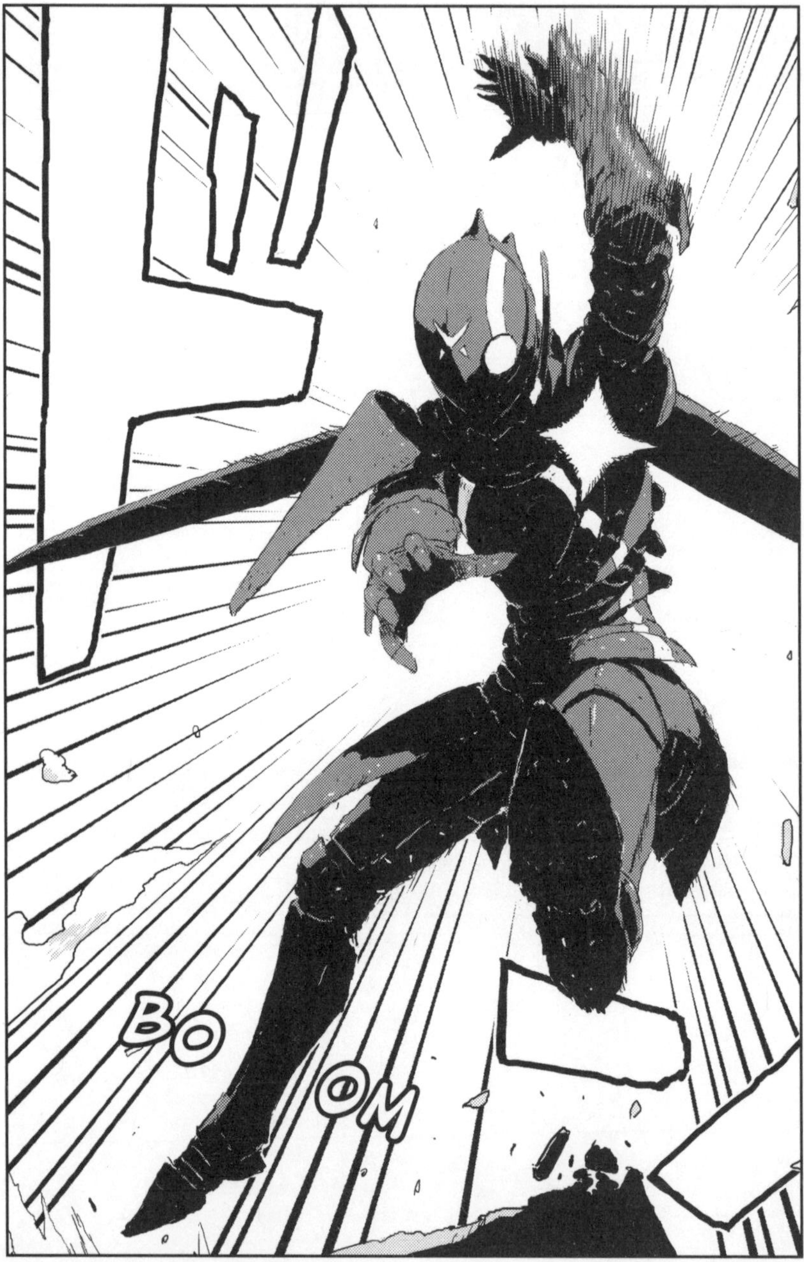
BOOM

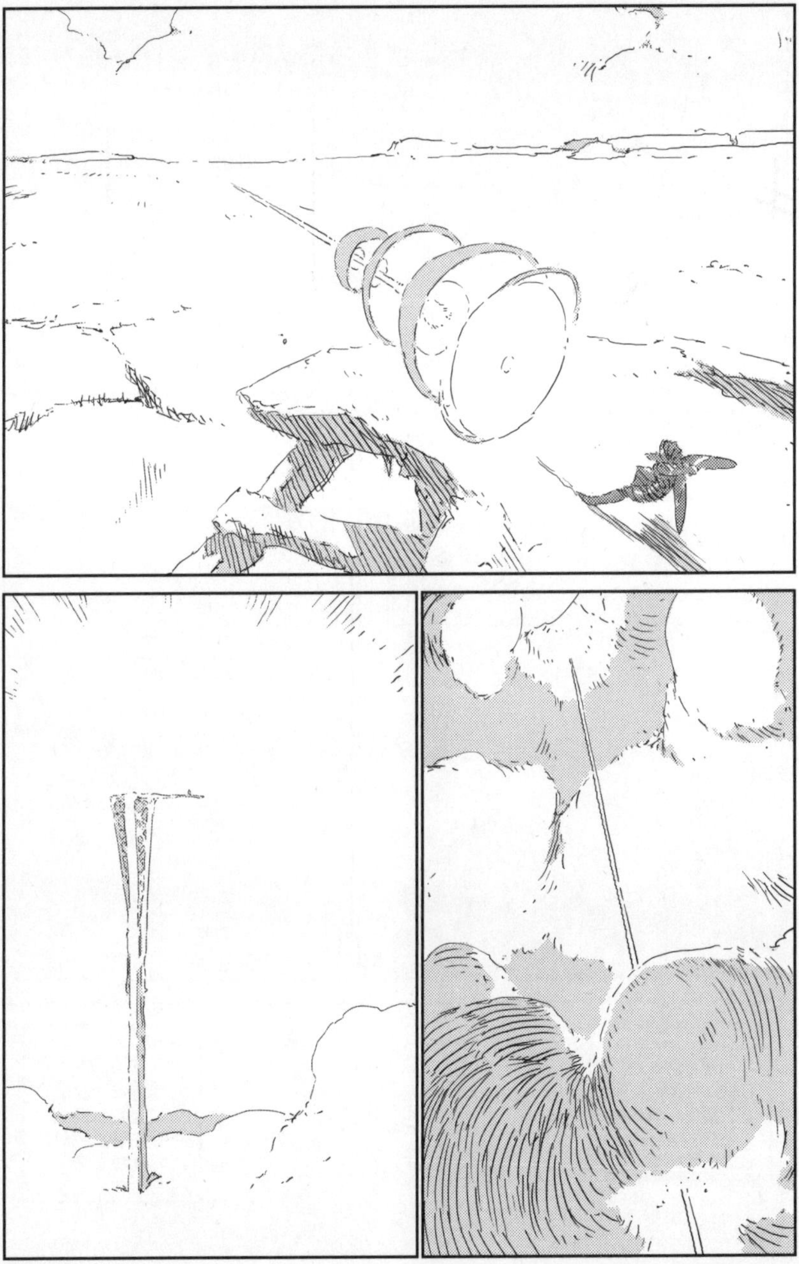

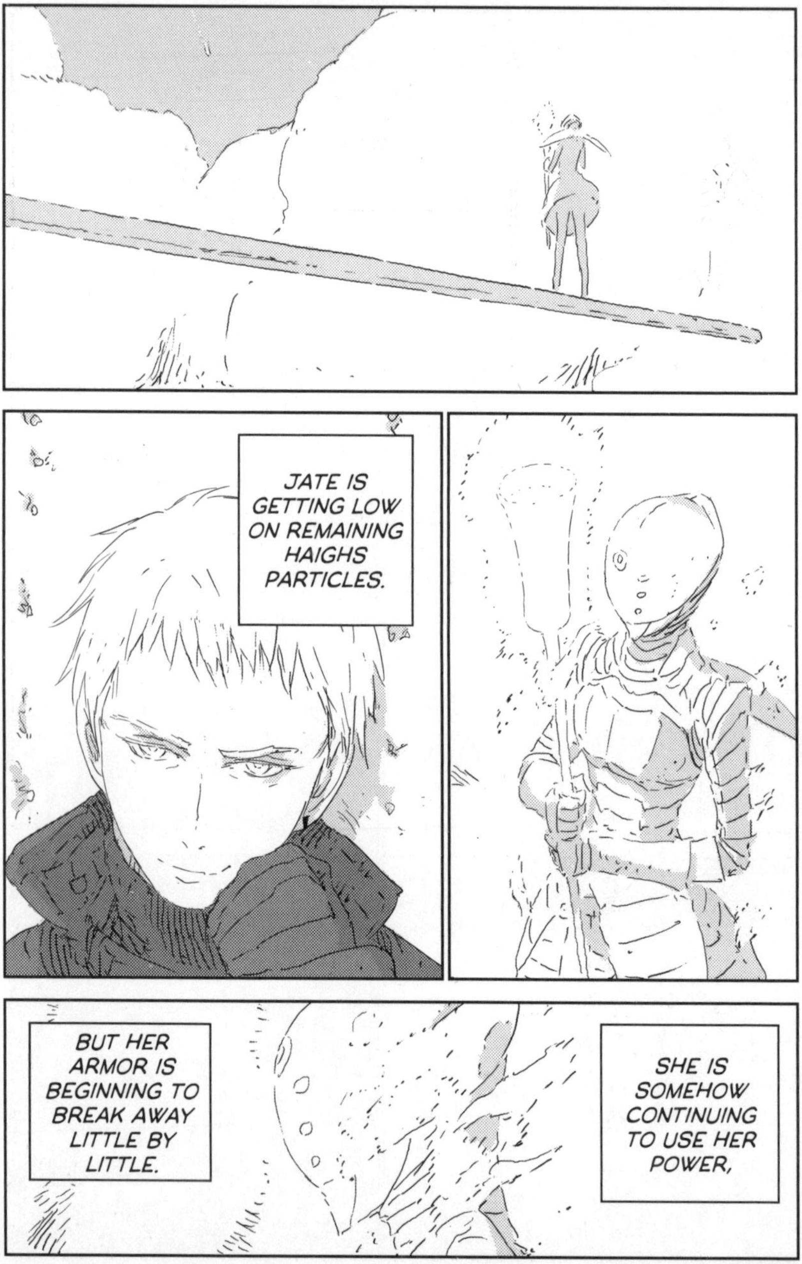
JATE IS GETTING LOW ON REMAINING HAIGHS PARTICLES.
SHE IS SOMEHOW CONTINUING TO USE HER POWER,
BUT HER ARMOR IS BEGINNING TO BREAK AWAY LITTLE BY LITTLE.

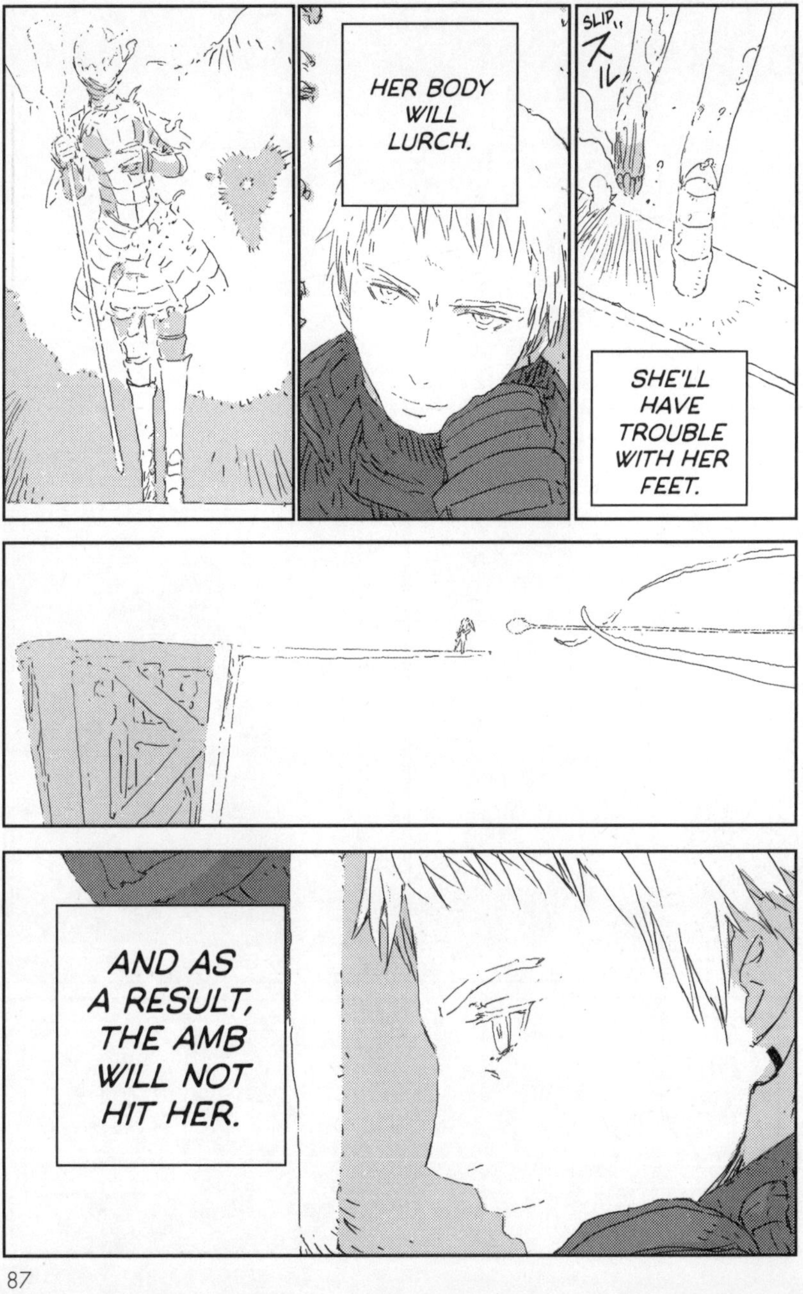
SLIP
スル
SHE'LL HAVE TROUBLE WITH HER FEET.
HER BODY WILL LURCH.
AND AS A RESULT, THE AMB WILL NOT HIT HER.

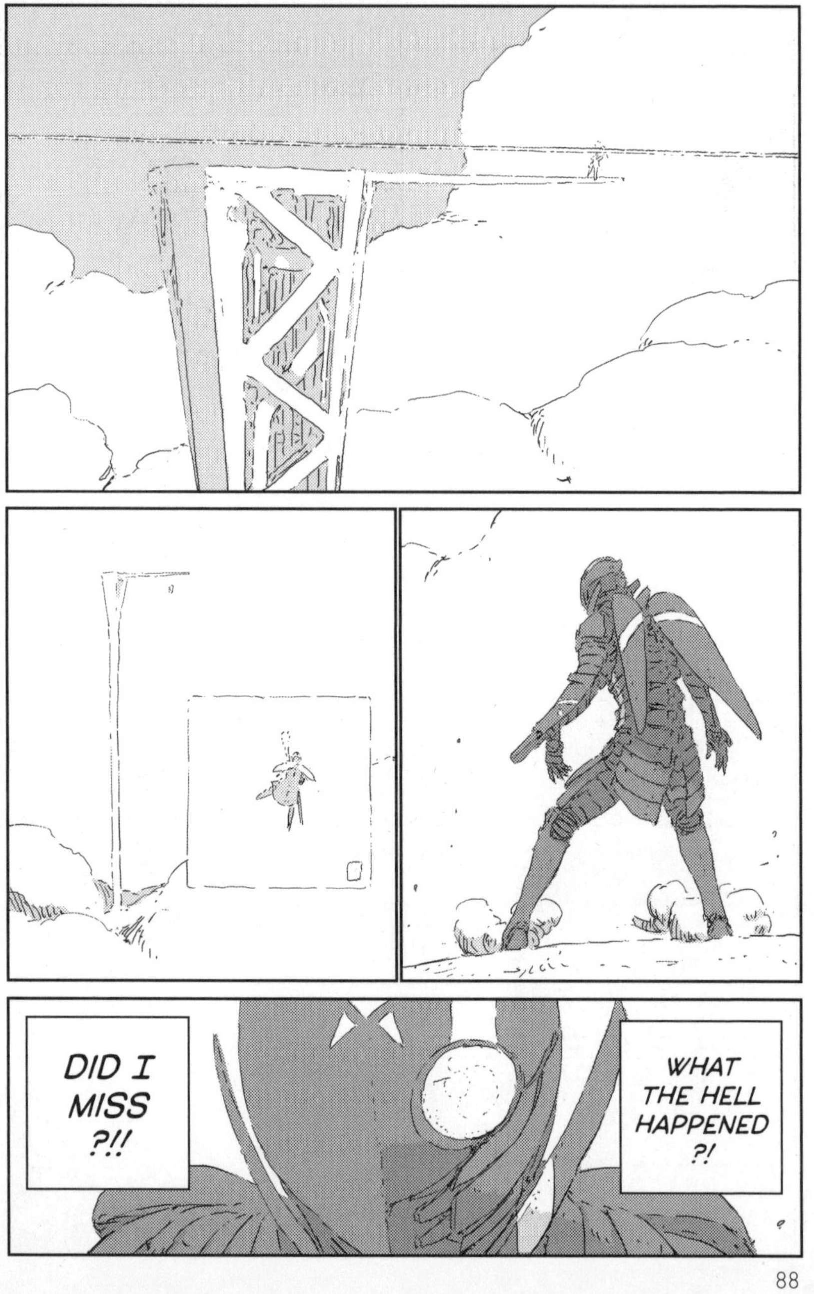
WHAT THE HELL HAPPENED ?!
DID I MISS ?!!

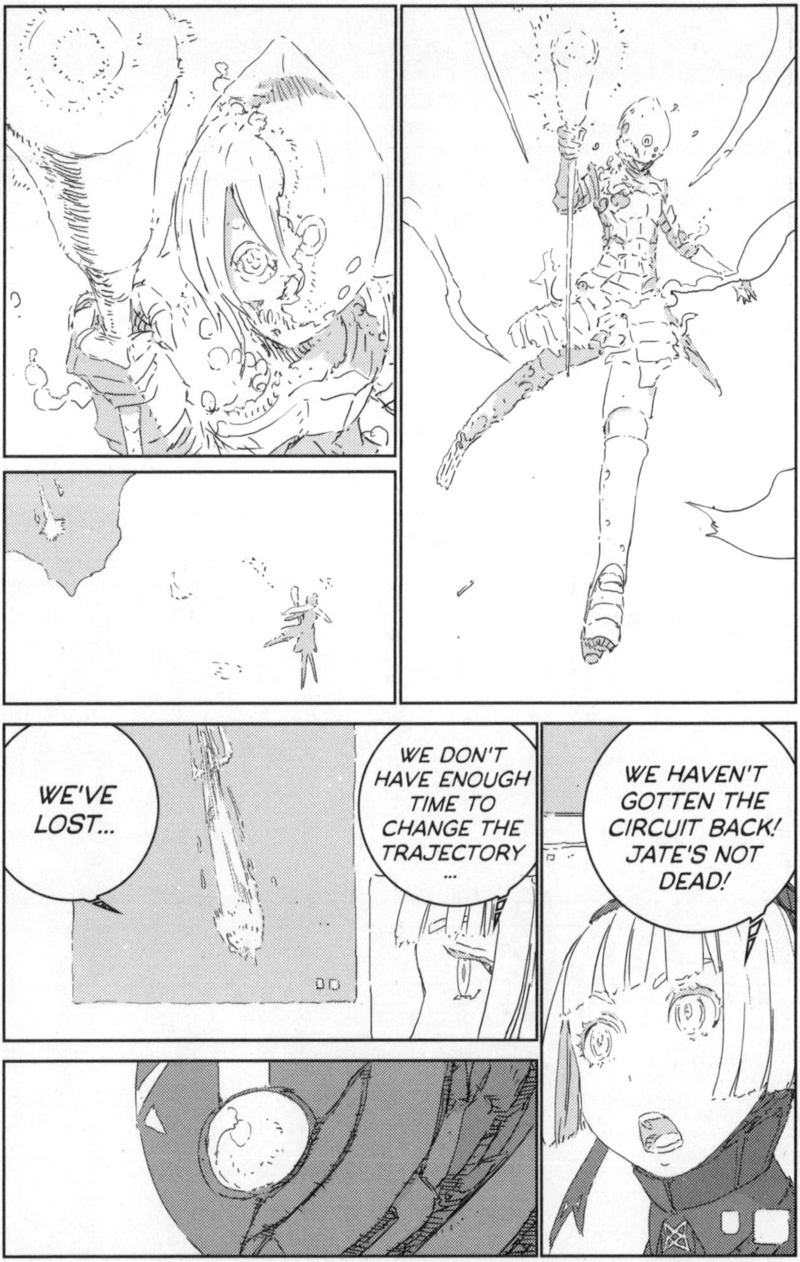
WE HAVEN'T GOTTEN THE CIRCUIT BACK! JATE'S NOT DEAD!
WE DON'T HAVE ENOUGH TIME TO CHANGE THE TRAJECTORY ...
WE'VE LOST...

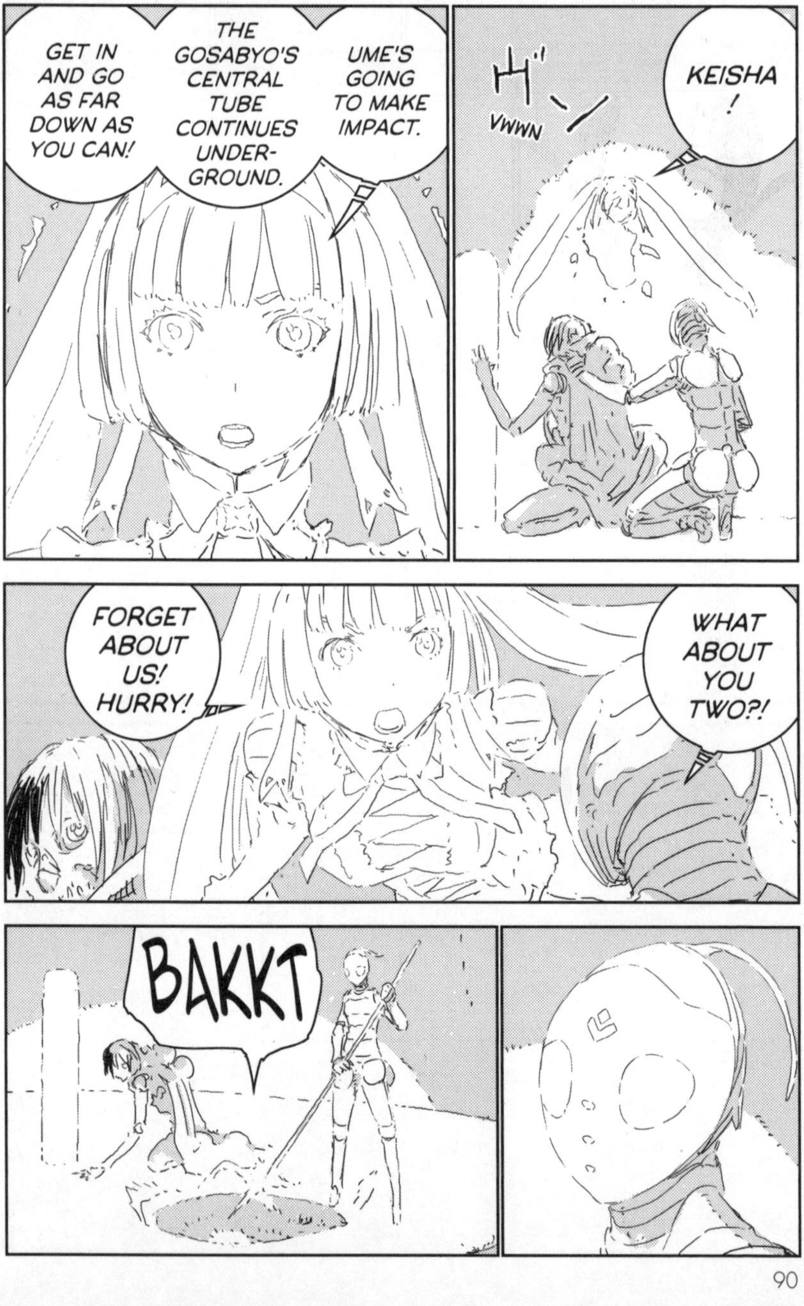

VWWN
KEISHA!
UME'S GOING TO MAKE IMPACT.
THE GOSABYO'S CENTRAL TUBE CONTINUES UNDER-GROUND.
GET IN AND GO AS FAR DOWN AS YOU CAN!
WHAT ABOUT YOU TWO?!
FORGET ABOUT US! HURRY!
BAKKT

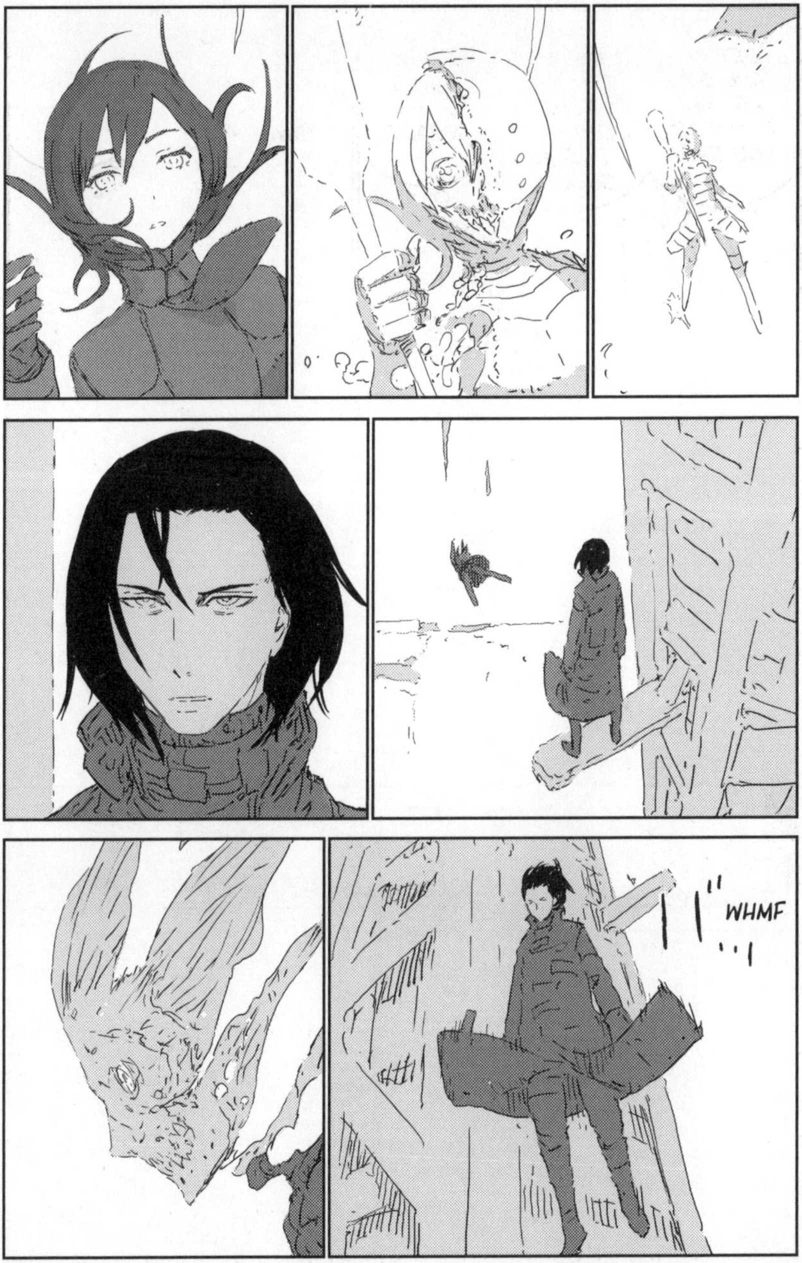
WHMF

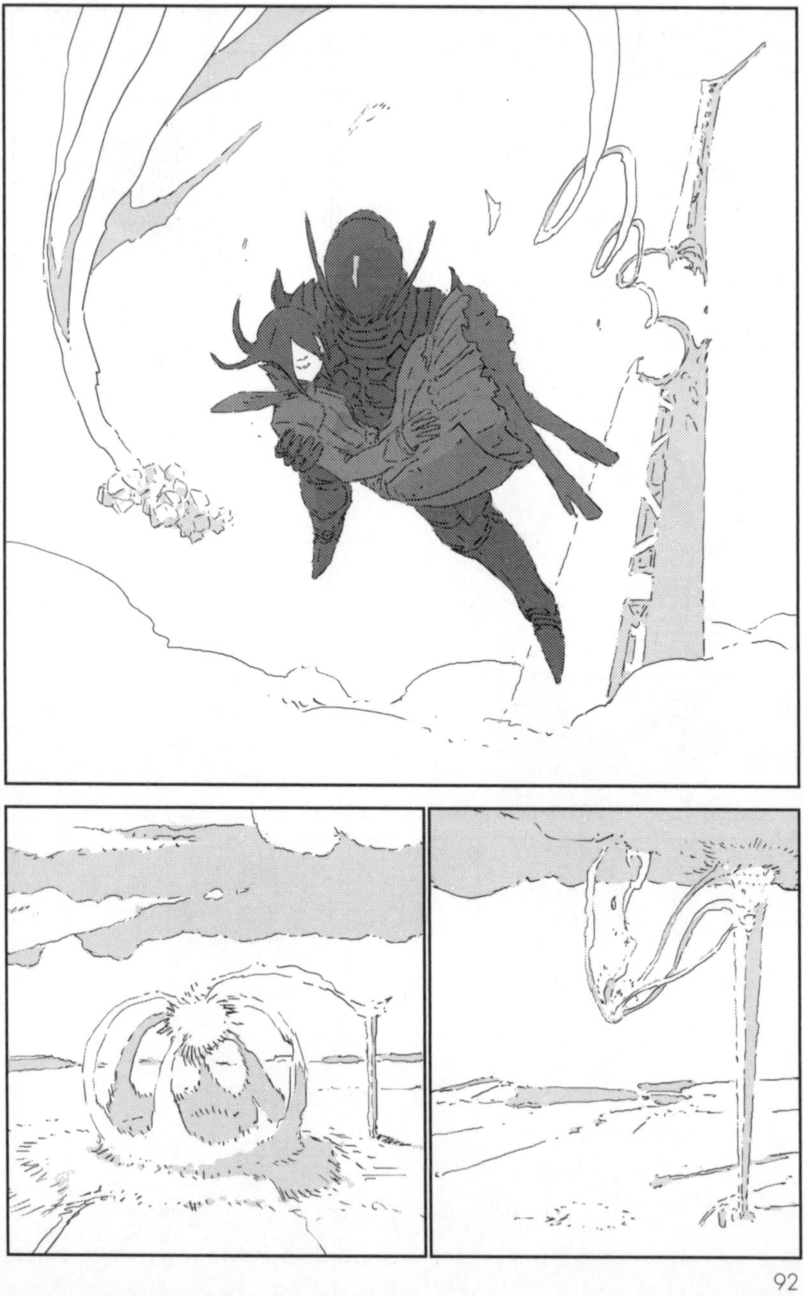

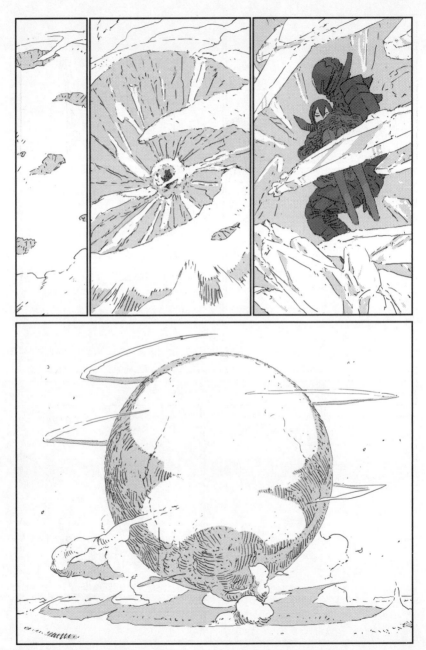

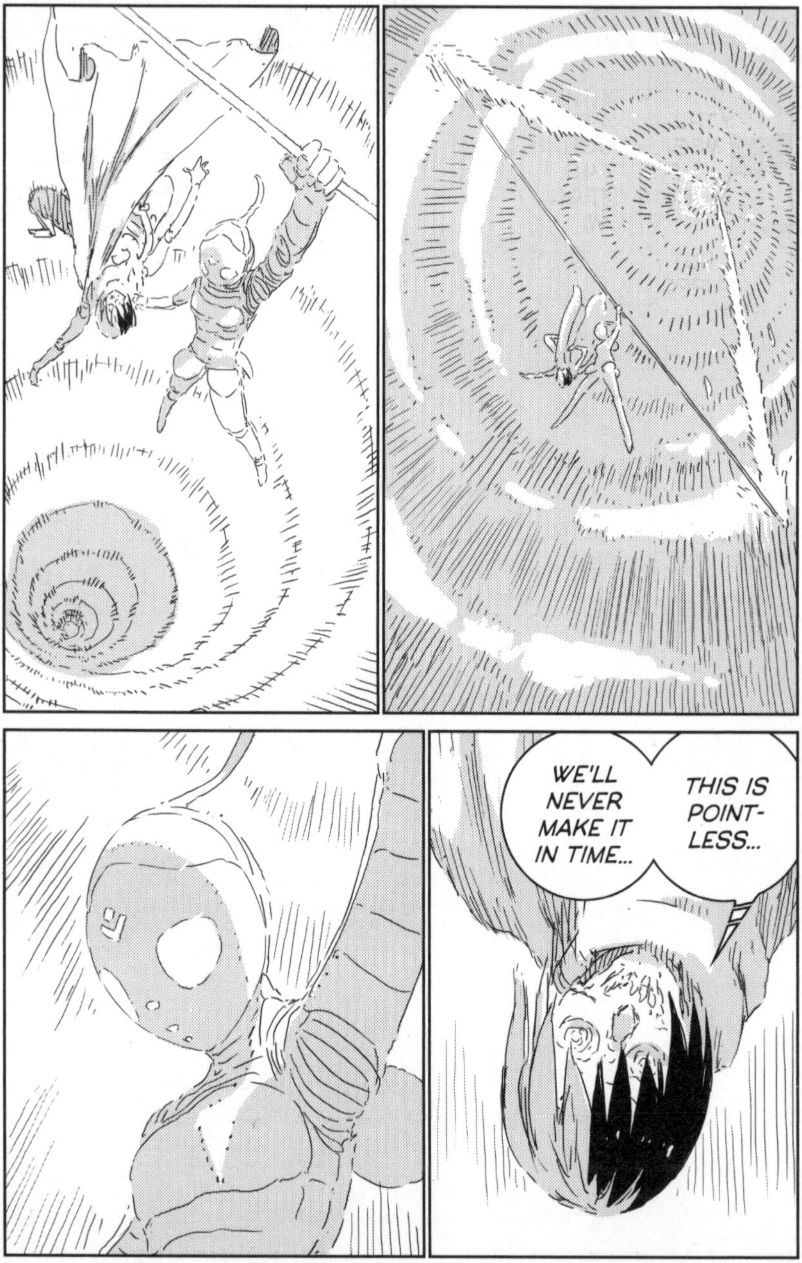
THIS IS POINT-LESS...
WE'LL NEVER MAKE IT IN TIME...

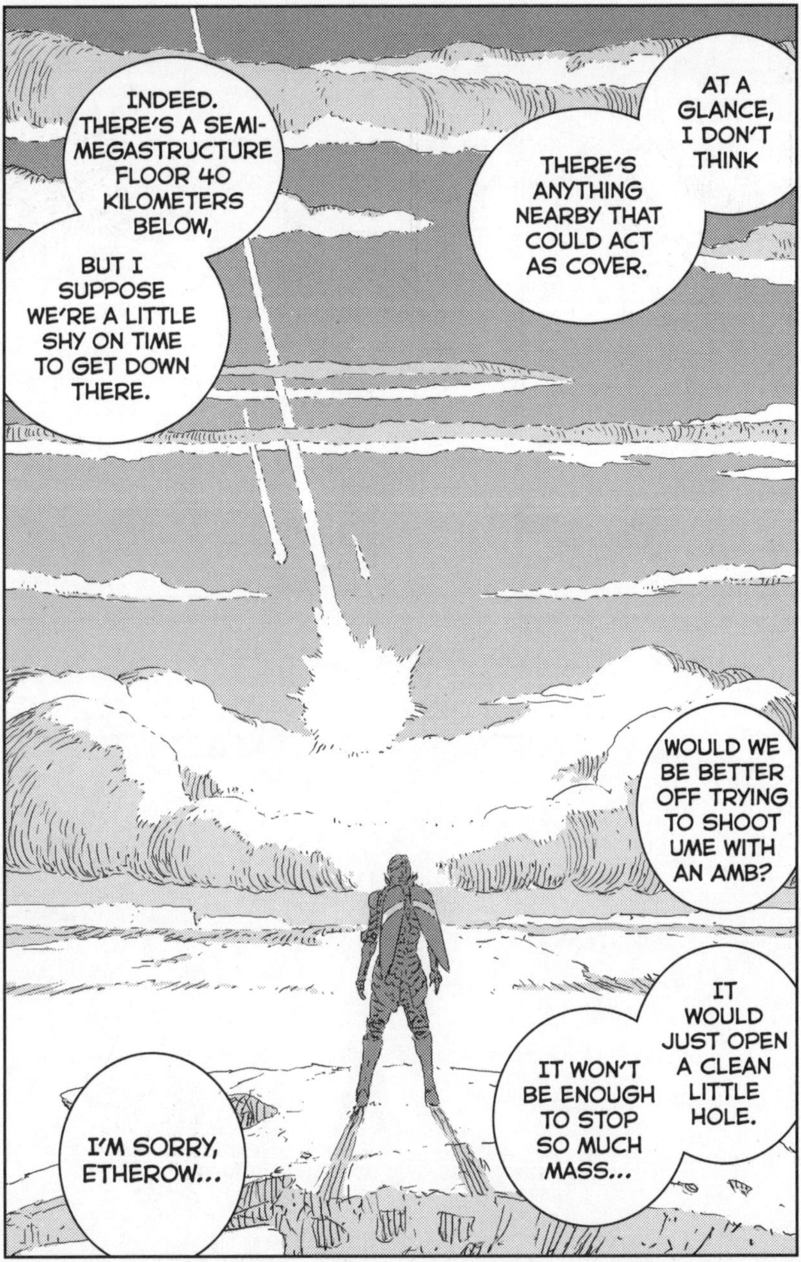
AT A GLANCE, I DON'T THINK
THERE'S ANYTHING NEARBY THAT COULD ACT AS COVER.
INDEED. THERE'S A SEMI-MEGASTRUCTURE FLOOR 40 KILOMETERS BELOW,
BUT I SUPPOSE WE'RE A LITTLE SHY ON TIME TO GET DOWN THERE.
WOULD WE BE BETTER OFF TRYING TO SHOOT UME WITH AN AMB?
IT WOULD JUST OPEN A CLEAN LITTLE HOLE.
IT WON'T BE ENOUGH TO STOP SO MUCH MASS...
I'M SORRY, ETHEROW...

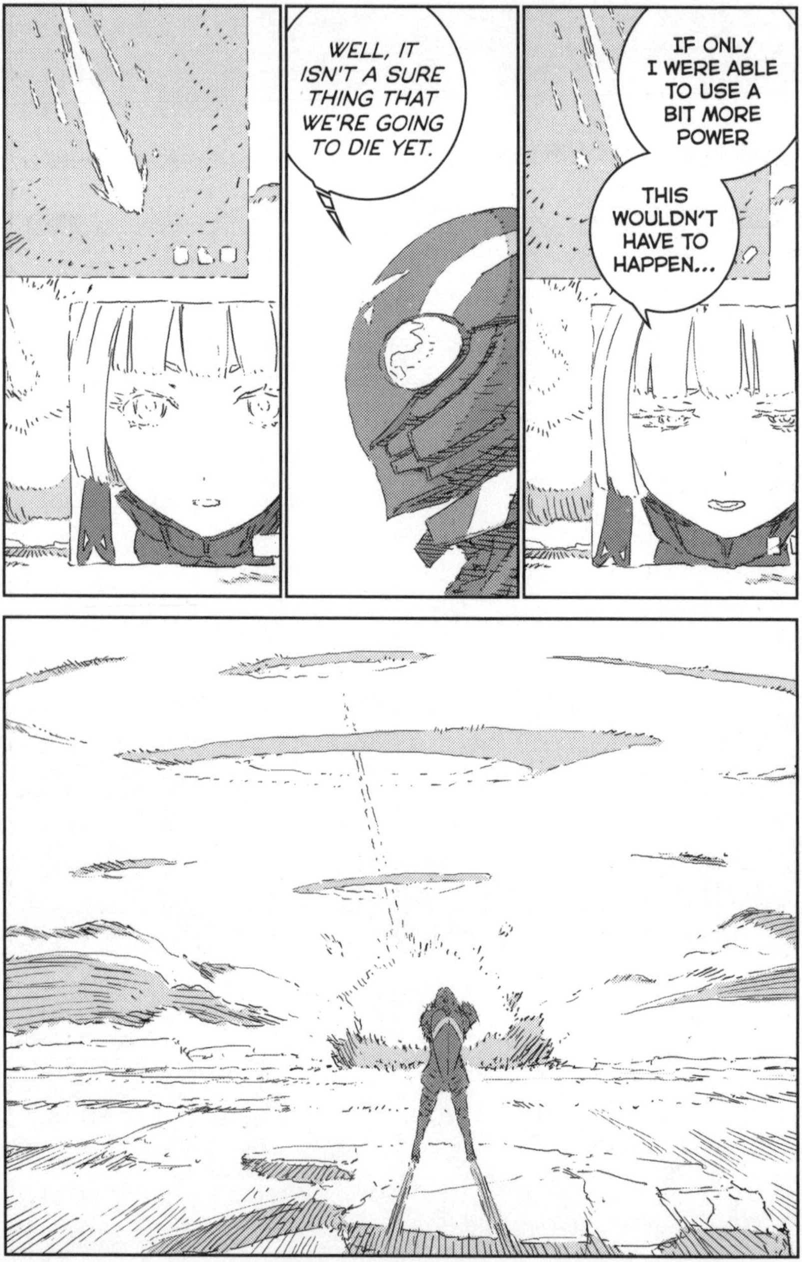
IF ONLY I WERE ABLE TO USE A BIT MORE POWER
THIS WOULDN'T HAVE TO HAPPEN...
WELL, IT ISN'T A SURE THING THAT WE'RE GOING TO DIE YET.

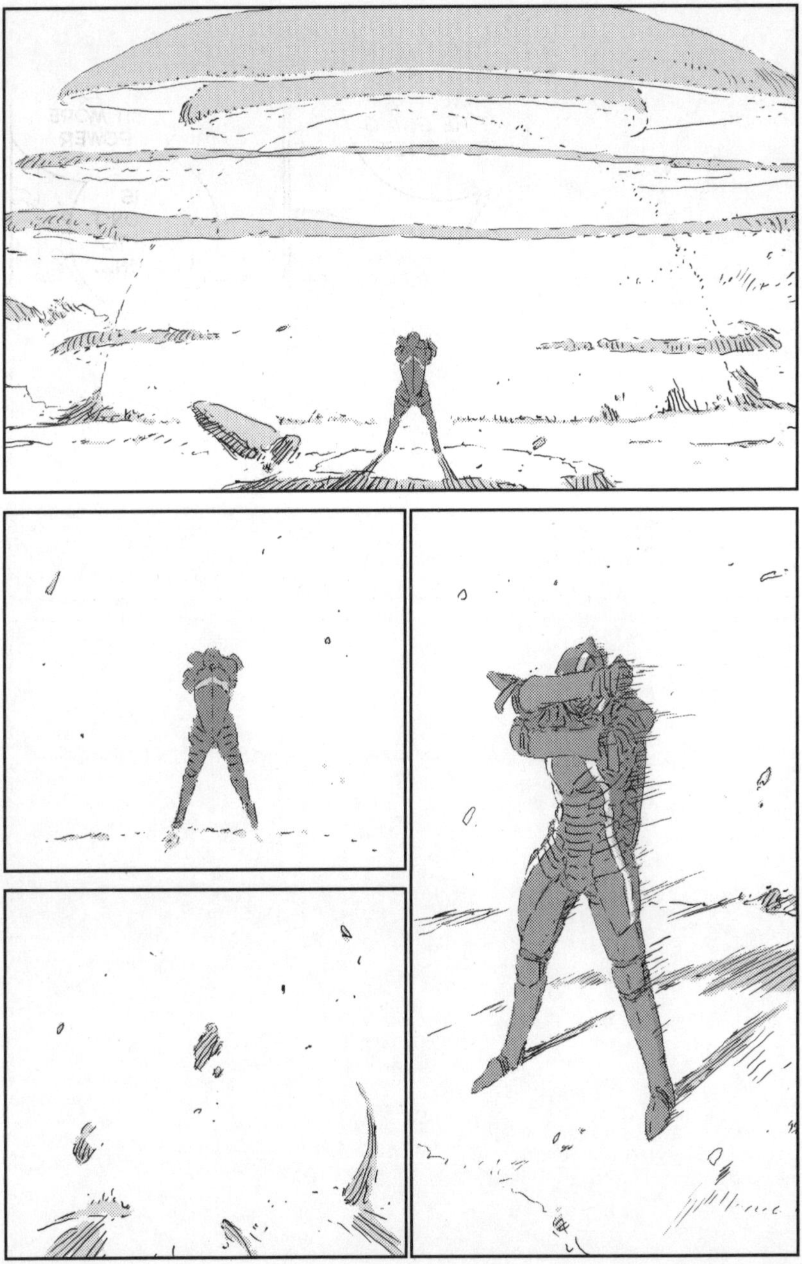

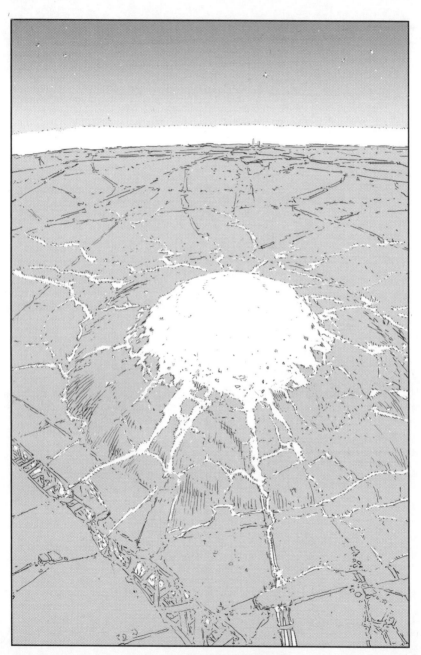

CHAPTER 21 END

APOSIMZ

CHAPTER 22

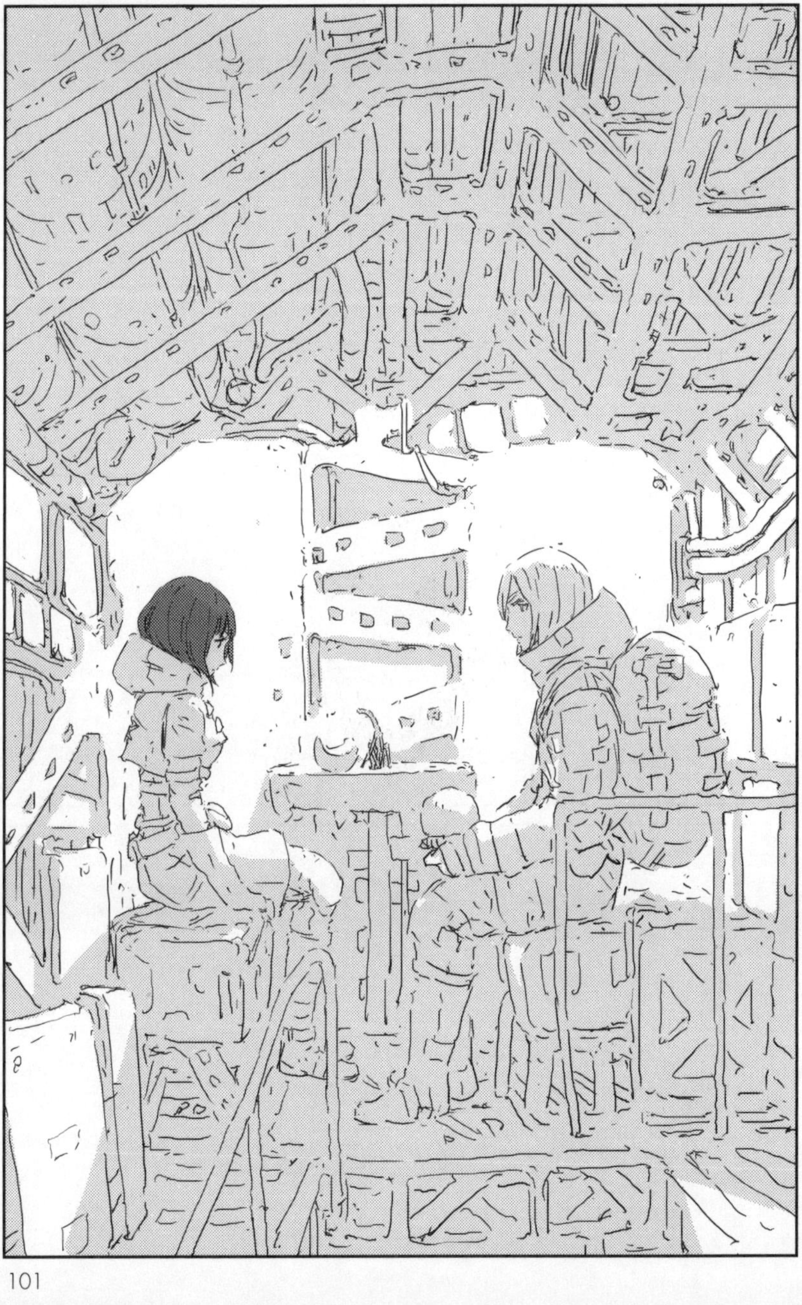

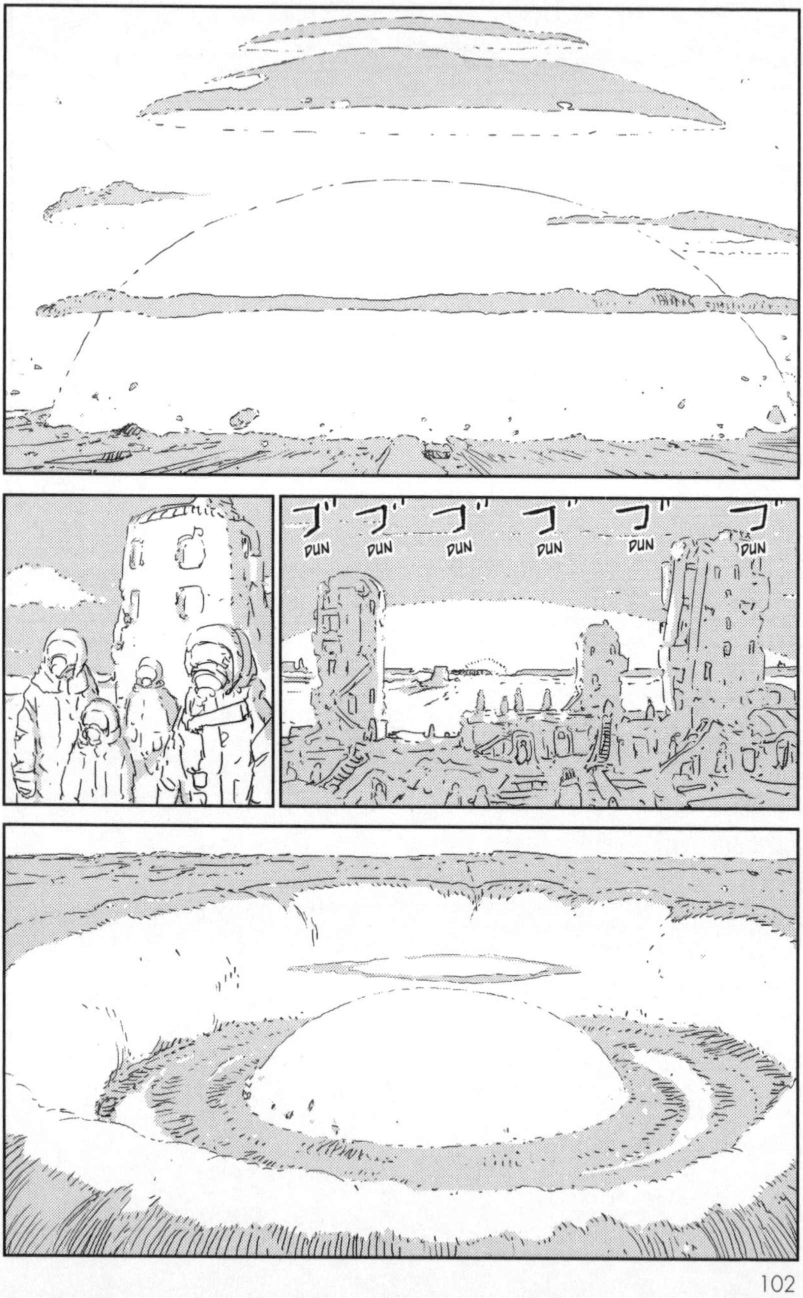
ゴ DUN
ゴ DUN
ゴ DUN
ゴ DUN
ゴ DUN
ゴ DUN

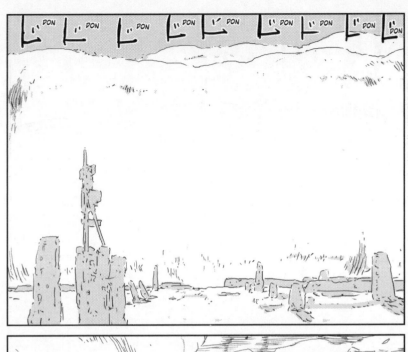

DON DON DON DON DON DON DON DON DON

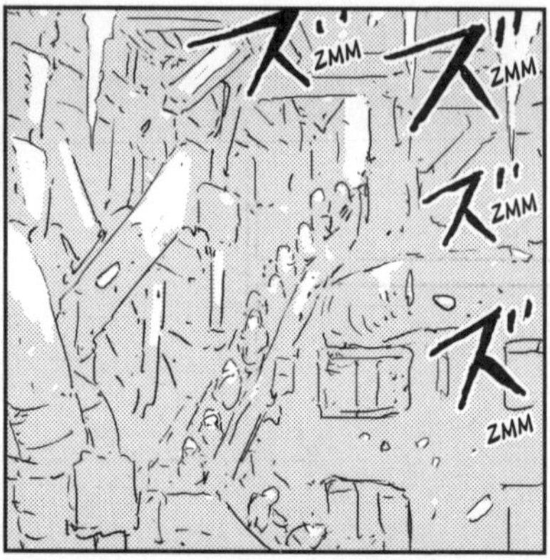
ズ ZMM
ズ ZMM
ズ ZMM
ズ ZMM
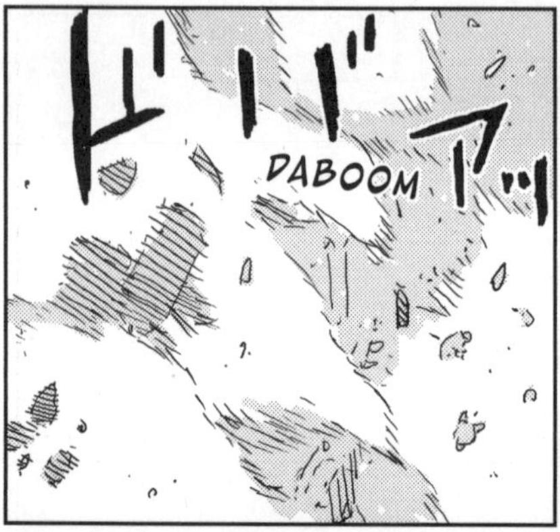
DABOOM
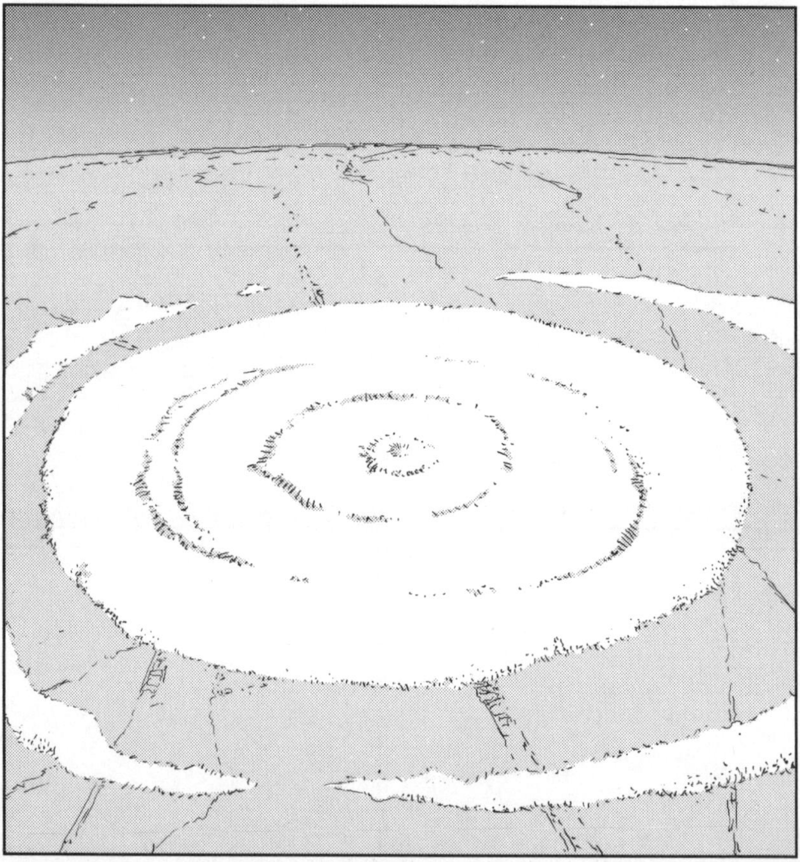

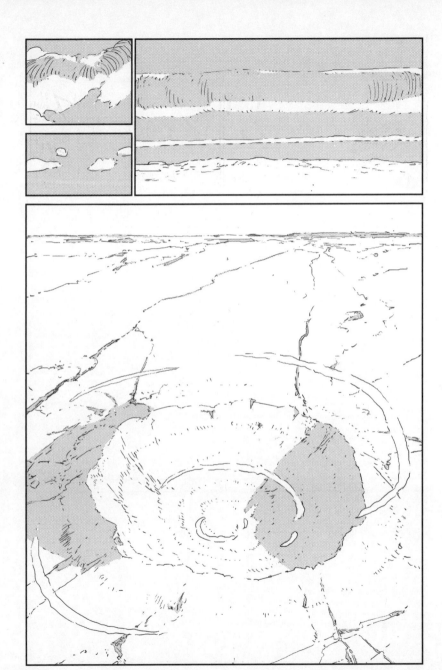

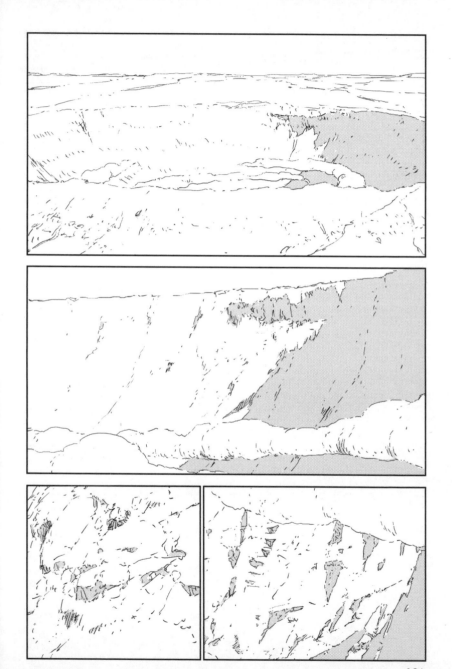

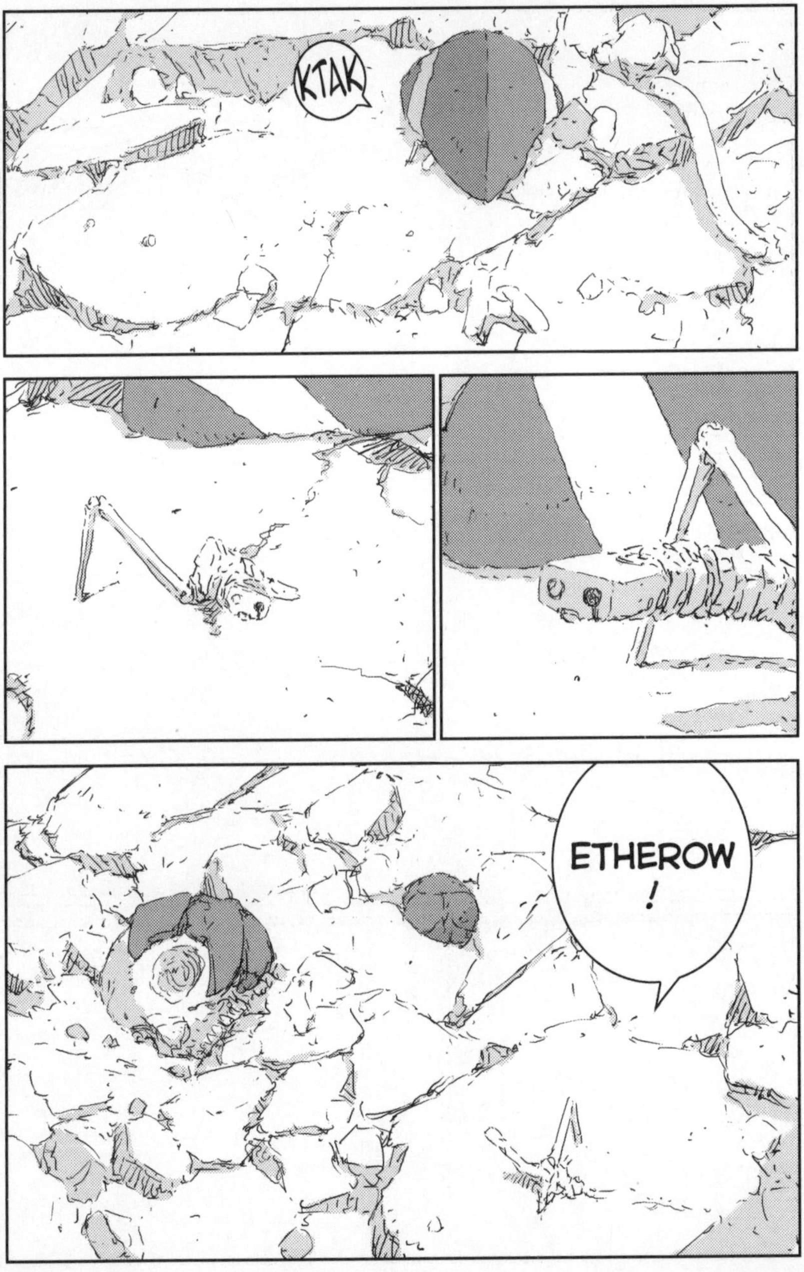
KTAK
ETHEROW
!

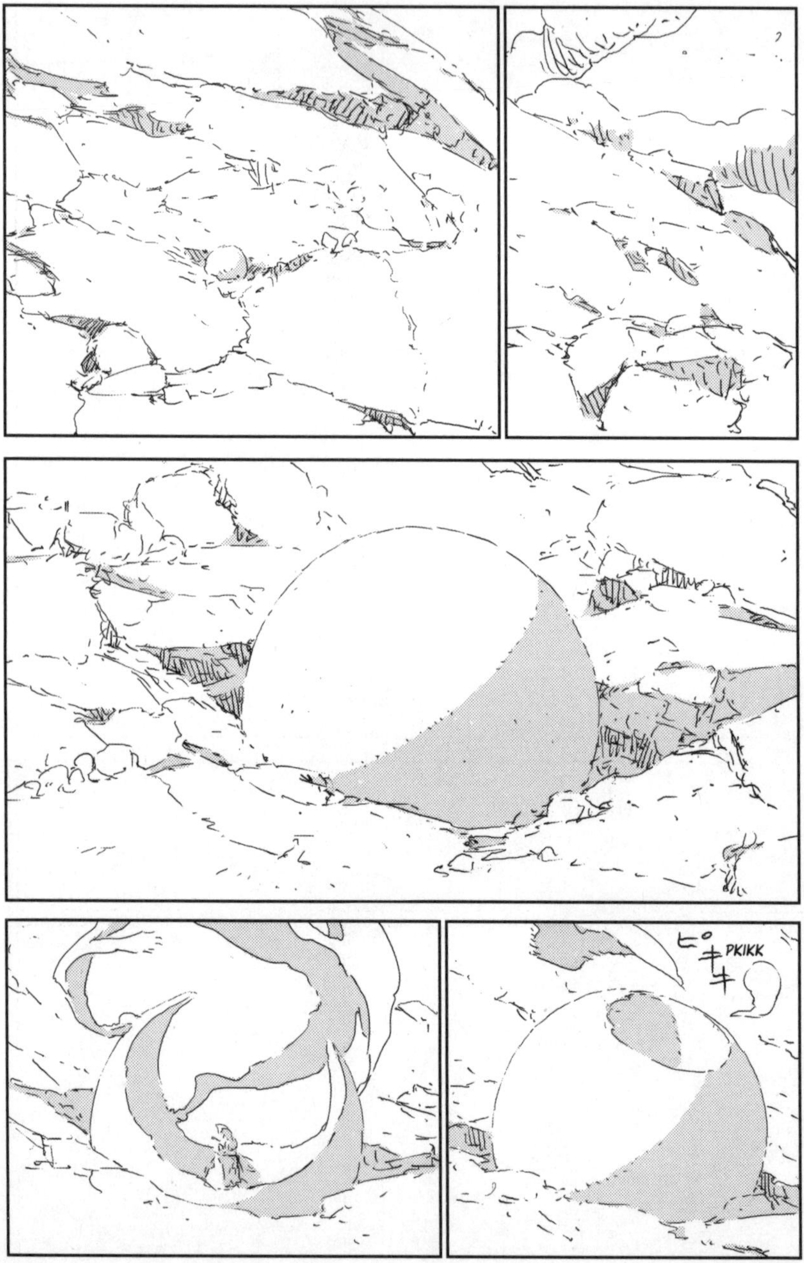
ピキキ PKIKK

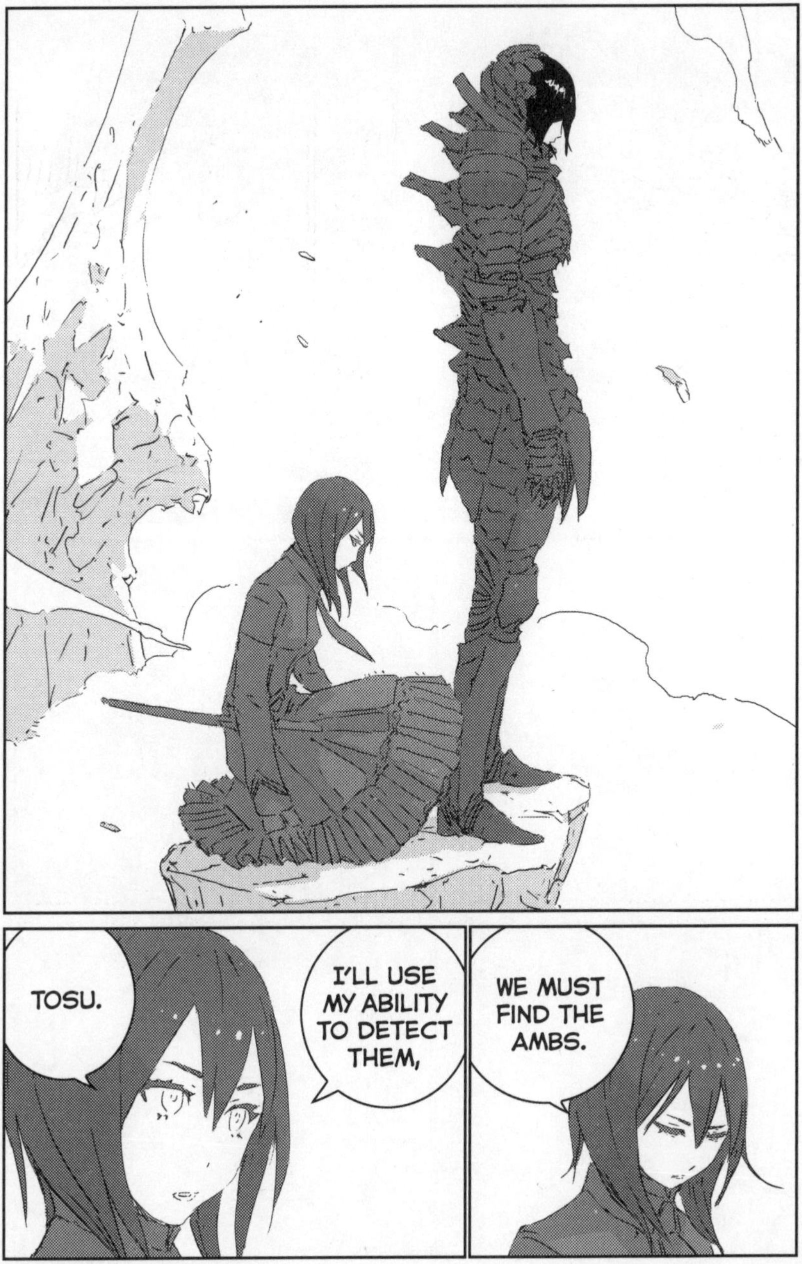
WE MUST FIND THE AMBS.
I'LL USE MY ABILITY TO DETECT THEM,
TOSU.

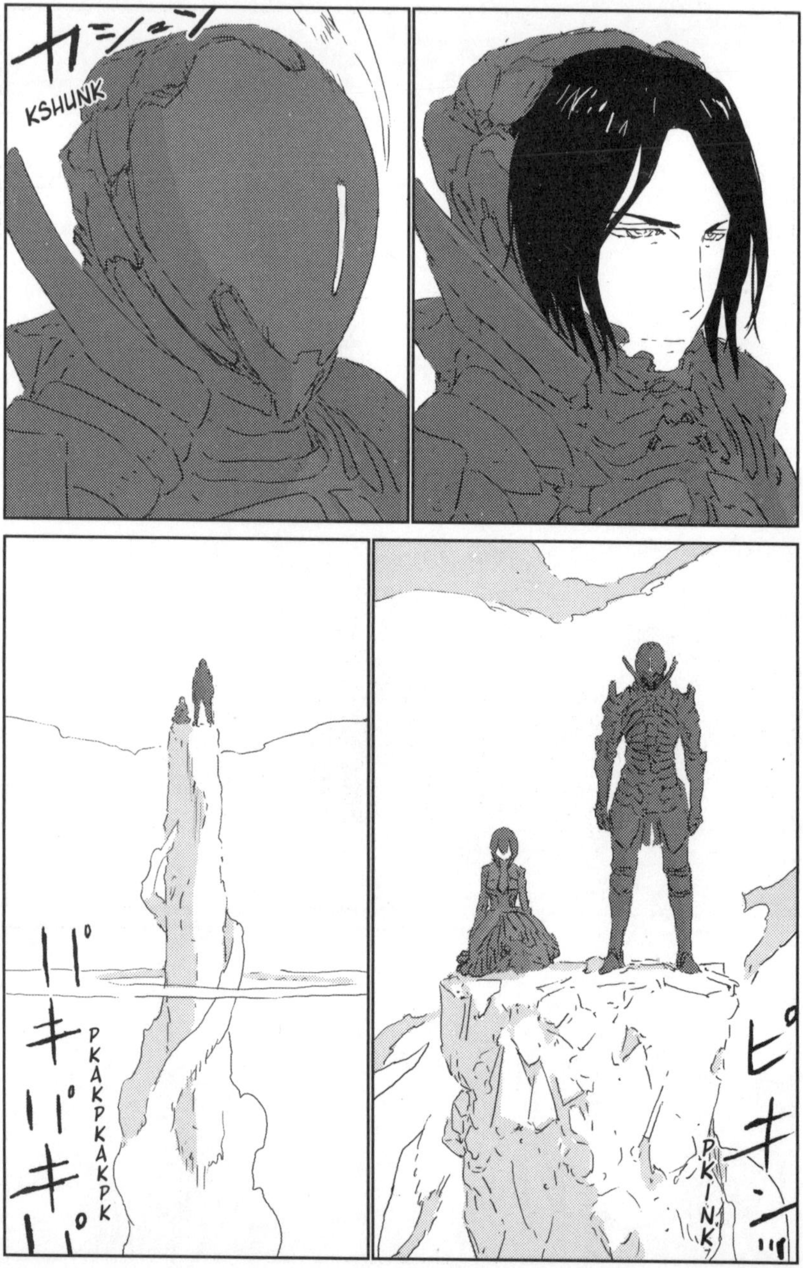
カシュン
KSHUNK
ピキーン…
PKINK
パキパキ
PKAKPKAKPK

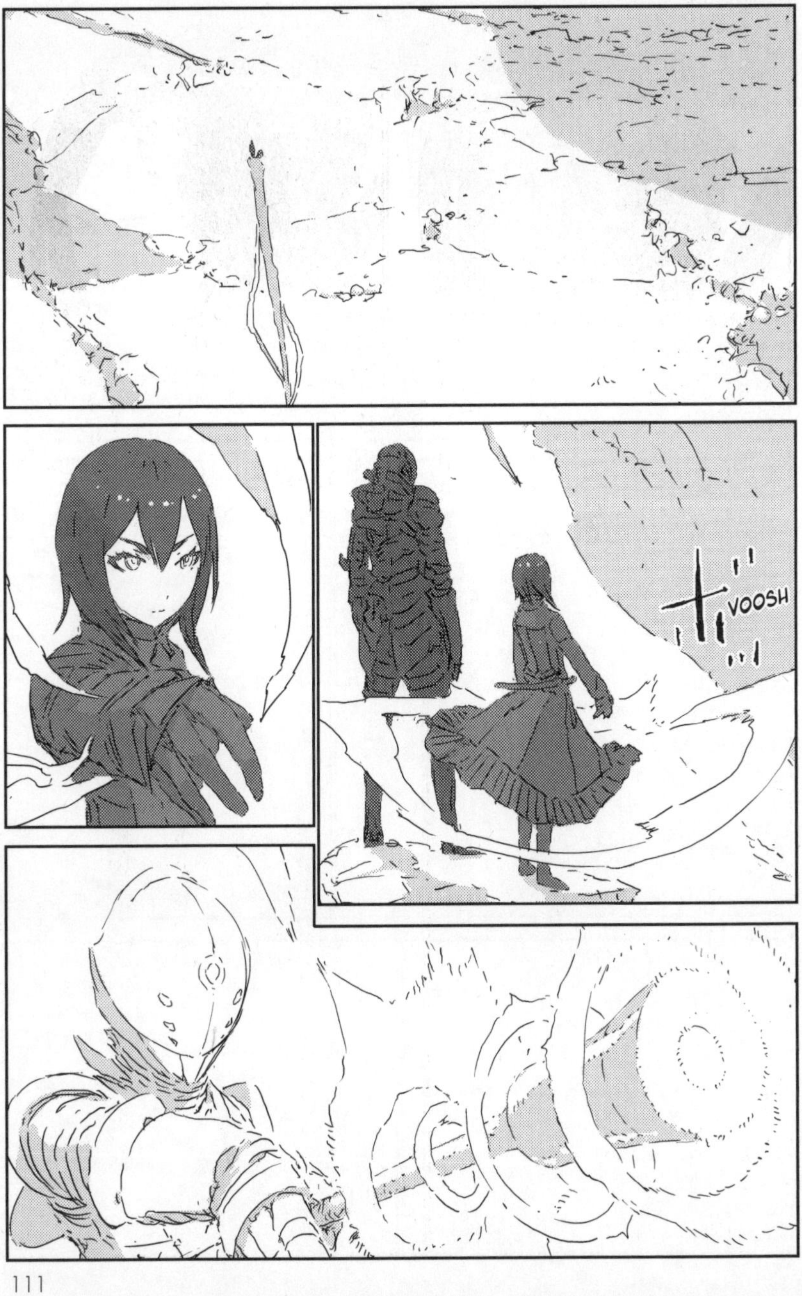
VOOSH

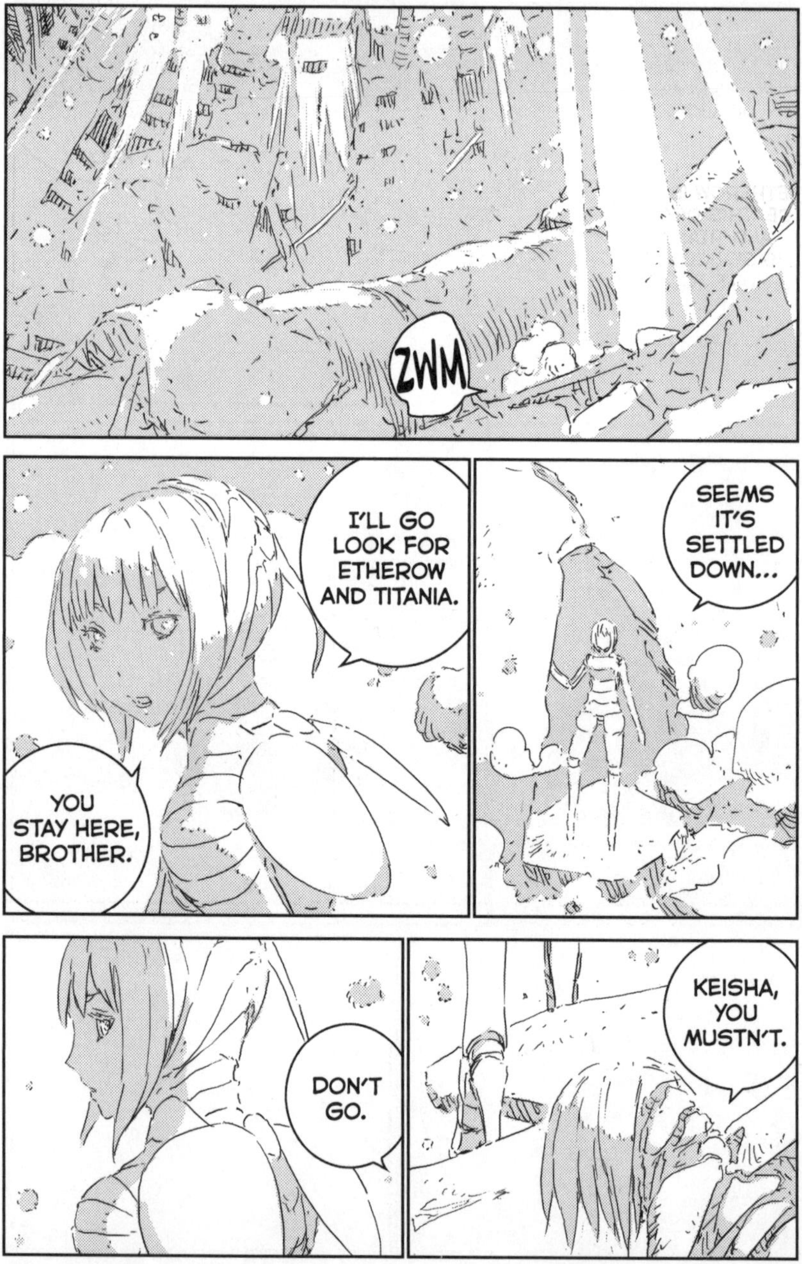
ZWM
SEEMS IT'S SETTLED DOWN...
I'LL GO LOOK FOR ETHEROW AND TITANIA.
YOU STAY HERE, BROTHER.
KEISHA, YOU MUSTN'T.
DON'T GO.

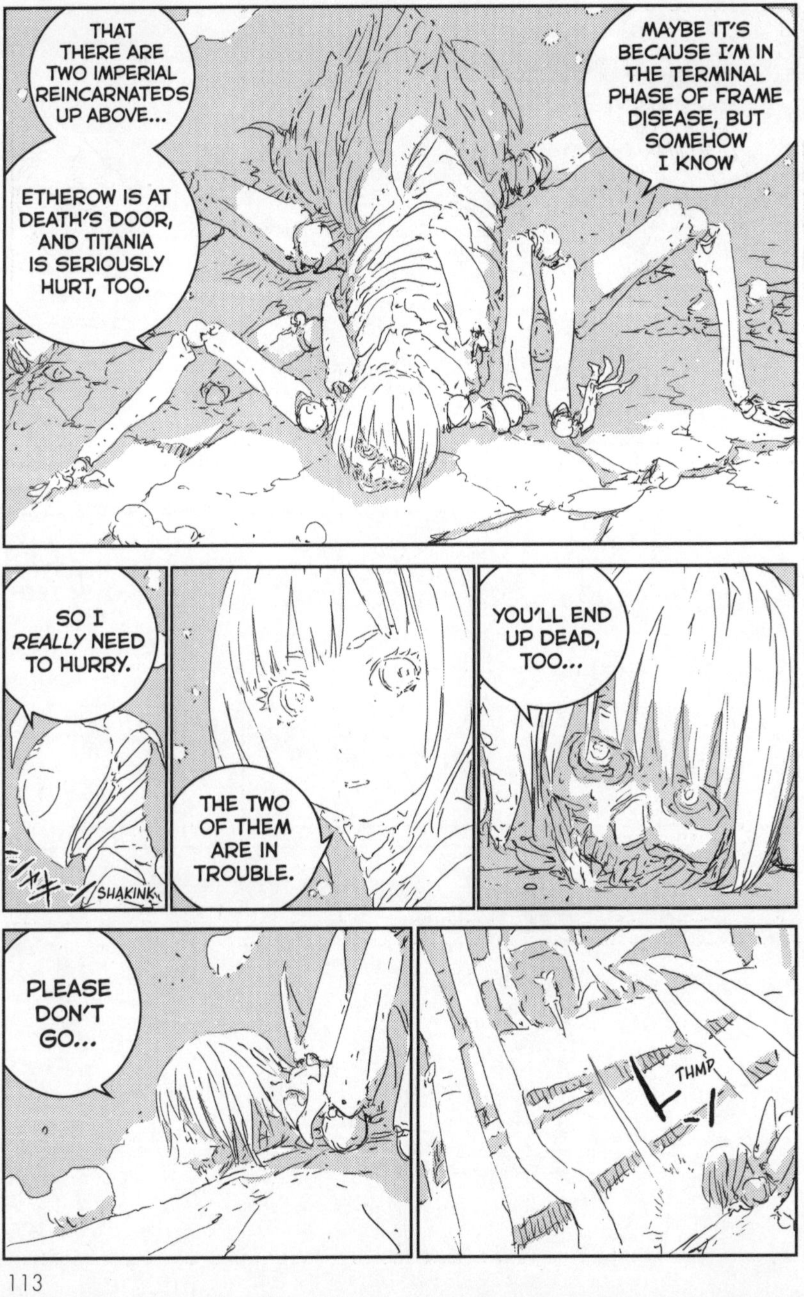
MAYBE IT'S BECAUSE I'M IN THE TERMINAL PHASE OF FRAME DISEASE, BUT SOMEHOW I KNOW
THAT THERE ARE TWO IMPERIAL REINCARNATEDS UP ABOVE...
ETHEROW IS AT DEATH'S DOOR, AND TITANIA IS SERIOUSLY HURT, TOO.
YOU'LL END UP DEAD, TOO...
THE TWO OF THEM ARE IN TROUBLE.
SO I *REALLY* NEED TO HURRY.
SHAKINK
THMP
PLEASE DON'T GO...

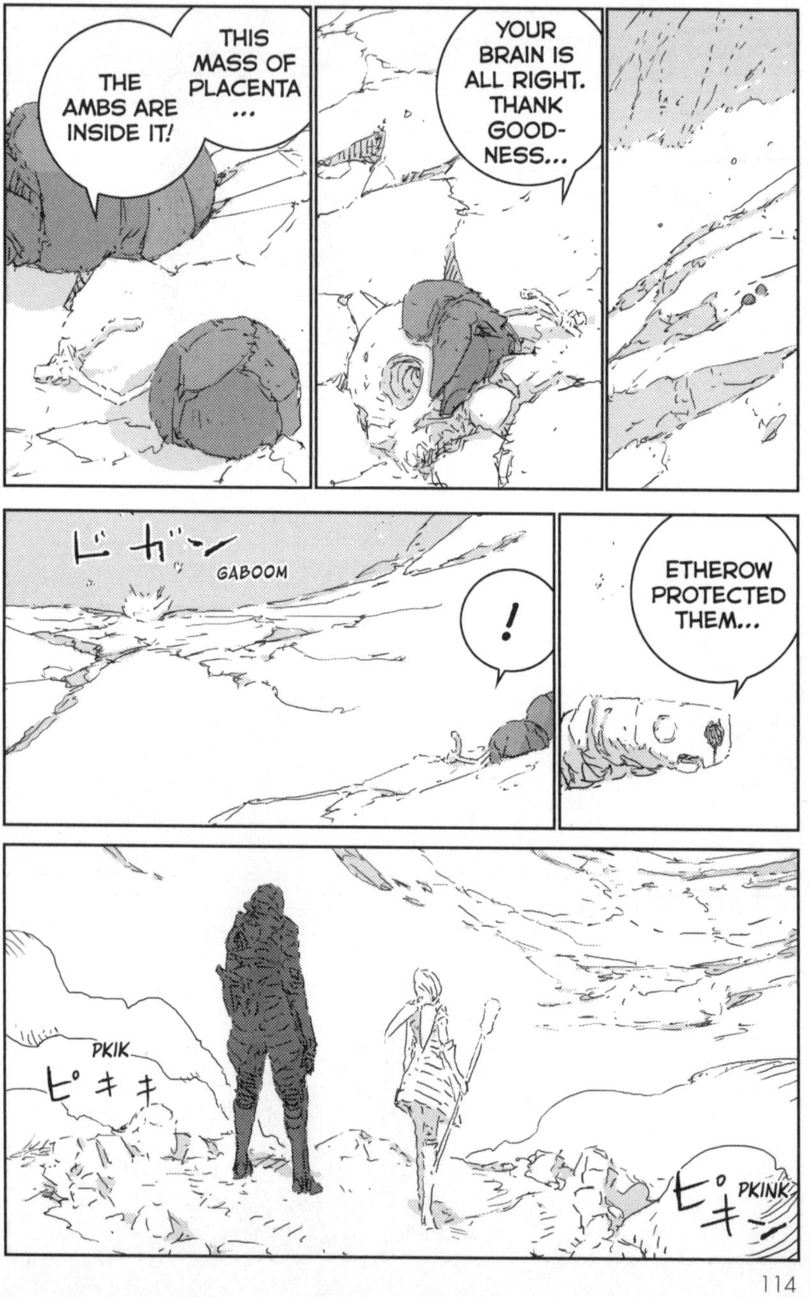
YOUR BRAIN IS ALL RIGHT. THANK GOOD-NESS...
THIS MASS OF PLACENTA ...
THE AMBS ARE INSIDE IT!
ETHEROW PROTECTED THEM...
ドガーン
GABOOM
!
ピキーン
PKINK
PKIK
ピキキ

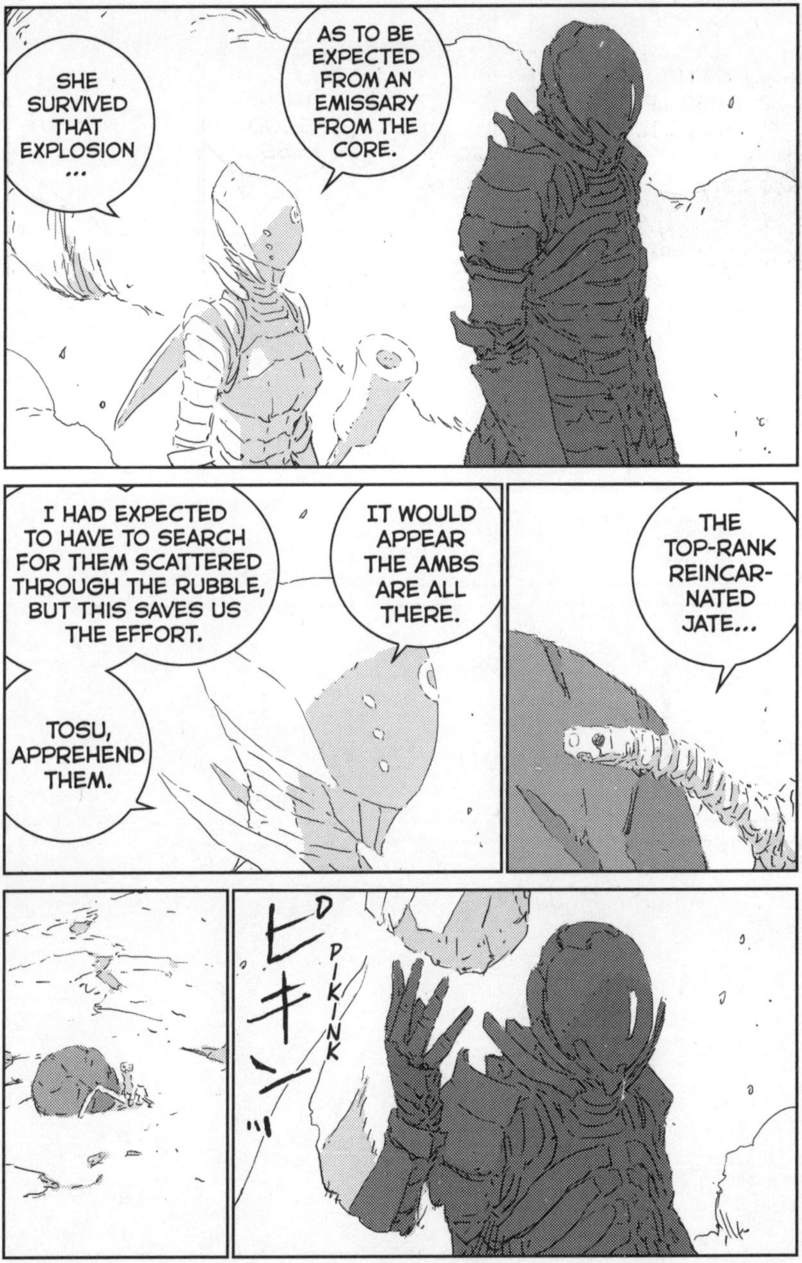
AS TO BE EXPECTED FROM AN EMISSARY FROM THE CORE.
SHE SURVIVED THAT EXPLOSION ...
THE TOP-RANK REINCAR-NATED JATE...
IT WOULD APPEAR THE AMBS ARE ALL THERE.
I HAD EXPECTED TO HAVE TO SEARCH FOR THEM SCATTERED THROUGH THE RUBBLE, BUT THIS SAVES US THE EFFORT.
TOSU, APPREHEND THEM.
ピキンッ
PIKINK

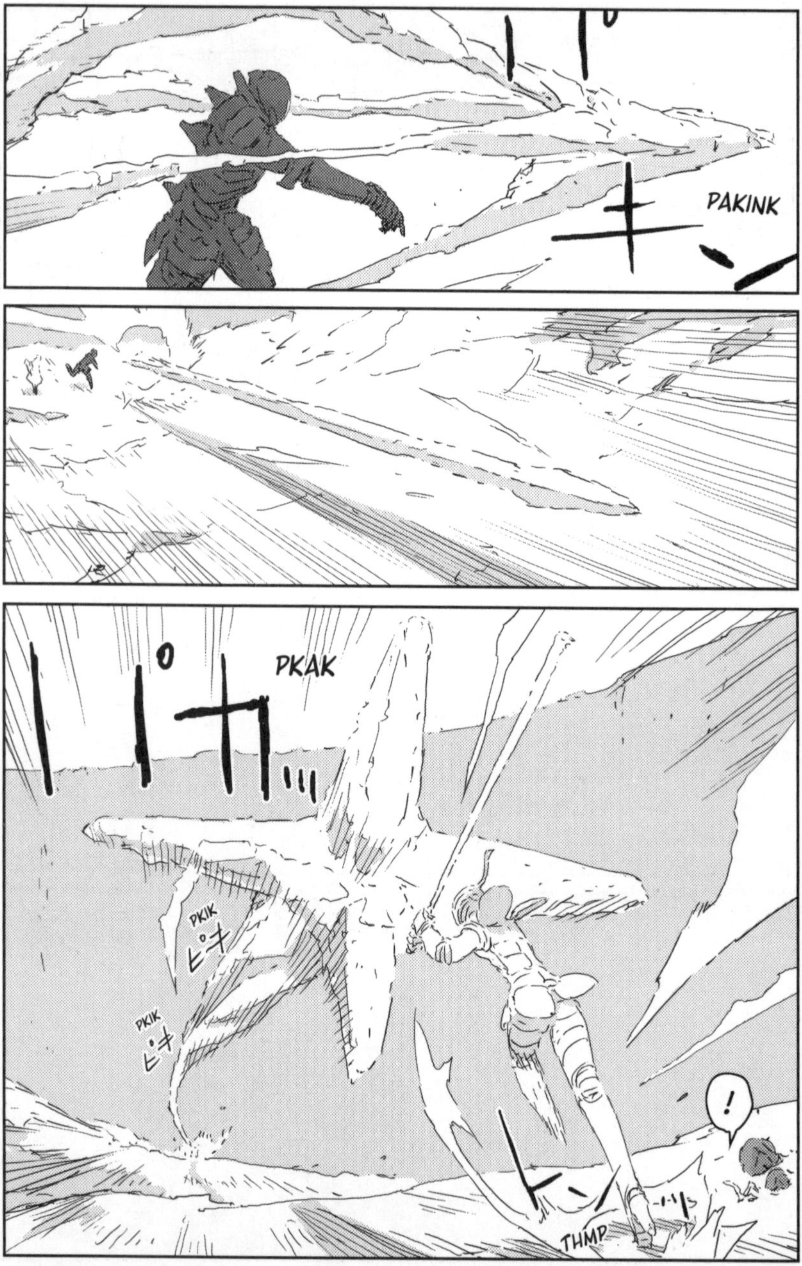
PAKINK
PKAK
PKIK
ピキ
PKIK
ピキ
!
THMP

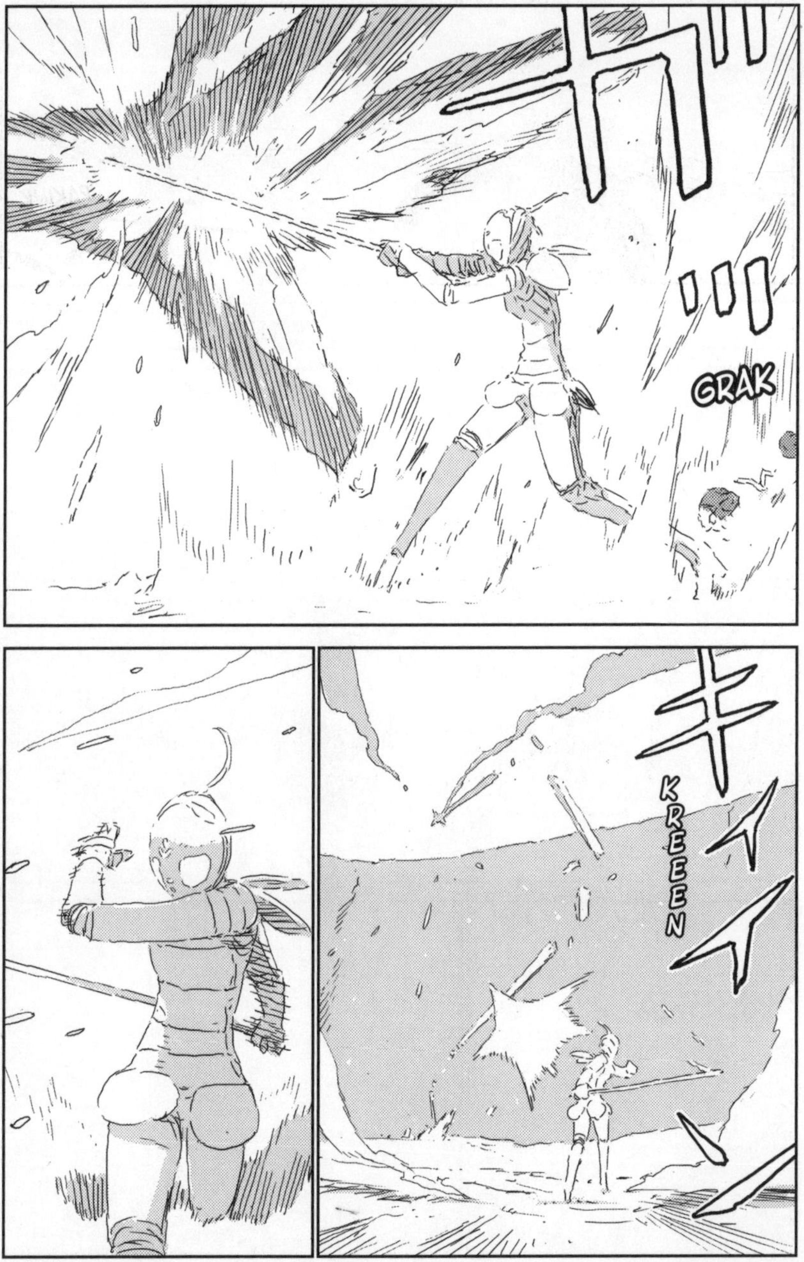
GRAK
KREEEN

GA   SHAAA   AANG

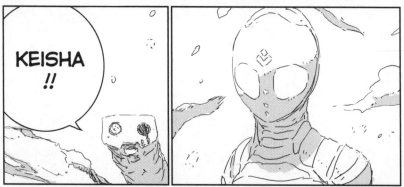

KEISHA
!!

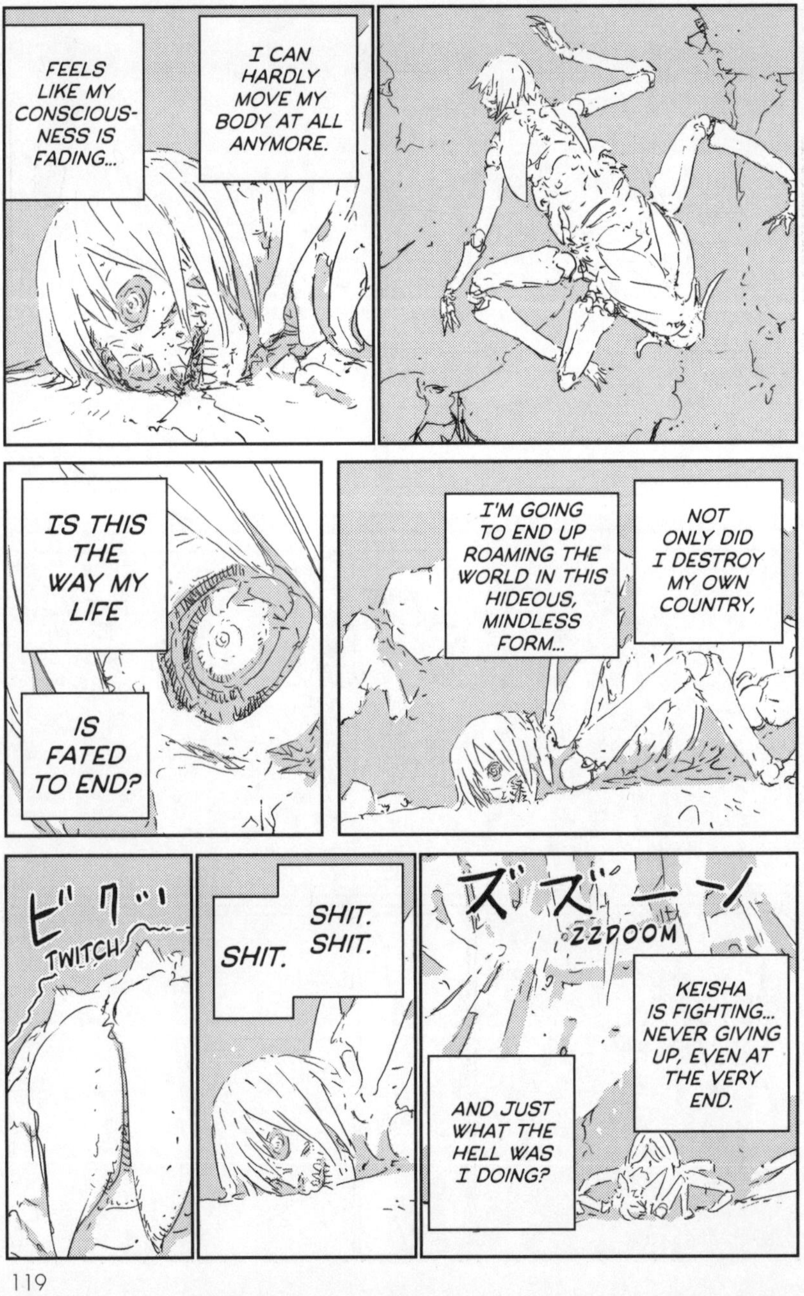
I CAN HARDLY MOVE MY BODY AT ALL ANYMORE.
FEELS LIKE MY CONSCIOUS-NESS IS FADING...
NOT ONLY DID I DESTROY MY OWN COUNTRY,
I'M GOING TO END UP ROAMING THE WORLD IN THIS HIDEOUS, MINDLESS FORM...
IS THIS THE WAY MY LIFE
IS FATED TO END?
ズズーーン
ZZDOOM
KEISHA IS FIGHTING... NEVER GIVING UP, EVEN AT THE VERY END.
AND JUST WHAT THE HELL WAS I DOING?
SHIT. SHIT.
SHIT.
ビクッ
TWITCH

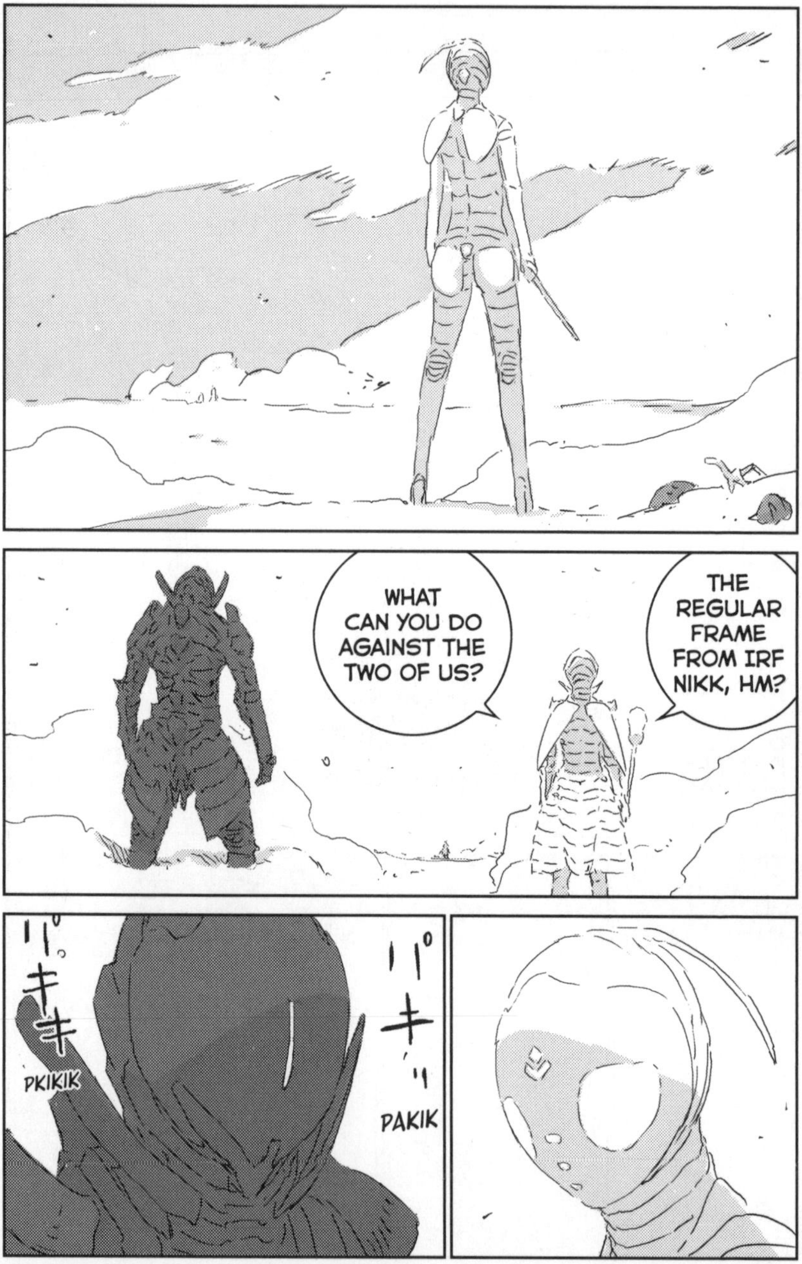
THE REGULAR FRAME FROM IRF NIKK, HM?
WHAT CAN YOU DO AGAINST THE TWO OF US?
パキッ
PAKIK
パッキキ
PKIKIK

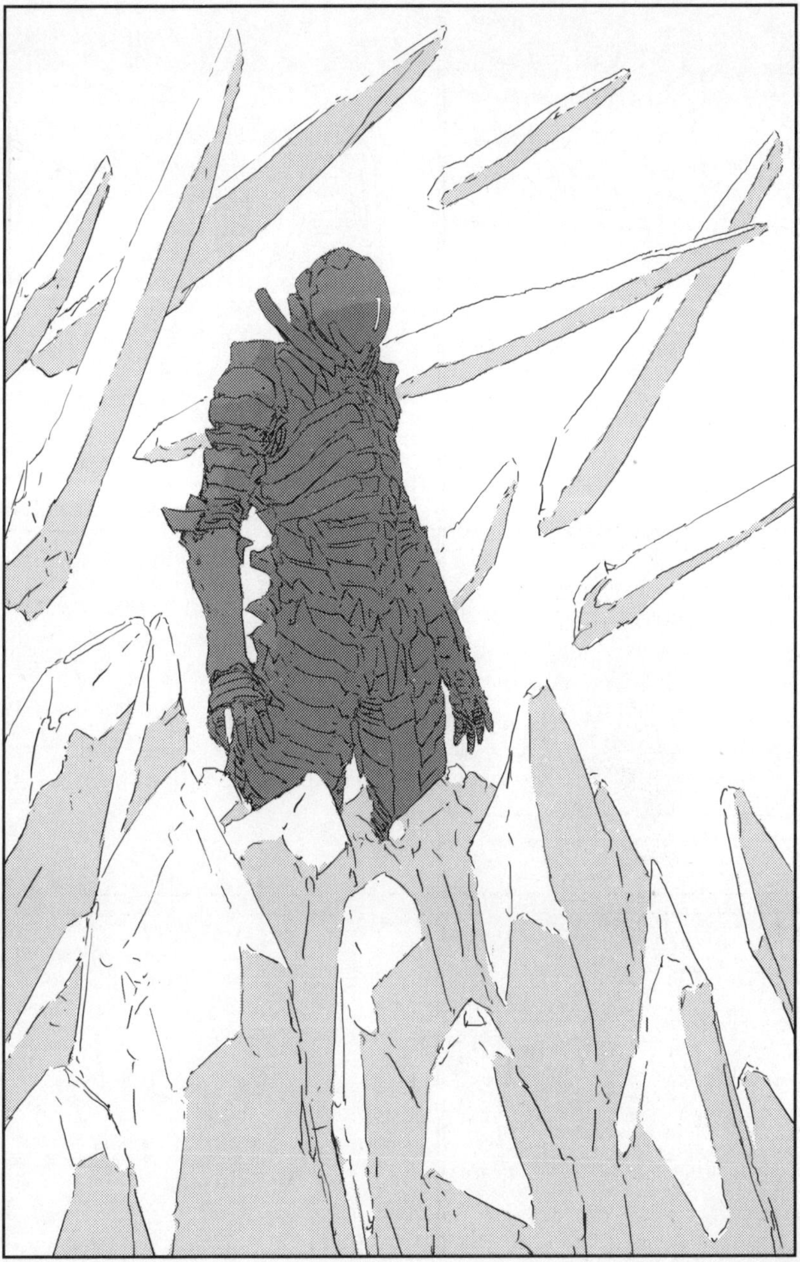

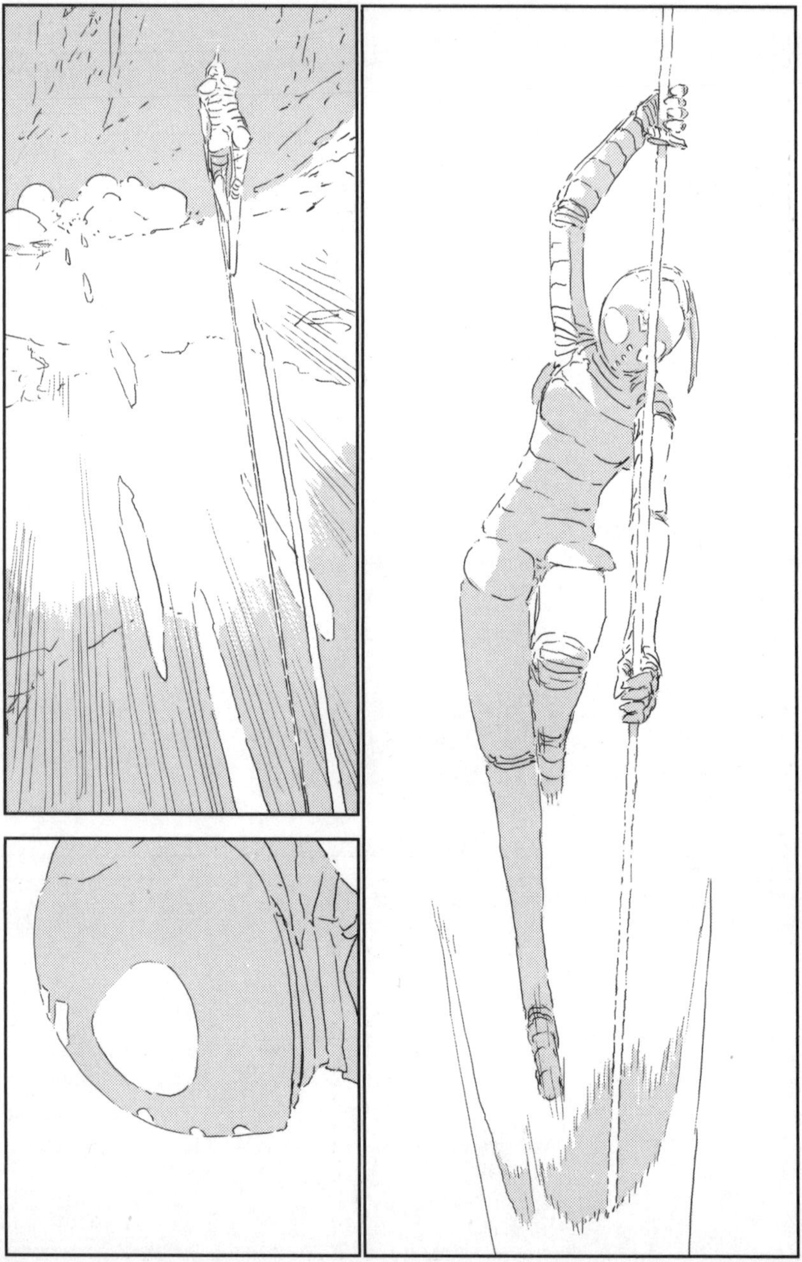

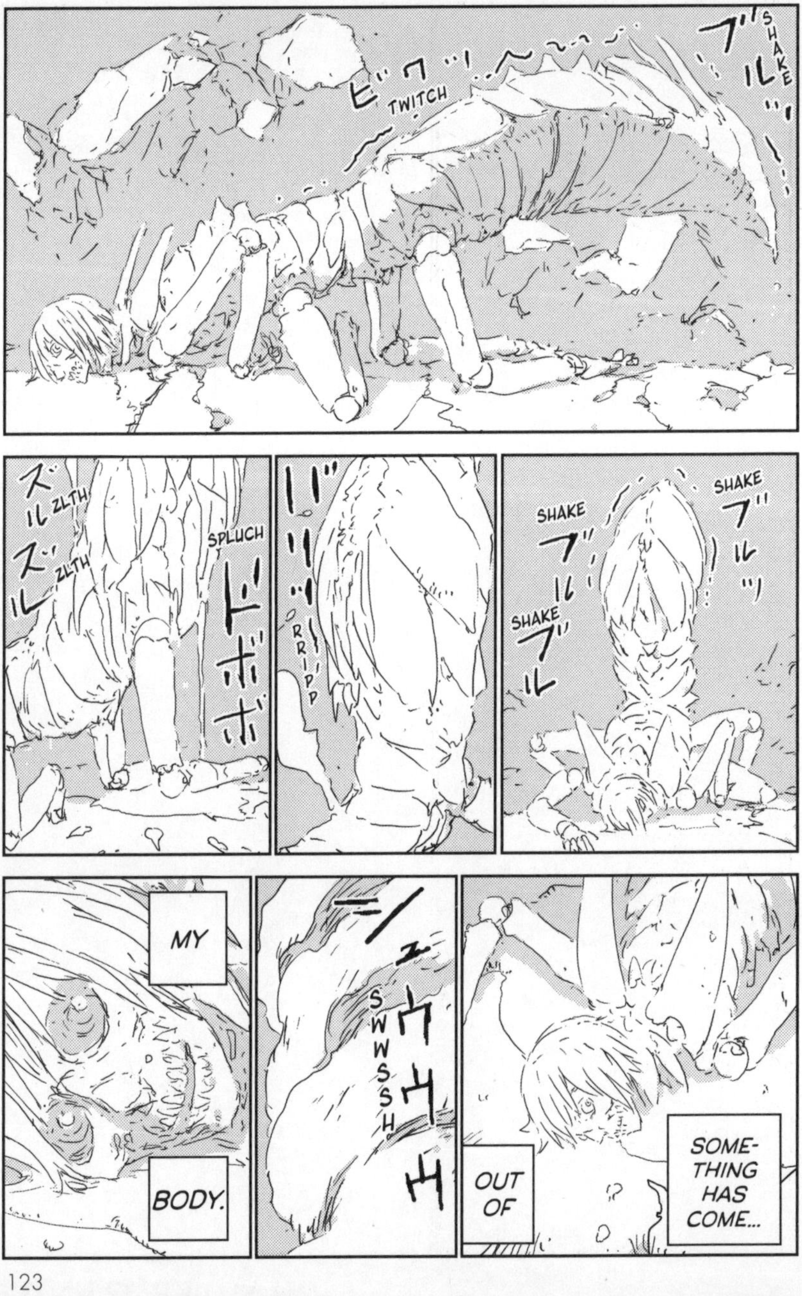
SHAKE
TWITCH
SHAKE
SHAKE
SHAKE
RRIPP
SPLUCH
ZLTH
ZLTH
SOME-THING HAS COME...
OUT OF
SWWSSH
MY
BODY.

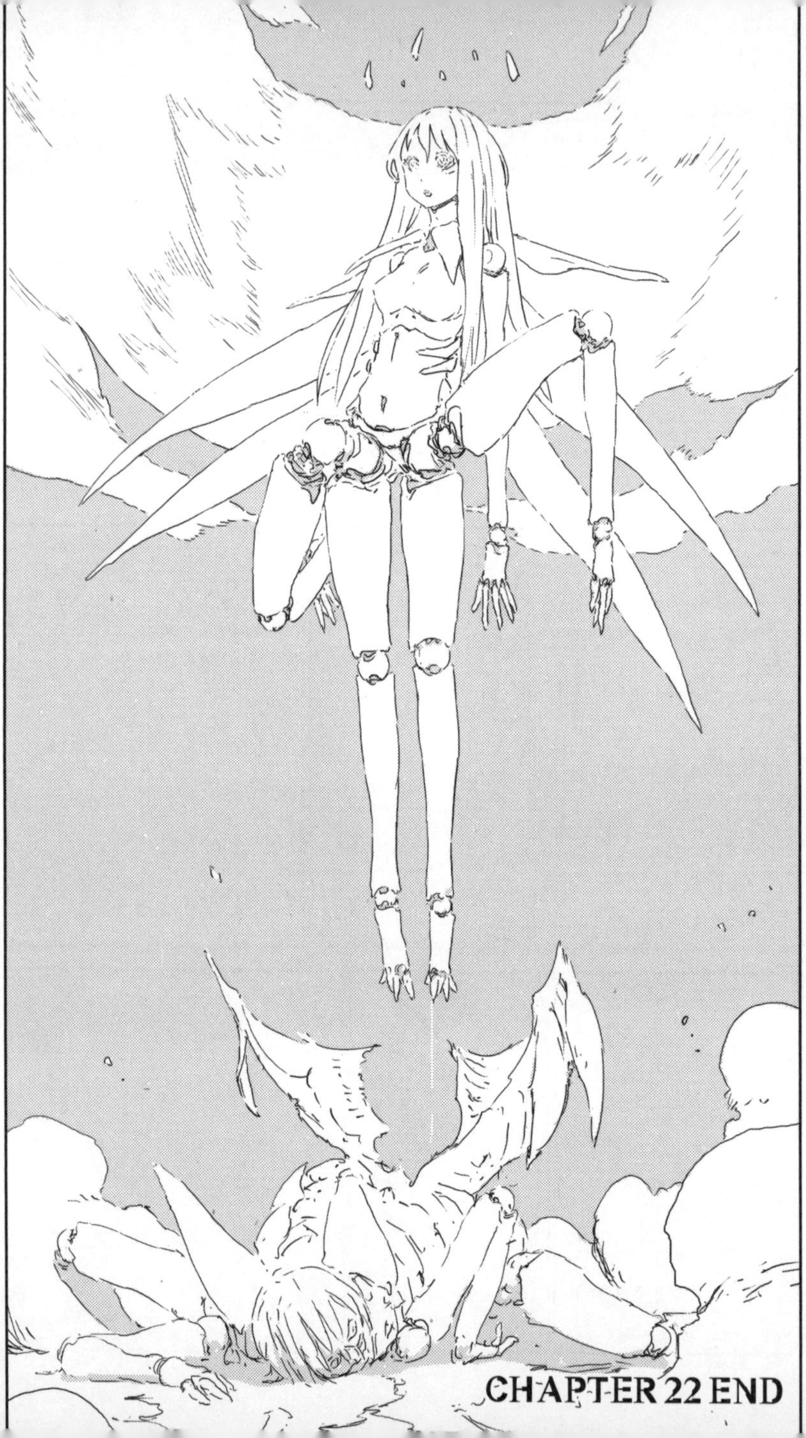
CHAPTER 22 END

APOSIMZ

X

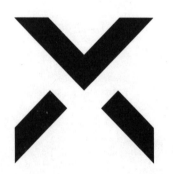

CHAPTER 22

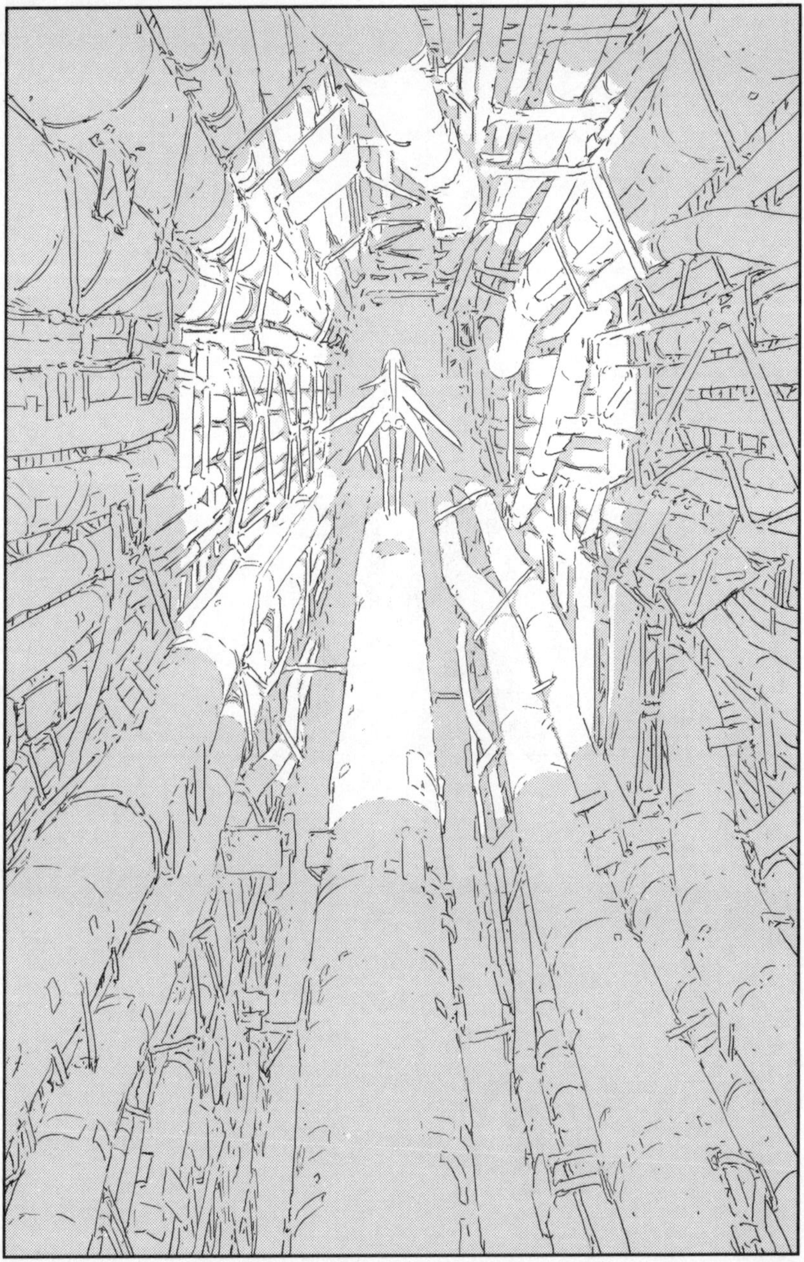

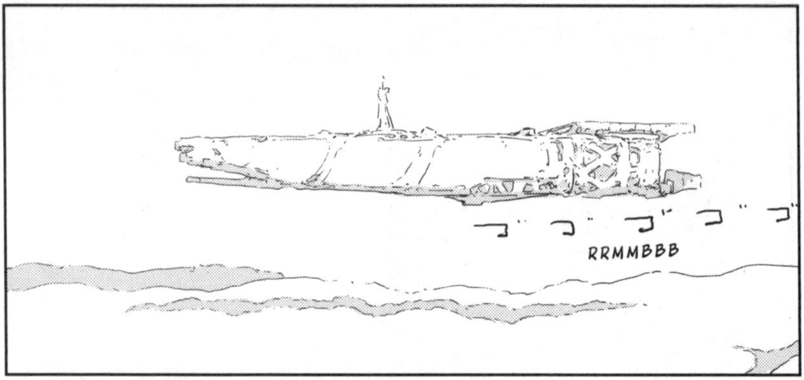
ゴゴゴゴゴ
RRMMBBB
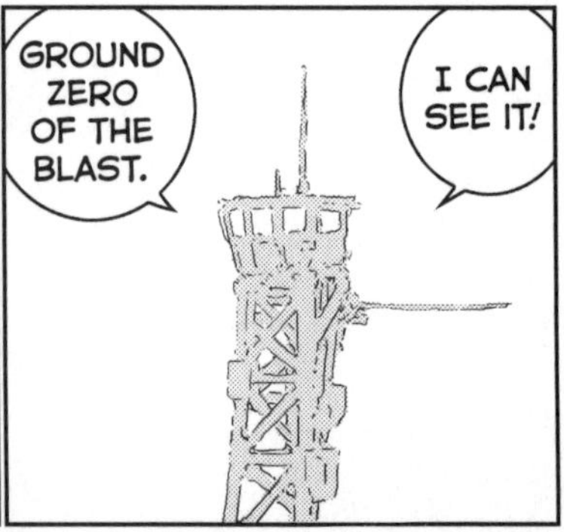
I CAN SEE IT!
GROUND ZERO OF THE BLAST.
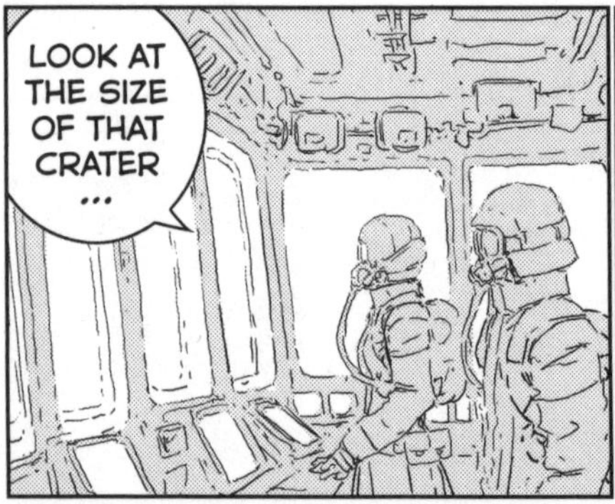
LOOK AT THE SIZE OF THAT CRATER ...
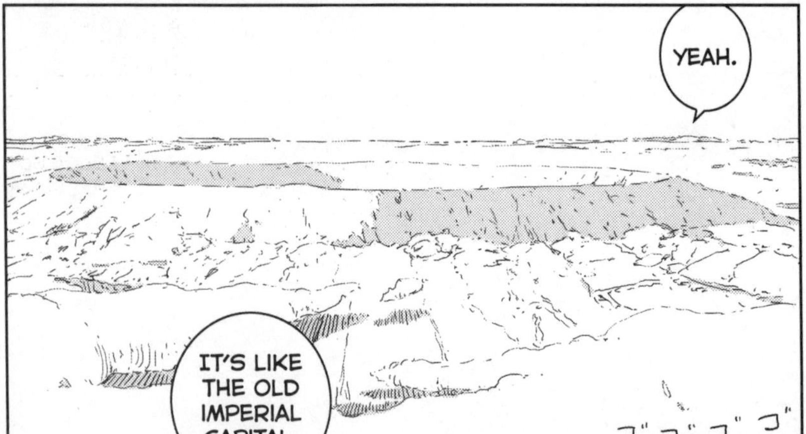
YEAH.
IT'S LIKE THE OLD IMPERIAL CAPITAL.
ゴゴゴゴ
RRMMBBLE

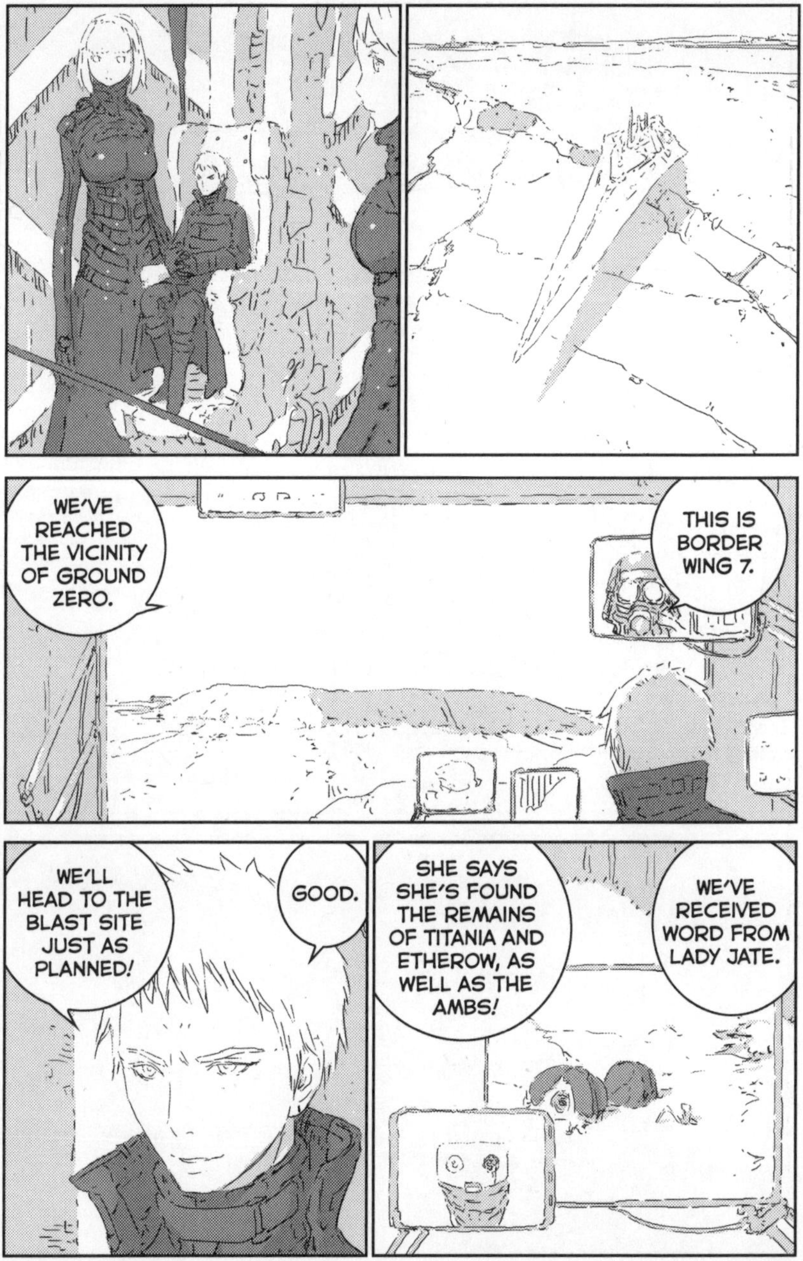
THIS IS BORDER WING 7.
WE'VE REACHED THE VICINITY OF GROUND ZERO.
WE'VE RECEIVED WORD FROM LADY JATE.
SHE SAYS SHE'S FOUND THE REMAINS OF TITANIA AND ETHEROW, AS WELL AS THE AMBS!
GOOD.
WE'LL HEAD TO THE BLAST SITE JUST AS PLANNED!

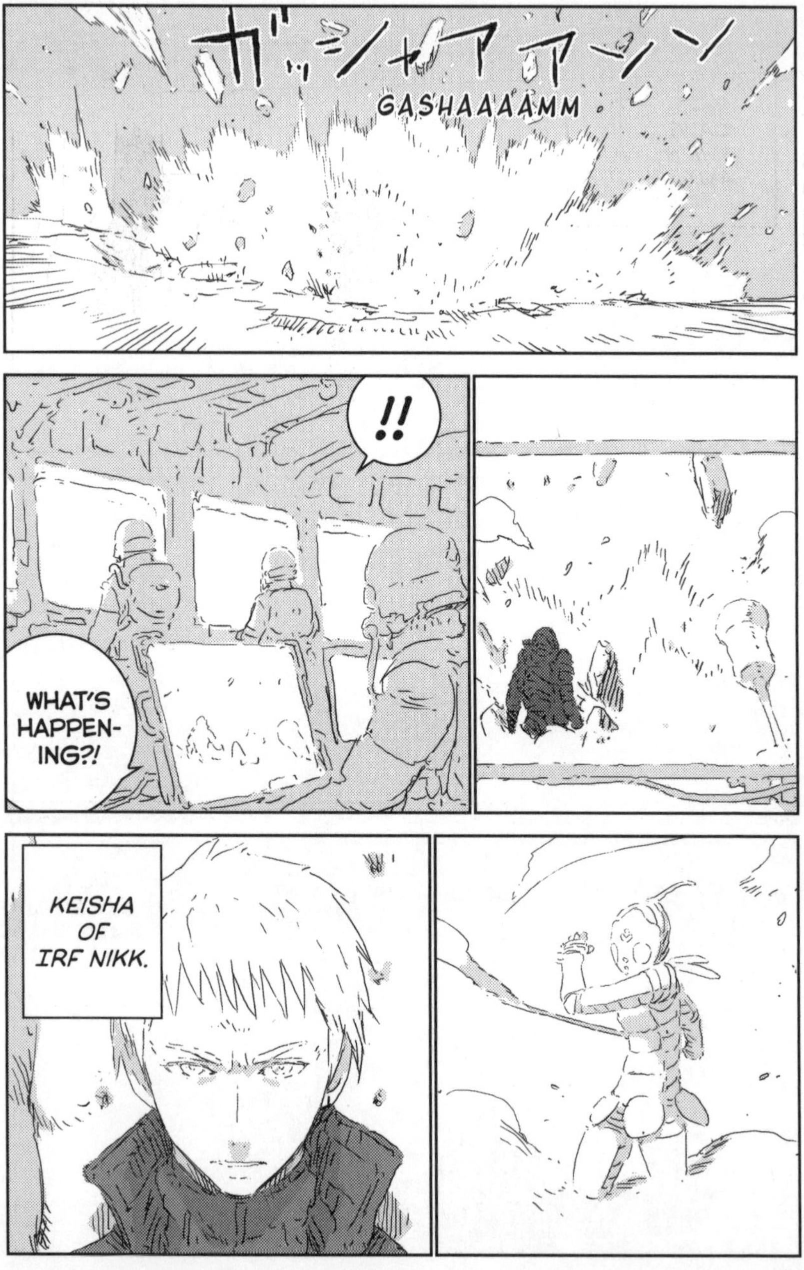
ガッシャアアーン
GASHAAAAMM
!!
WHAT'S HAPPENING?!
KEISHA OF IRF NIKK.

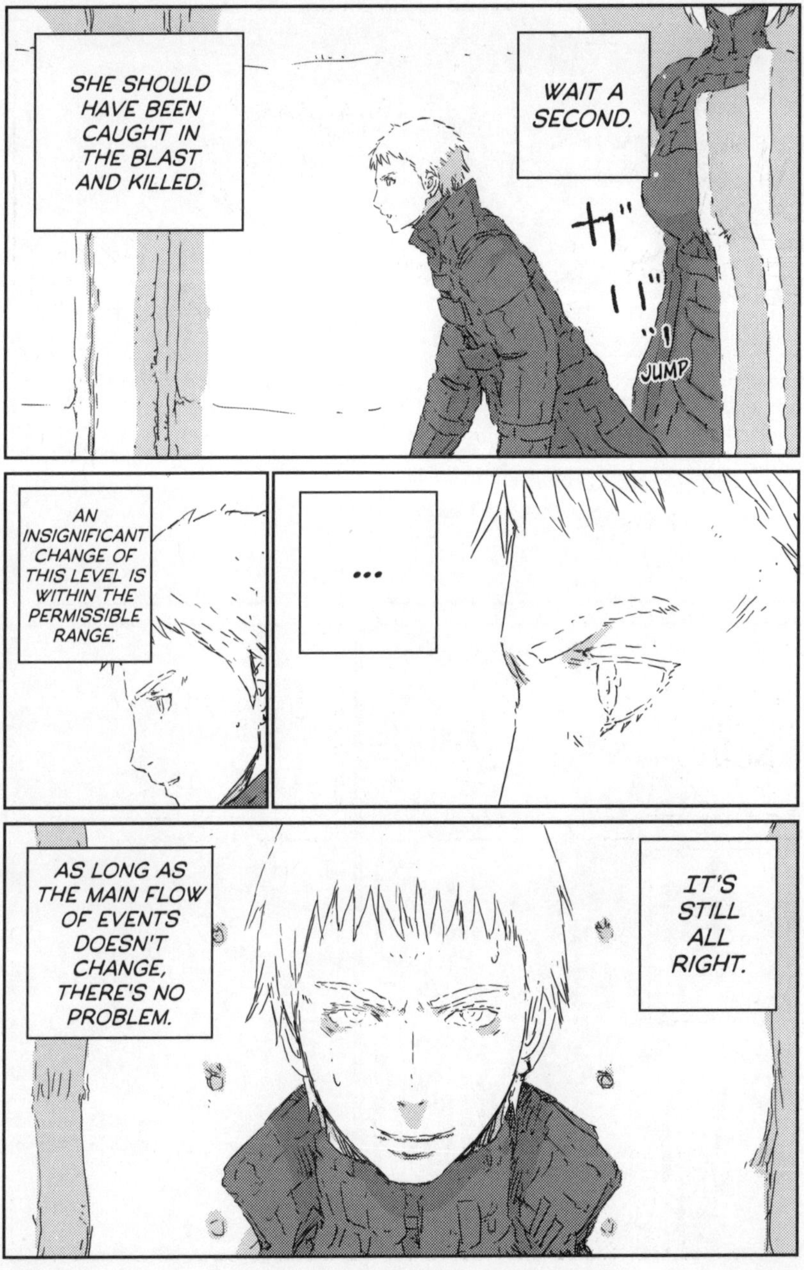

WAIT A SECOND.
SHE SHOULD HAVE BEEN CAUGHT IN THE BLAST AND KILLED.
JUMP
...
AN INSIGNIFICANT CHANGE OF THIS LEVEL IS WITHIN THE PERMISSIBLE RANGE.
IT'S STILL ALL RIGHT.
AS LONG AS THE MAIN FLOW OF EVENTS DOESN'T CHANGE, THERE'S NO PROBLEM.

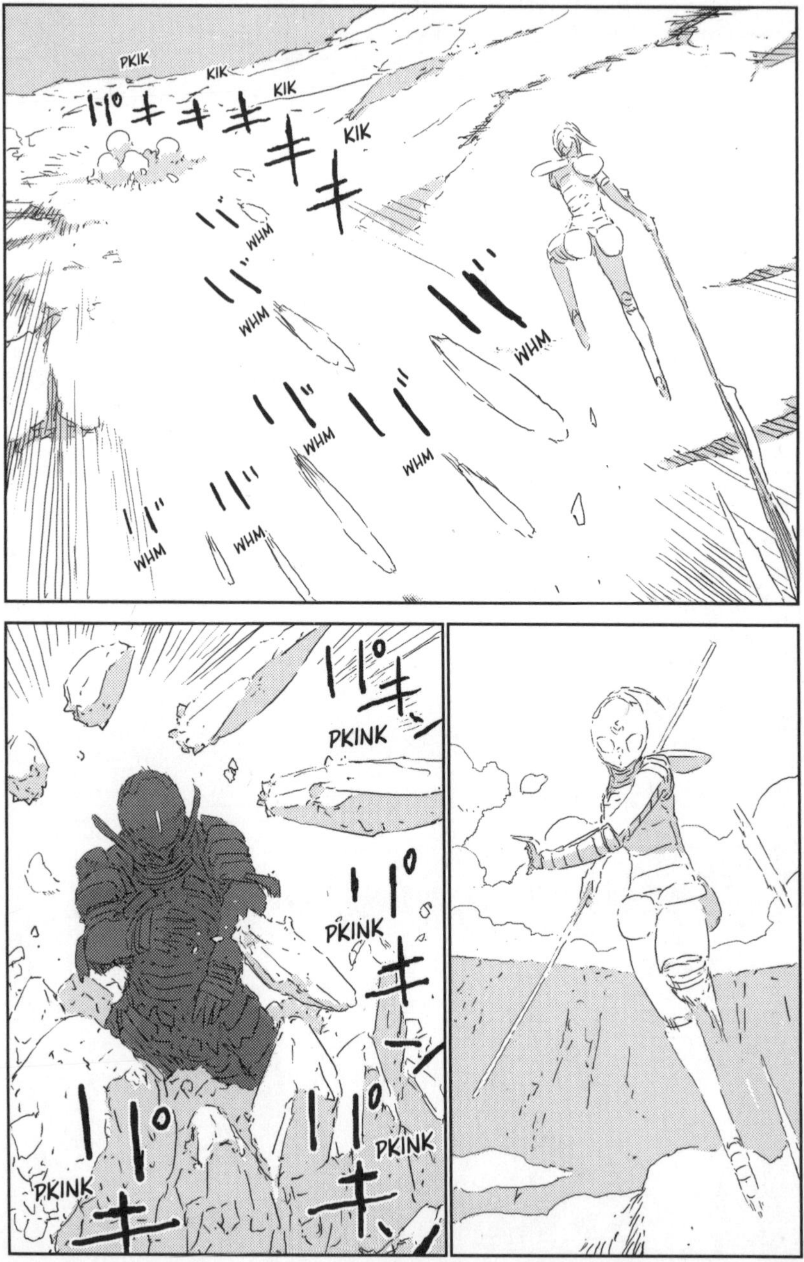
パキキキキキ
PKIK
KIK
KIK
KIK
バババババババ
WHM
WHM
WHM
WHM
WHM
WHM
WHM
パキン
PKINK
パキン
PKINK
パキン
PKINK
パキン
PKINK

I SWEAR I'LL KILL YOU!
BZZT
BZZAP
BJZZT
TZZT
THMP
SHE DOVE INTO THIS QUITE FEAR-LESSLY.
VMP
SHE MUST KNOW SHE CAN'T WIN TWO-TO-ONE.

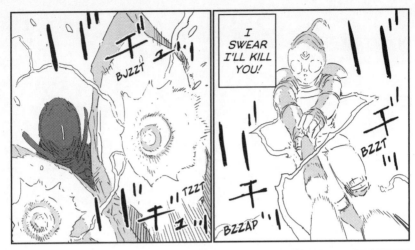

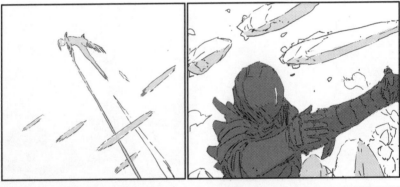

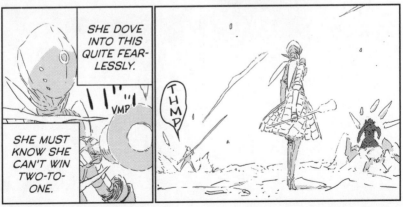

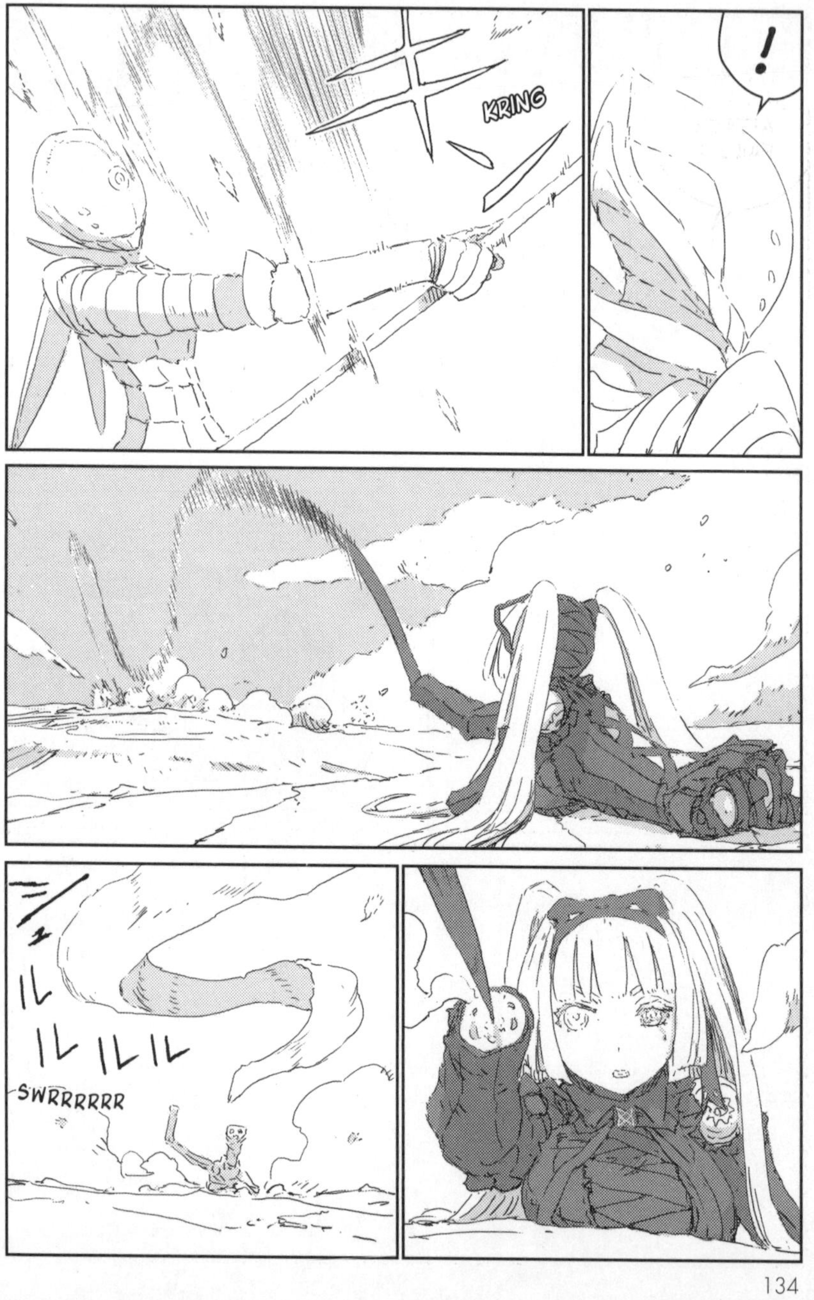
!
KRING
シュルルルル
SWRRRRRR

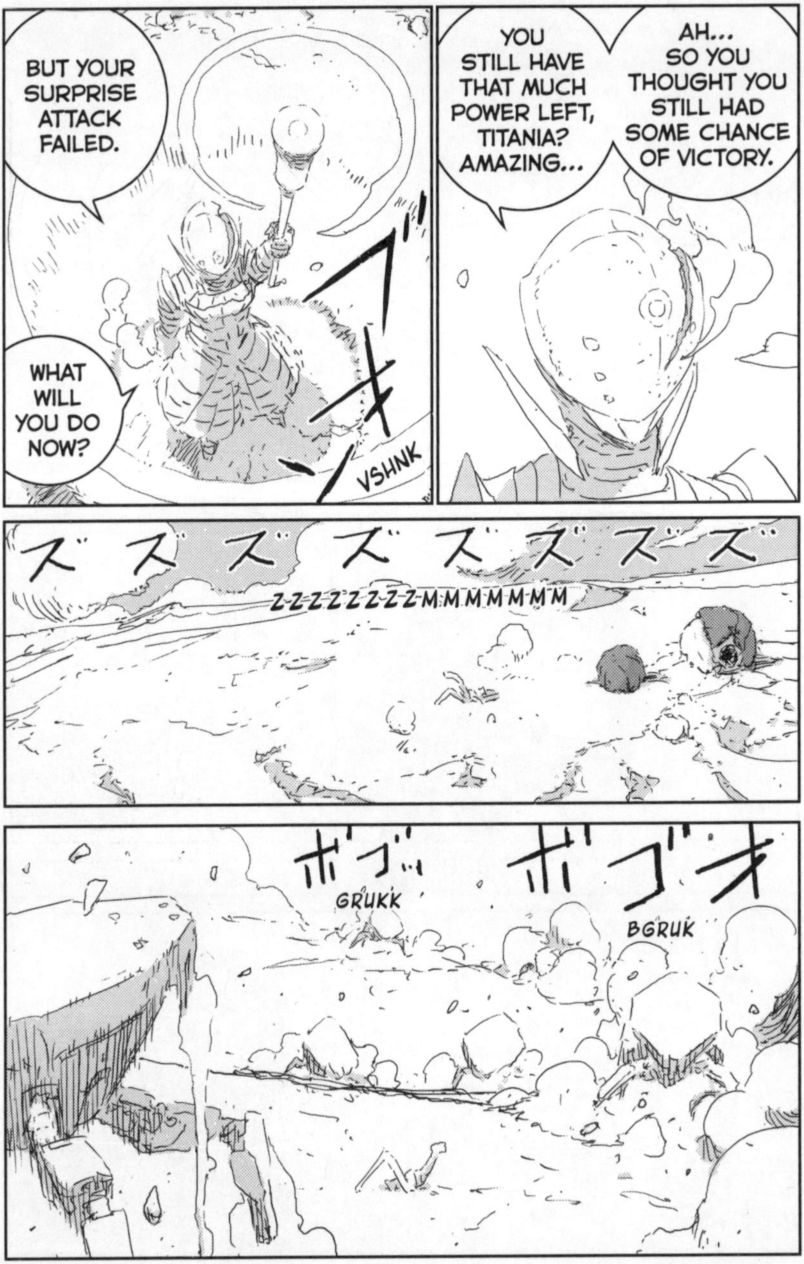
AH... SO YOU THOUGHT YOU STILL HAD SOME CHANCE OF VICTORY.
YOU STILL HAVE THAT MUCH POWER LEFT, TITANIA? AMAZING...
BUT YOUR SURPRISE ATTACK FAILED.
WHAT WILL YOU DO NOW?
VSHNK
ズズズズズズズズ
ZZZZZZZZMMMMMMM
ボゴオ
BGRUK
ボゴッ
GRUKK

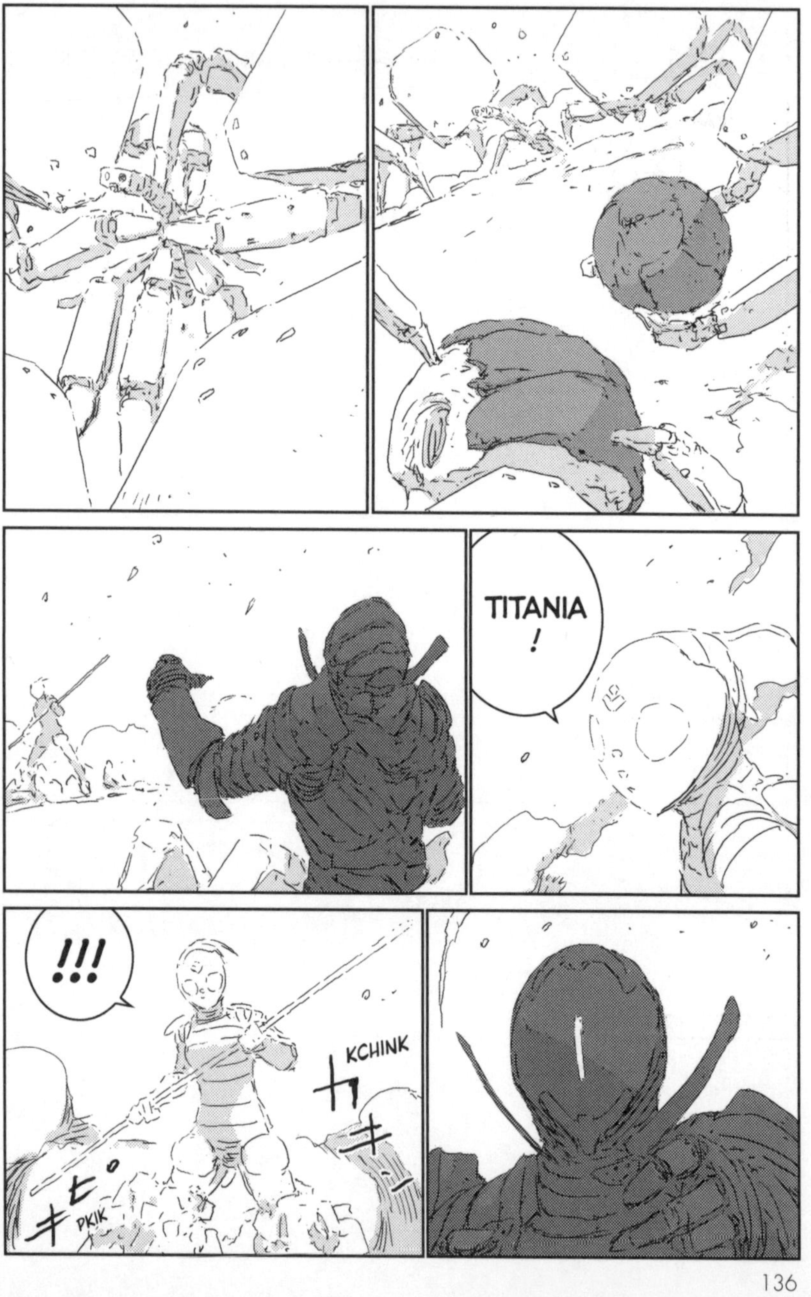
TITANIA!
!!!
KCHINK
PKIK

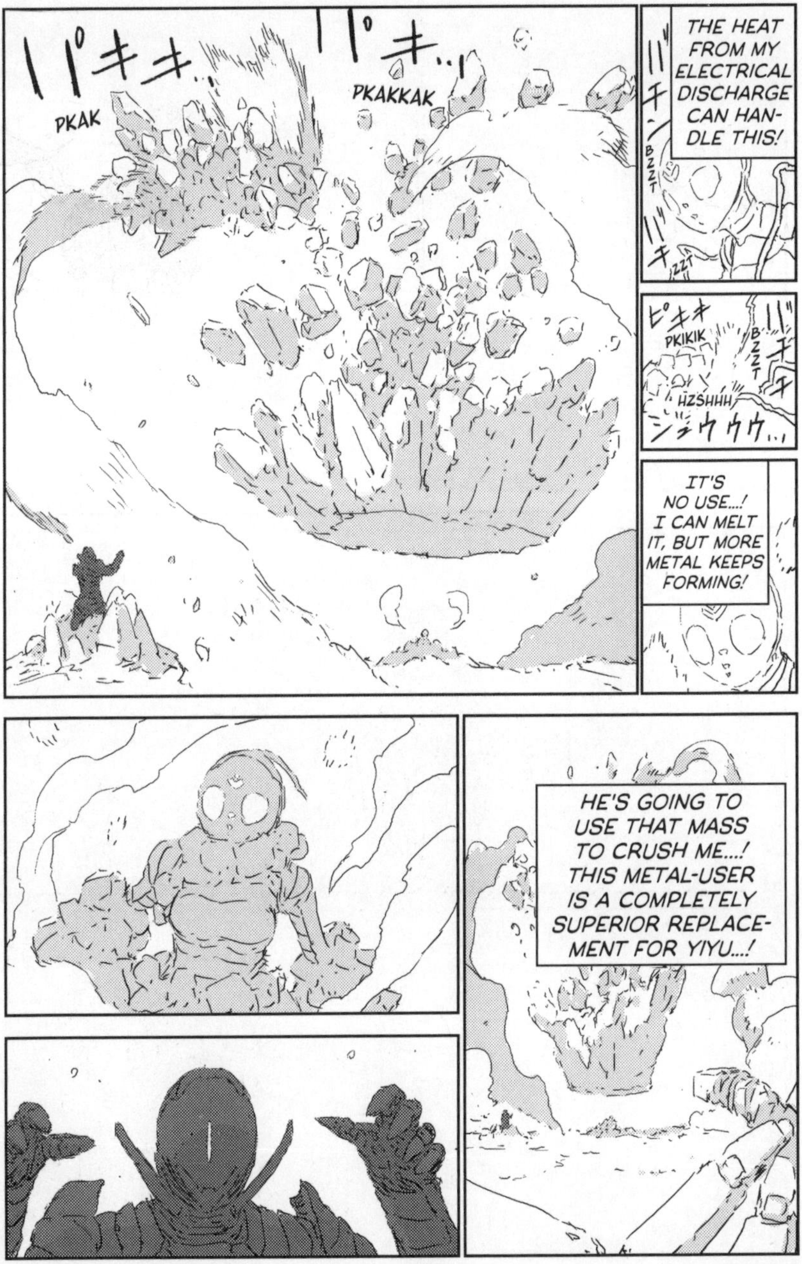
THE HEAT FROM MY ELECTRICAL DISCHARGE CAN HANDLE THIS!
バチ
BZZT
バチ
ZZT
ピキキ
PKIKIK
バチチ
BZZT
HZSHHH
ジュウウウ
IT'S NO USE...! I CAN MELT IT, BUT MORE METAL KEEPS FORMING!
パキキ
PKAK
パキ
PKAKKAK
HE'S GOING TO USE THAT MASS TO CRUSH ME...! THIS METAL-USER IS A COMPLETELY SUPERIOR REPLACEMENT FOR YIYU...!

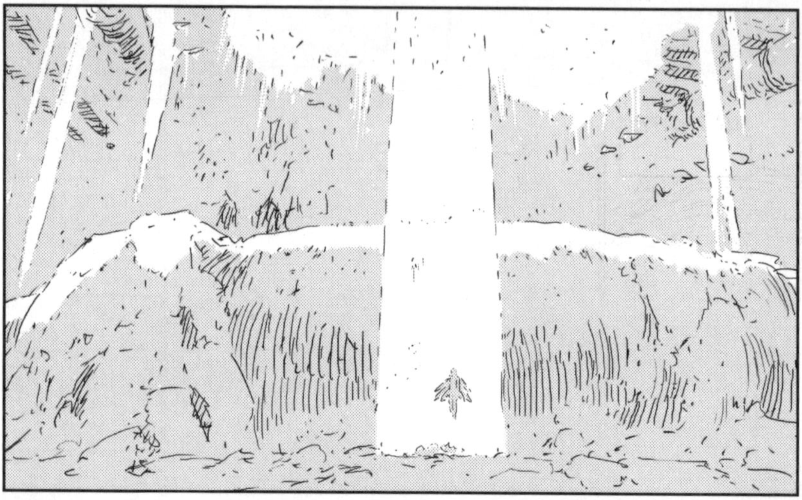

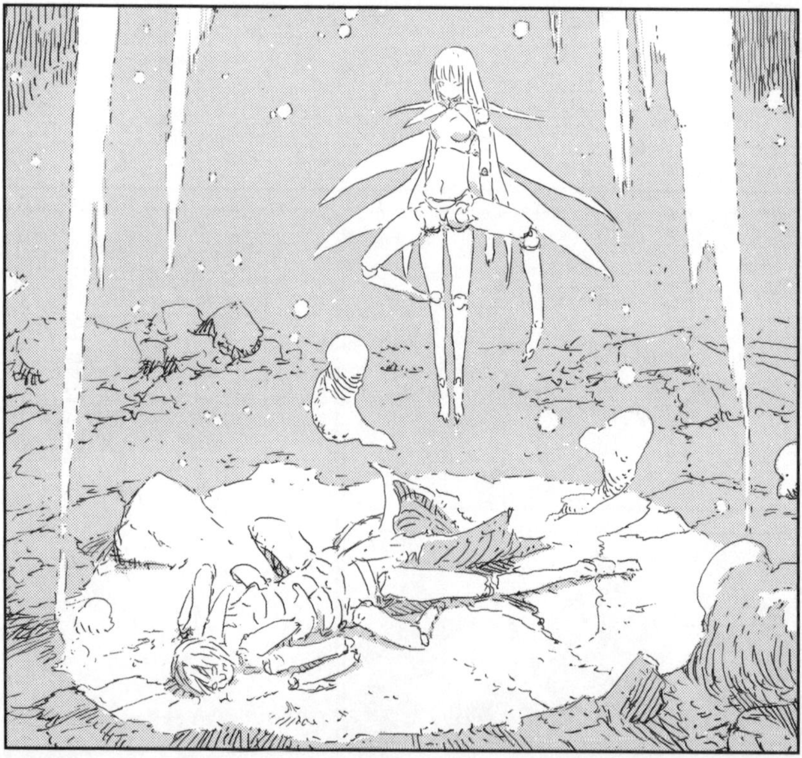

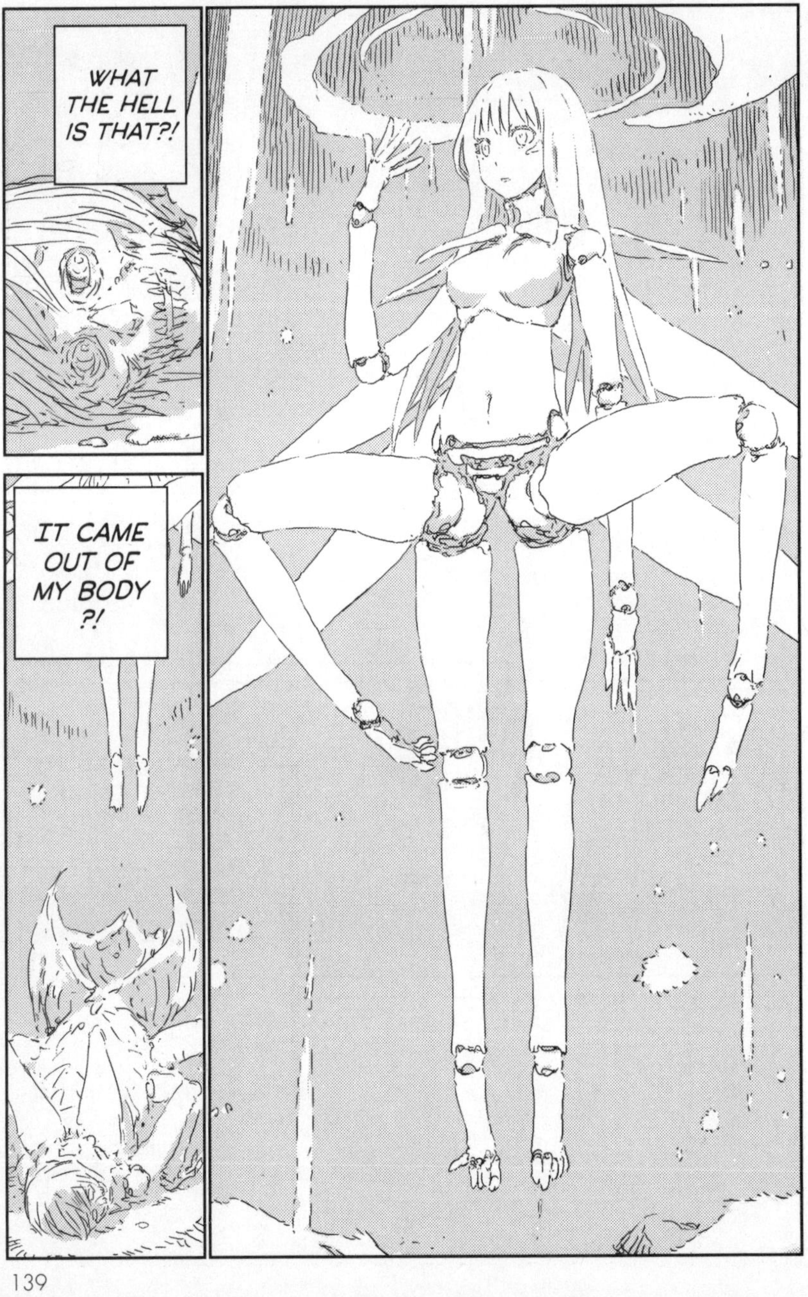
WHAT THE HELL IS THAT?!
IT CAME OUT OF MY BODY ?!

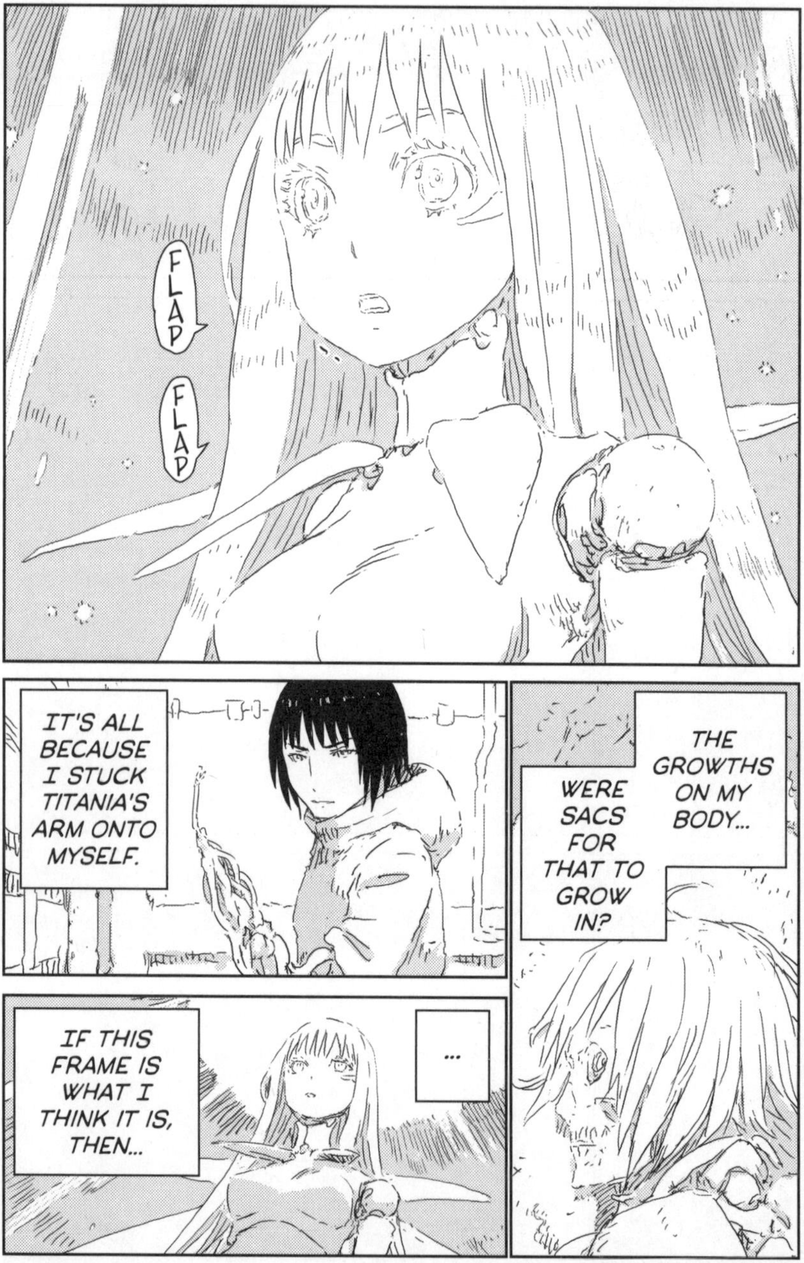
FLAP
FLAP
FLAP
FLAP
THE GROWTHS ON MY BODY...
WERE SACS FOR THAT TO GROW IN?
IT'S ALL BECAUSE I STUCK TITANIA'S ARM ONTO MYSELF.
...
IF THIS FRAME IS WHAT I THINK IT IS, THEN...

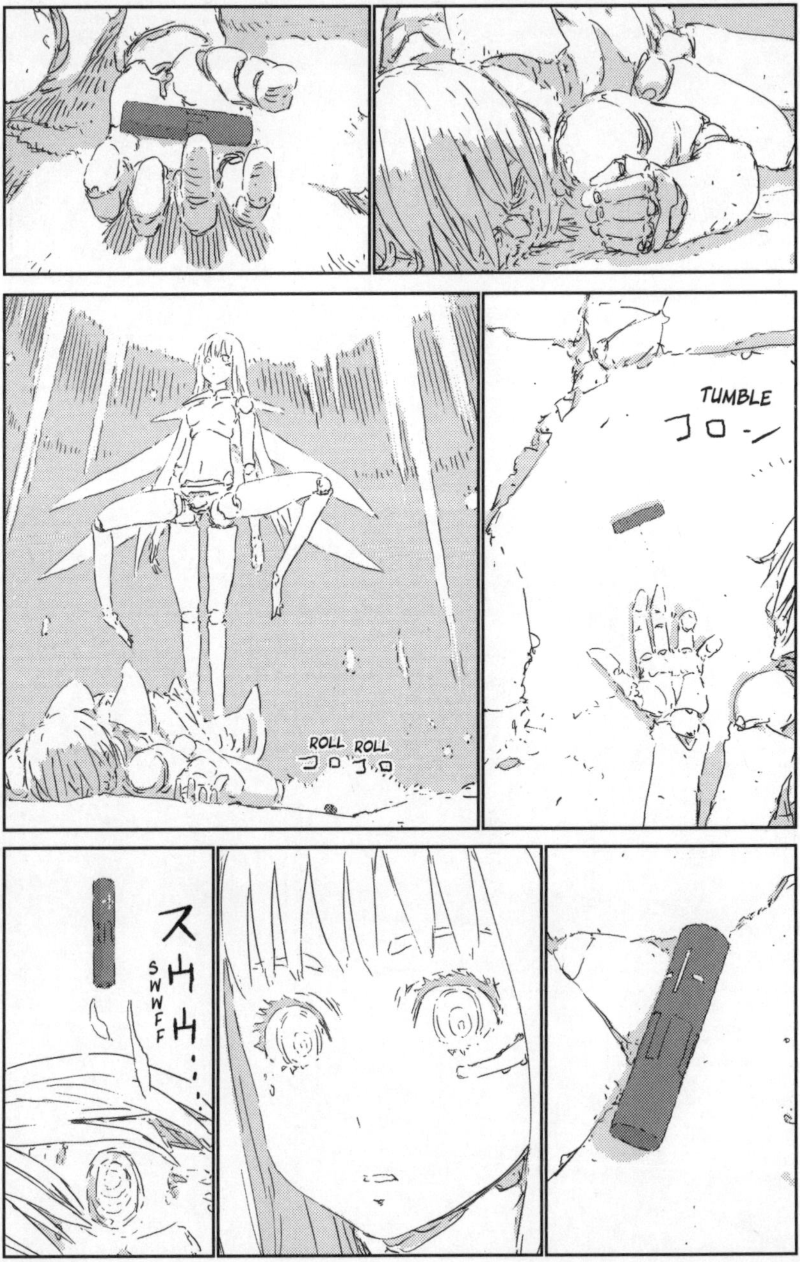
TUMBLE
コローン
ROLL ROLL
コロコロ
ス
SWWFF

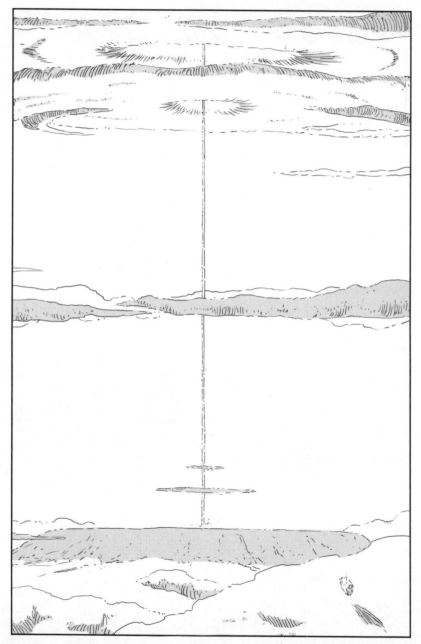

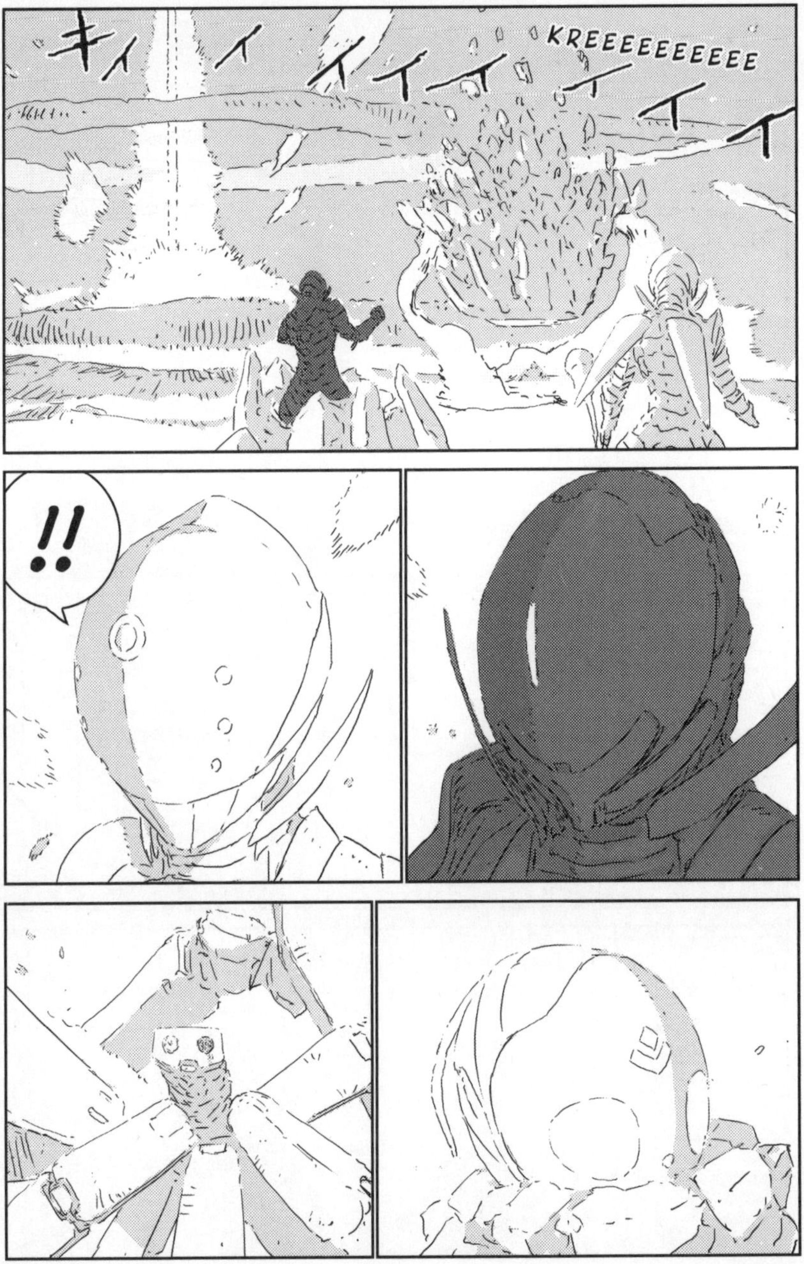
キィイイイイイイ
KREEEEEEEEEEE
!!

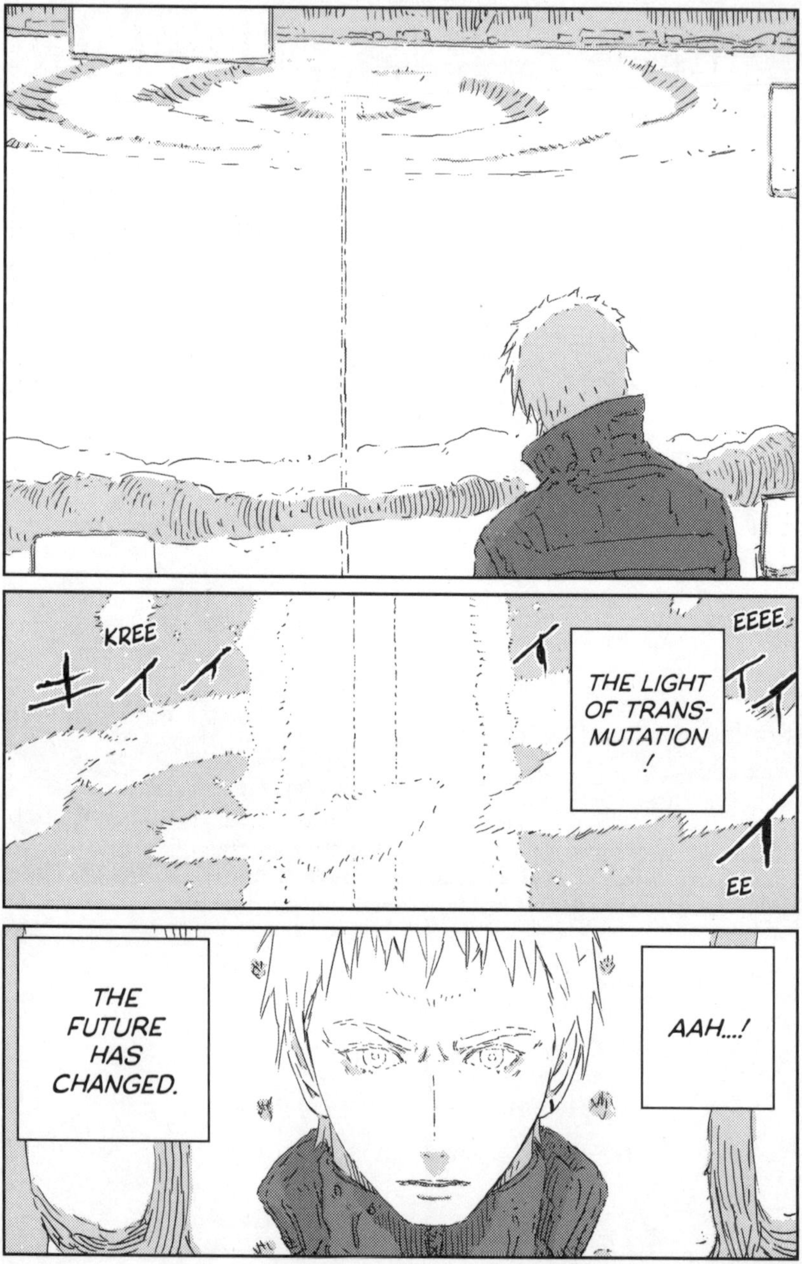
EEEE
THE LIGHT OF TRANS-MUTATION !
EE
KREE
キイイ
イイイ
AAH...!
THE FUTURE HAS CHANGED.

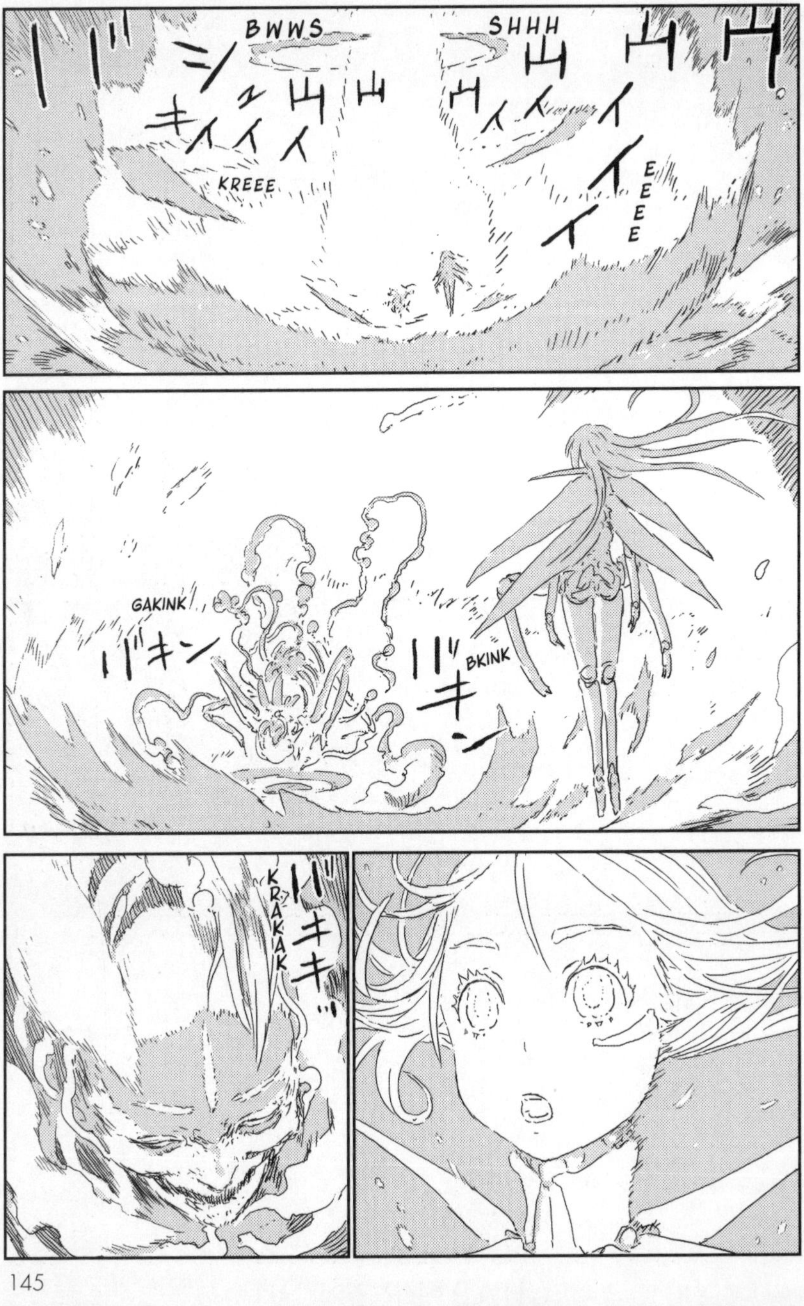
SHHH
EEEE
BWWS
KREEE
BKINK
GAKINK
KRAKAK

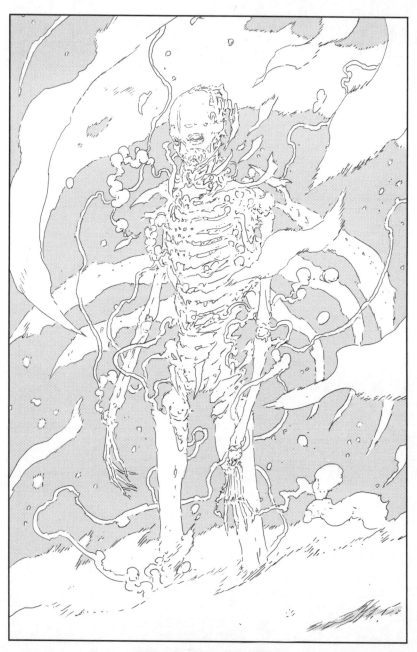

CHAPTER 23 END

APOSIMZ

CHAPTER 24

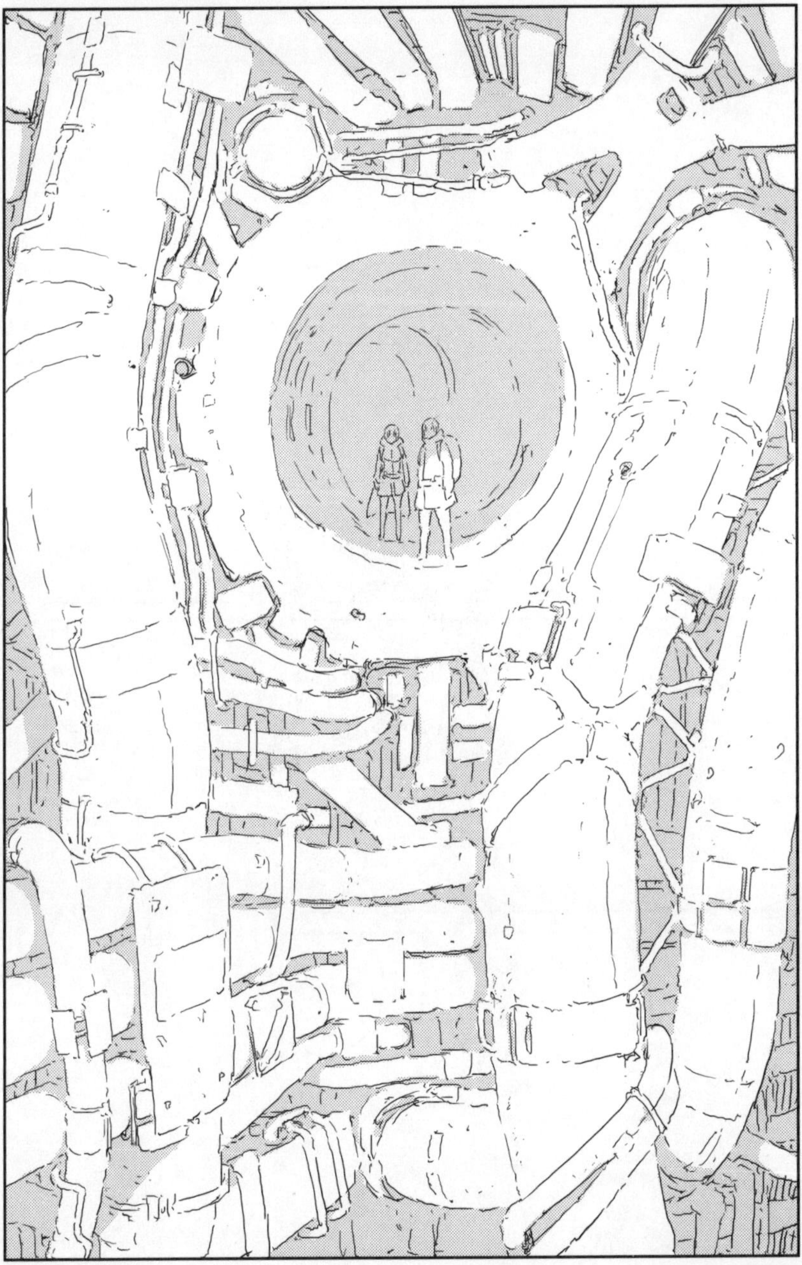

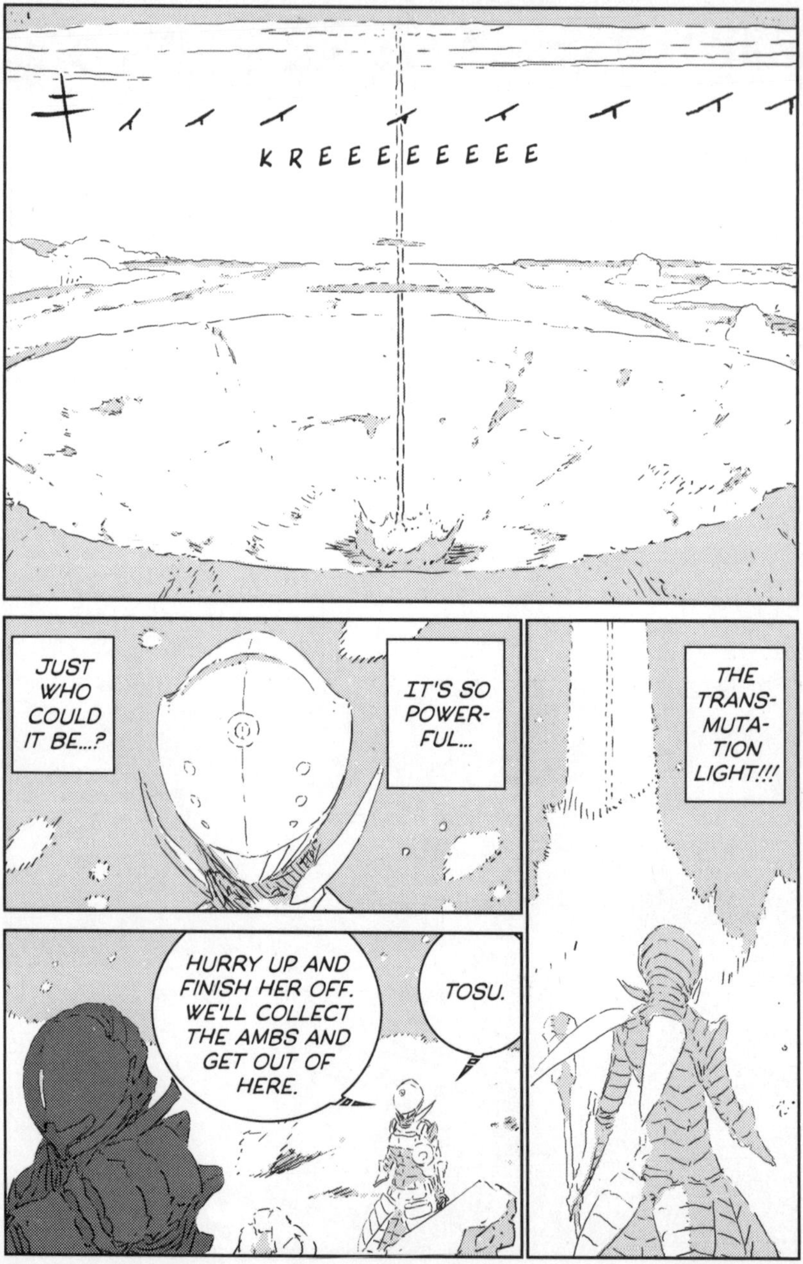
キィィィィィィィィ
KREEEEEEEEE
THE TRANSMUTATION LIGHT!!!
IT'S SO POWERFUL...
JUST WHO COULD IT BE...?
TOSU.
HURRY UP AND FINISH HER OFF. WE'LL COLLECT THE AMBS AND GET OUT OF HERE.

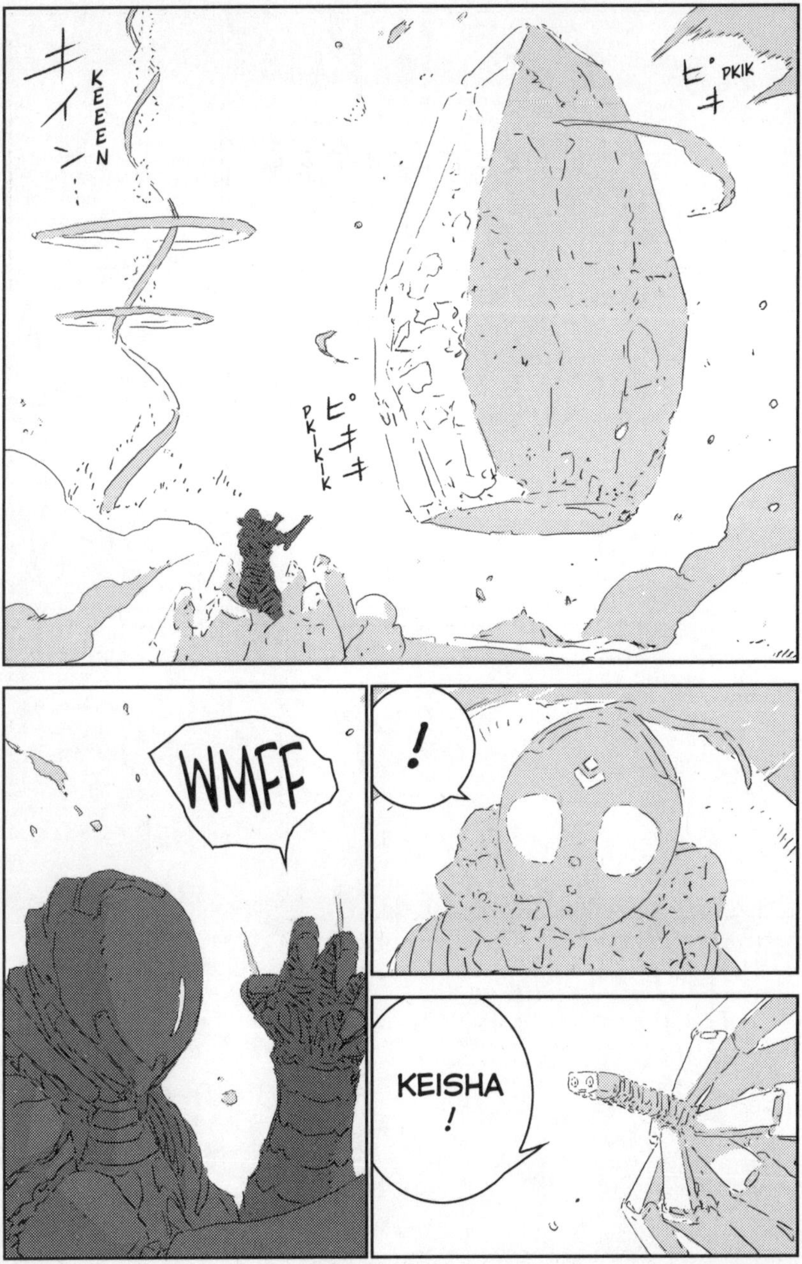
ピキ PKIK
キイン KEEEN
ピキキ PKIKIK
!
KEISHA!
WMFF

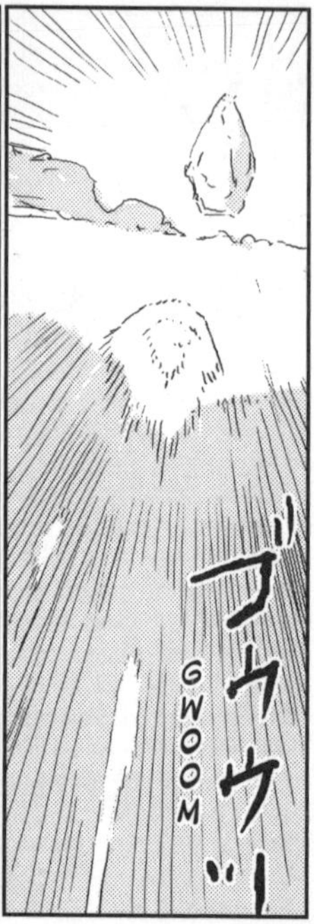
GWOOM

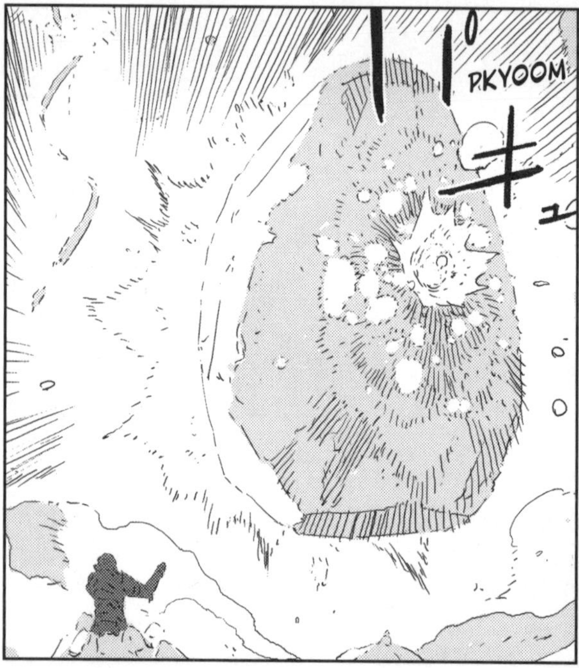
PKYOOM

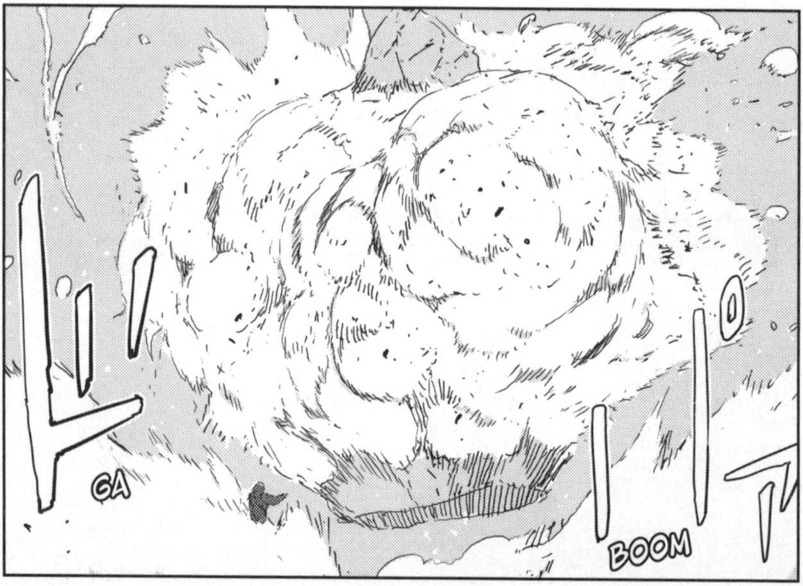
GA
BOOM

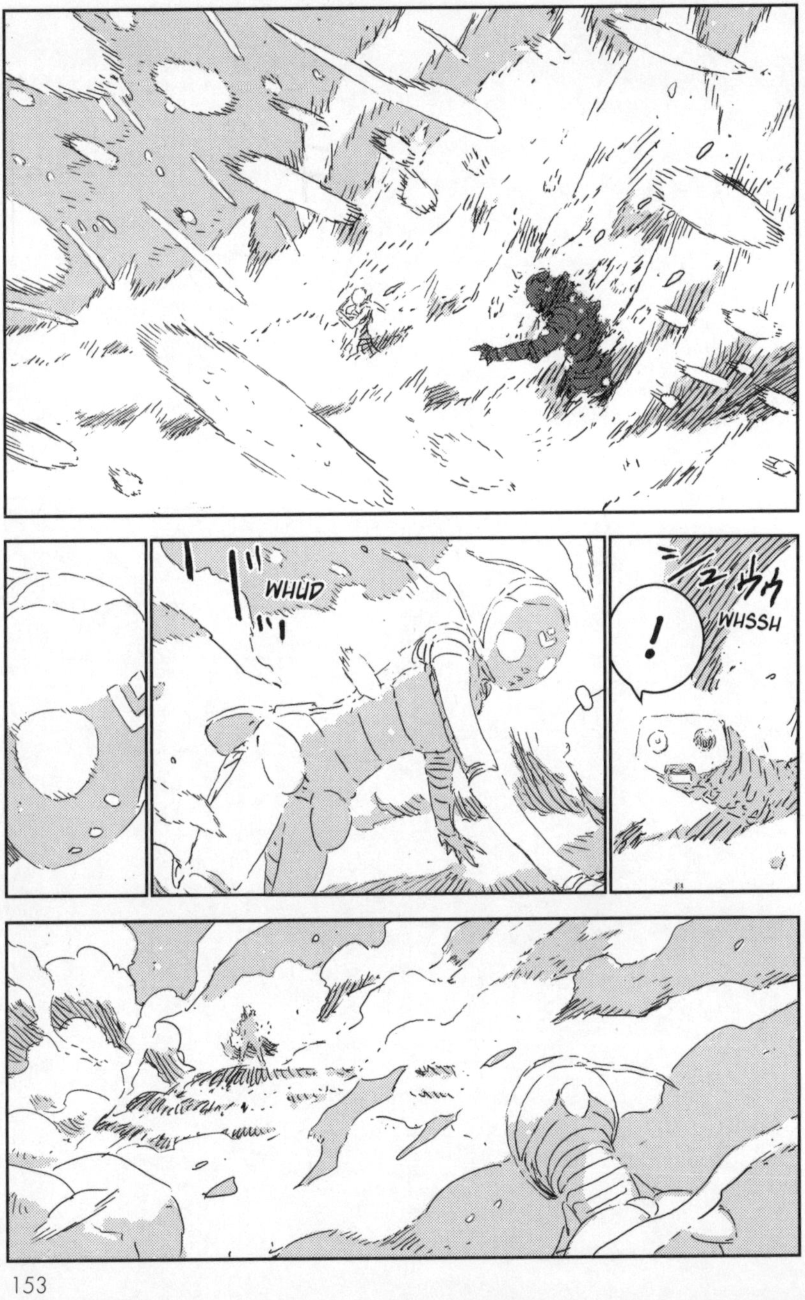
!
WHSSH
WHUD

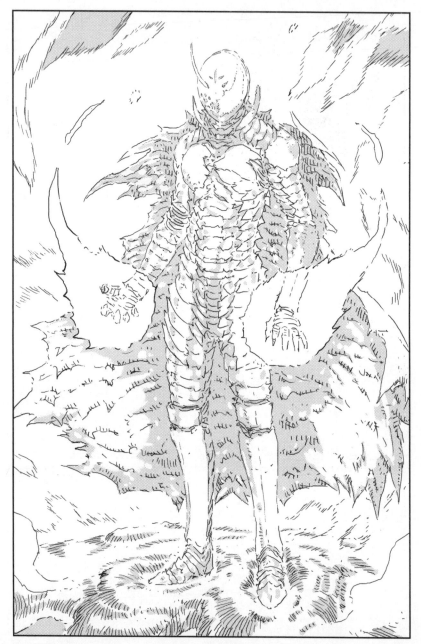

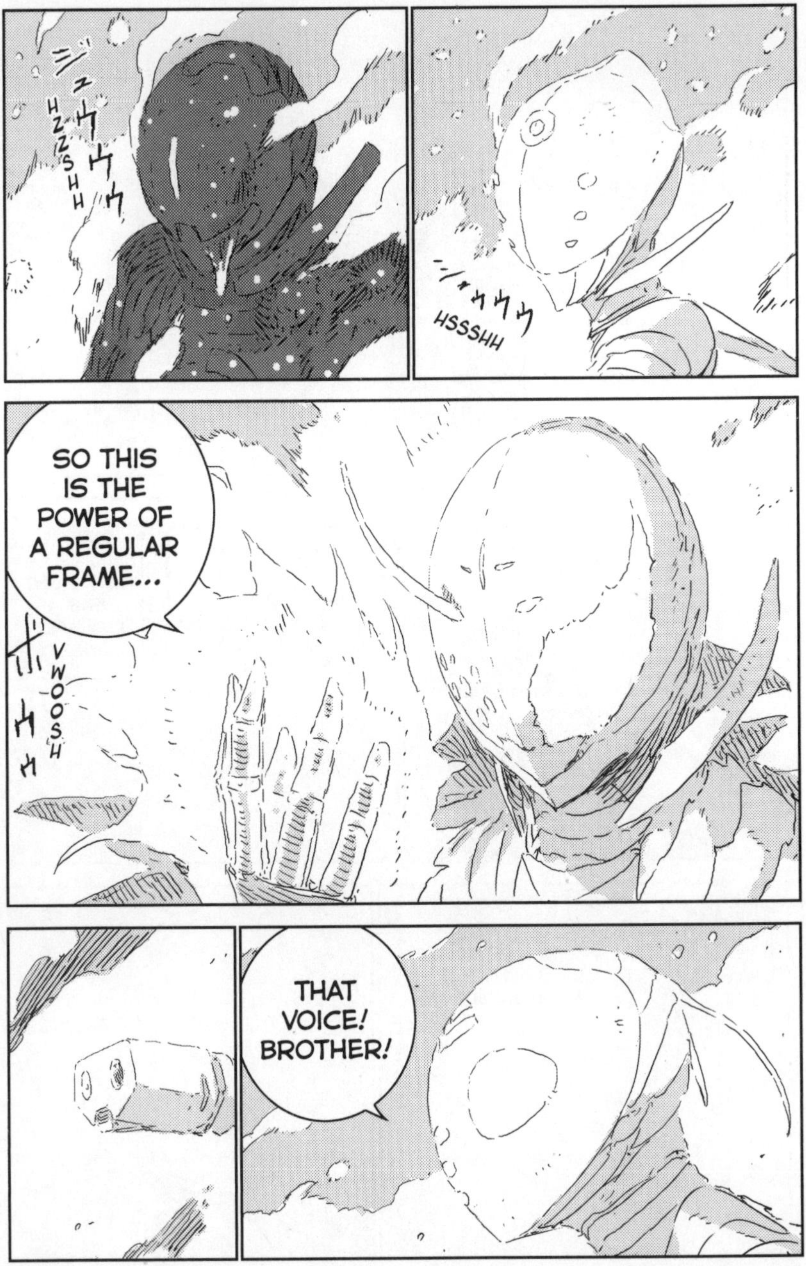
HSSSHH
HZZSHH
SO THIS IS THE POWER OF A REGULAR FRAME...
VWOOSH
THAT VOICE! BROTHER!

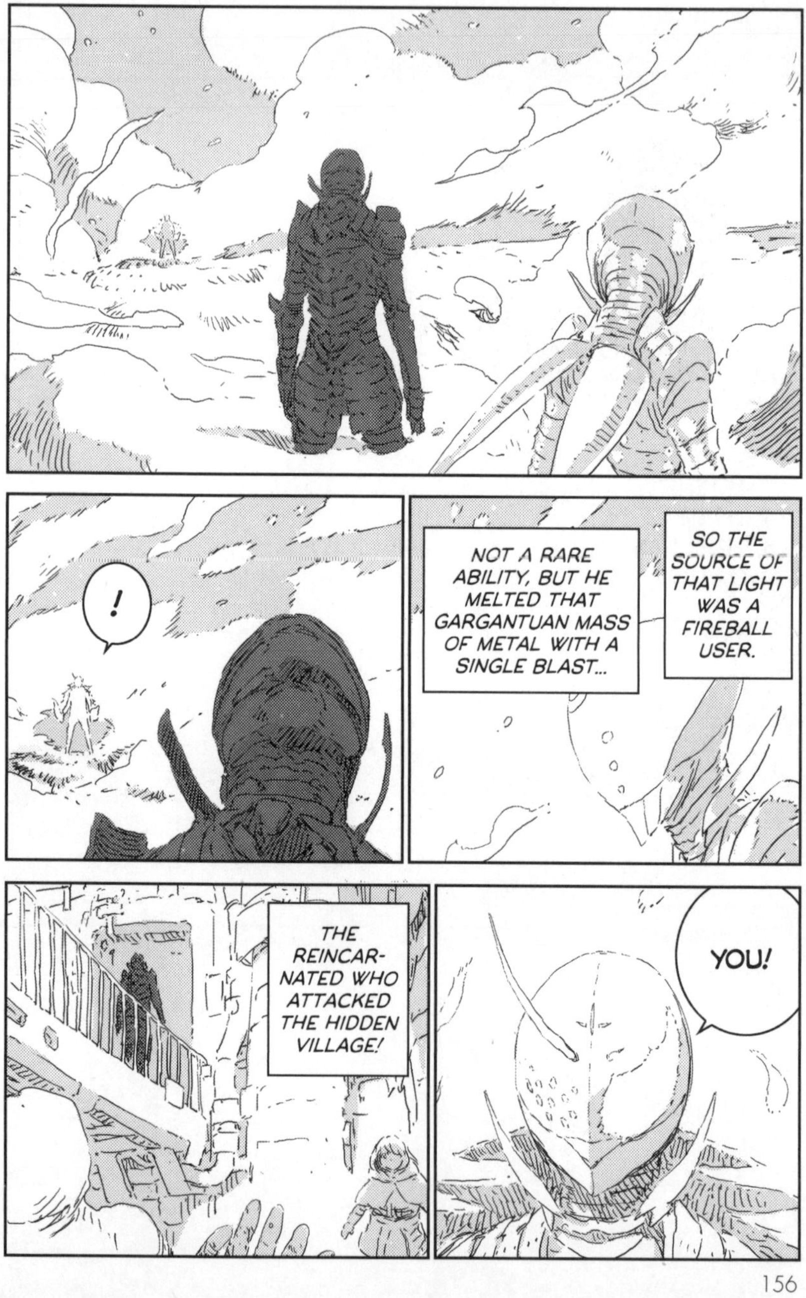
SO THE SOURCE OF THAT LIGHT WAS A FIREBALL USER.
NOT A RARE ABILITY, BUT HE MELTED THAT GARGANTUAN MASS OF METAL WITH A SINGLE BLAST...
!
YOU!
THE REINCAR-NATED WHO ATTACKED THE HIDDEN VILLAGE!

YOU MADE A REAL FOOL OF ME THERE.
ピキ
PKIK
ピキキ
PKIKIK

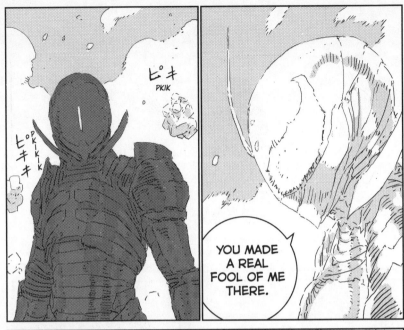

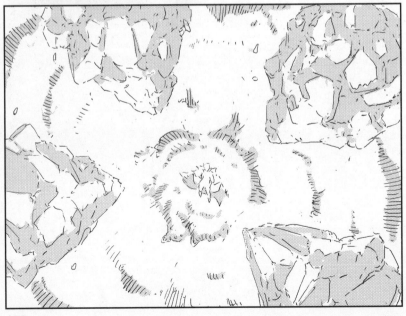

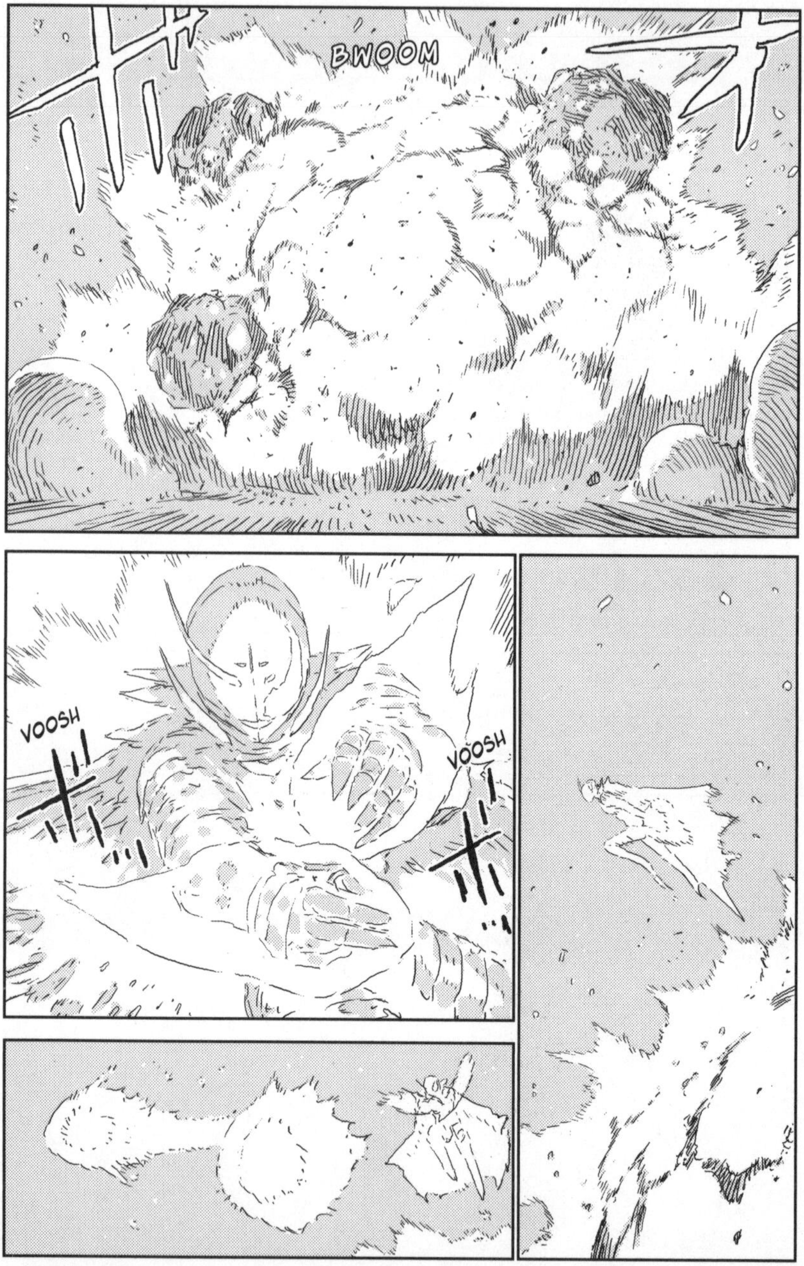
BWOOM
VOOSH
VOOSH

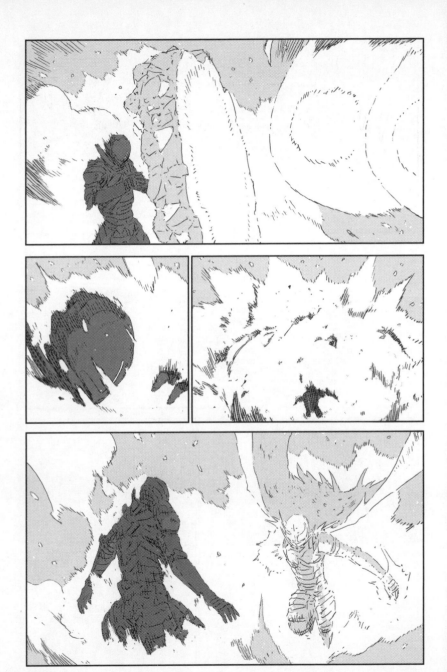

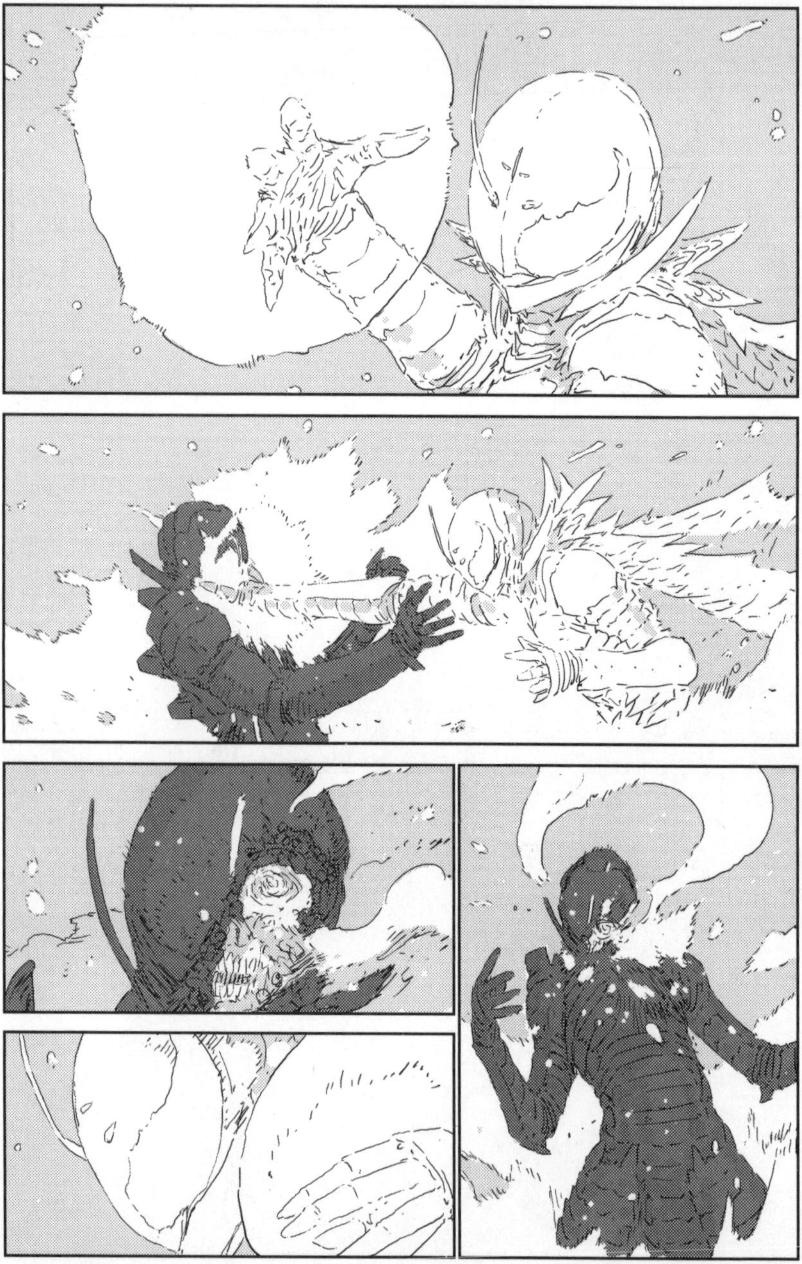

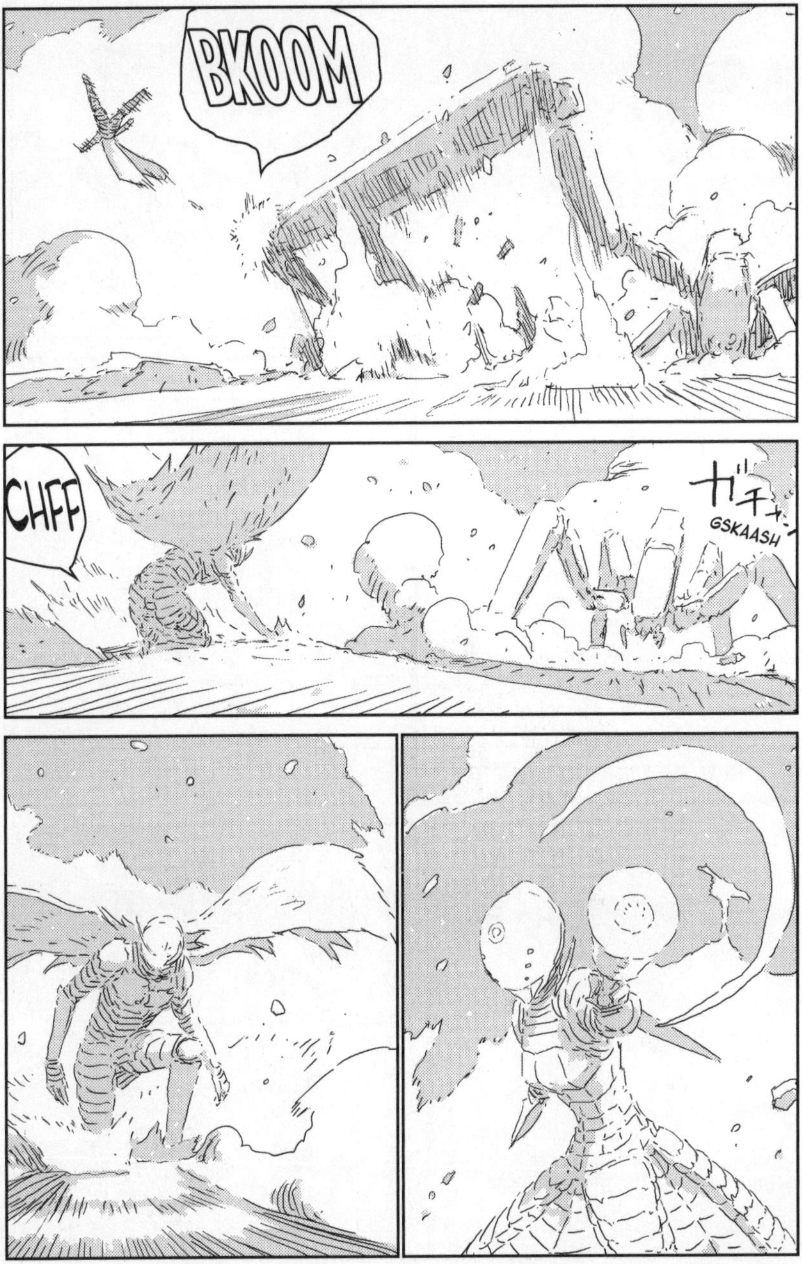
BKOOM
ガチャ
GSKAASH
CHFF

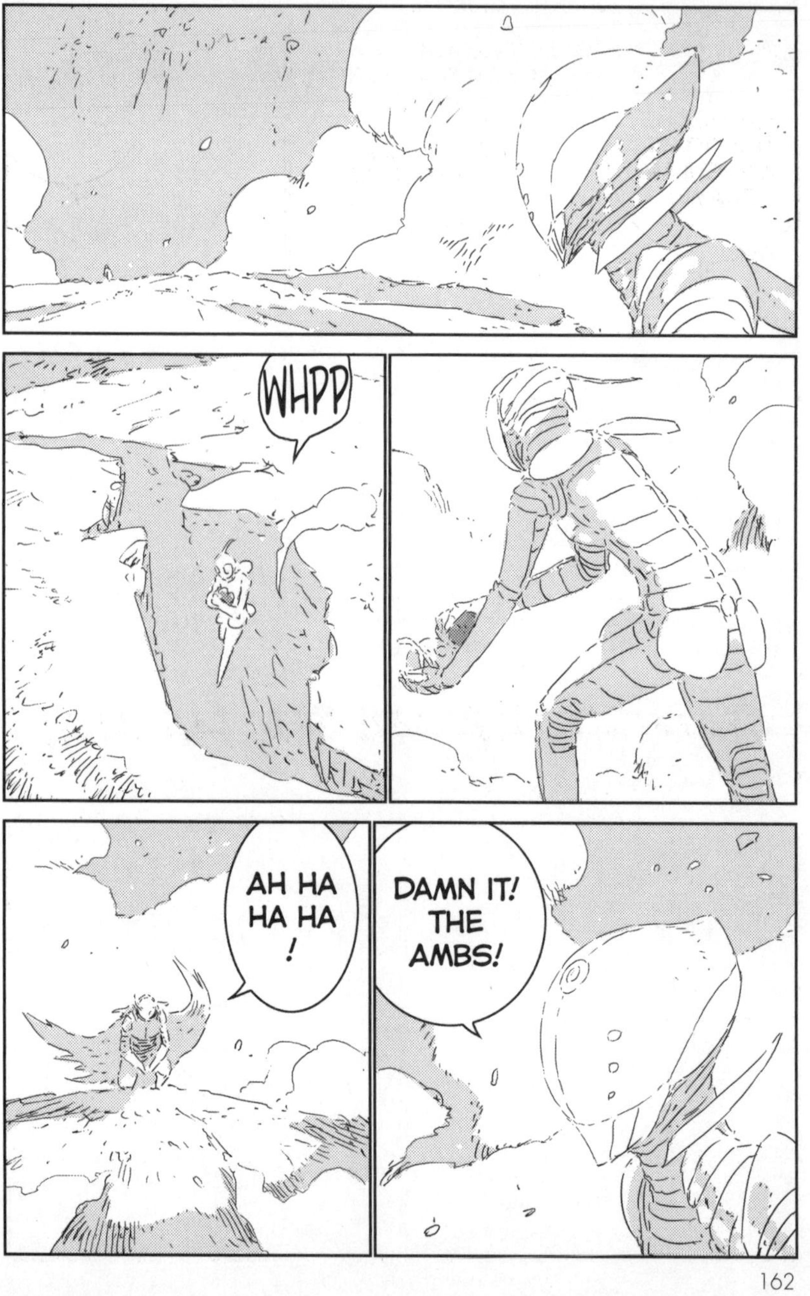
WHPP
DAMN IT! THE AMBS!
AH HA HA HA !

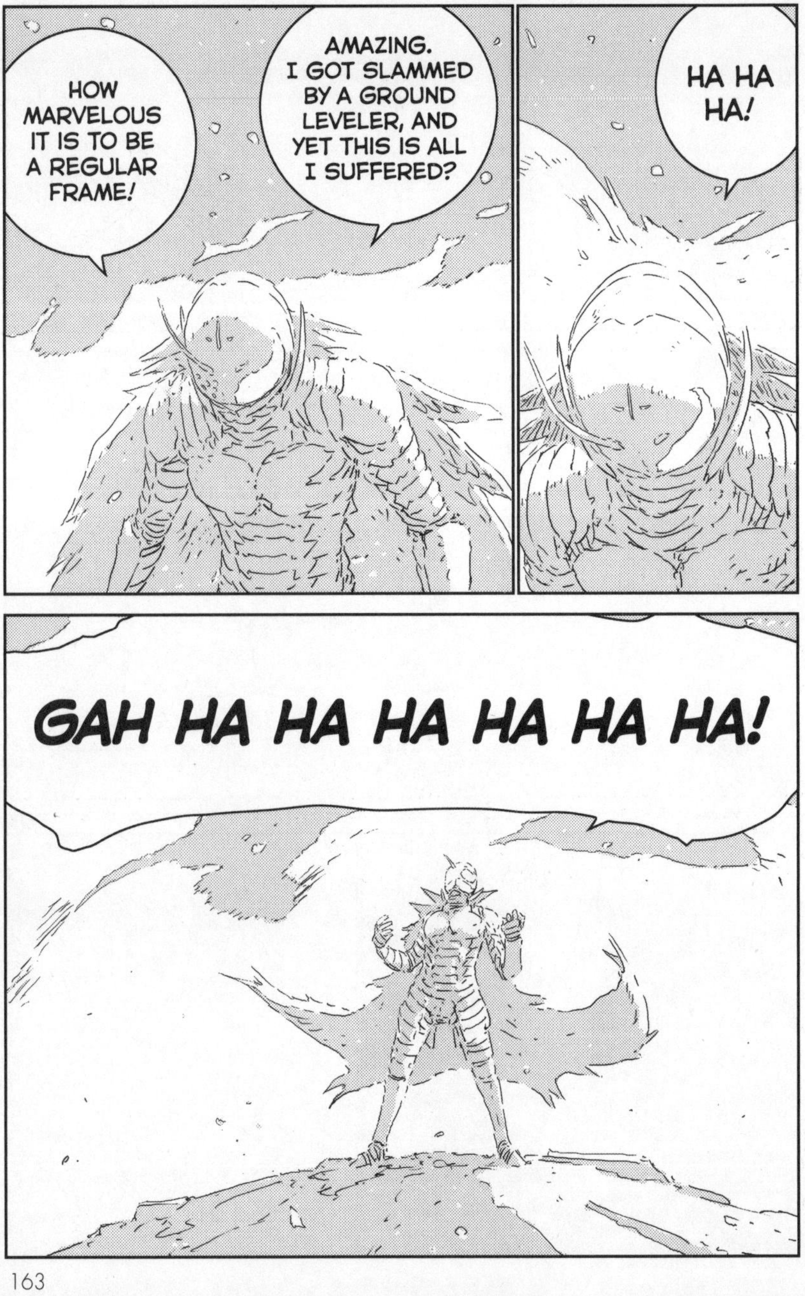
HA HA HA!
AMAZING. I GOT SLAMMED BY A GROUND LEVELER, AND YET THIS IS ALL I SUFFERED?
HOW MARVELOUS IT IS TO BE A REGULAR FRAME!
GAH HA HA HA HA HA HA!

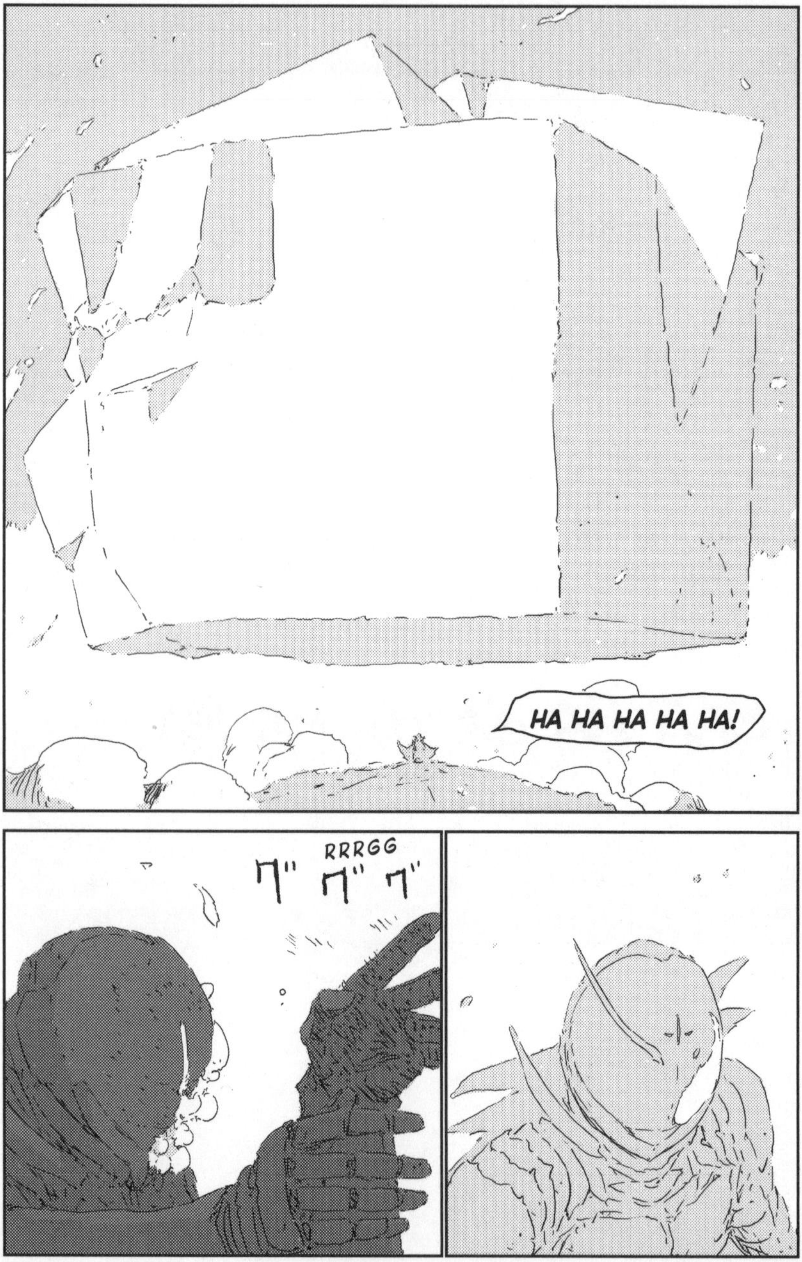
HA HA HA HA HA!
RRRGG

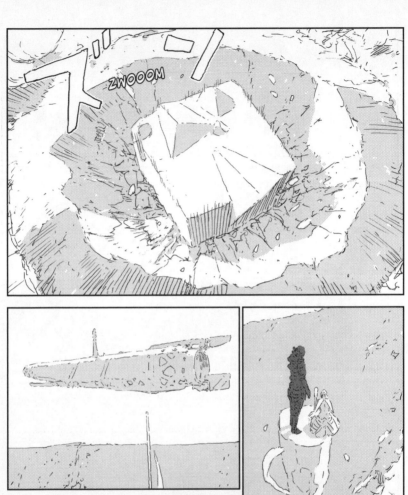

ZWOOOM

ZCHSSHH
MMB
RRR
ZHADOOOM
ZCHSSHH
ZMM
ZMM
ZZZMMM

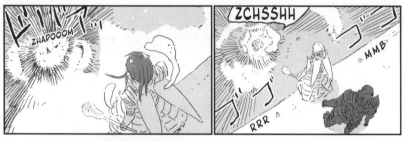

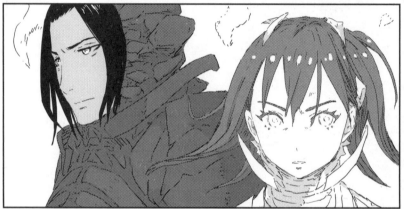

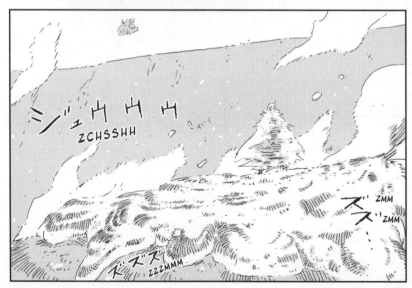

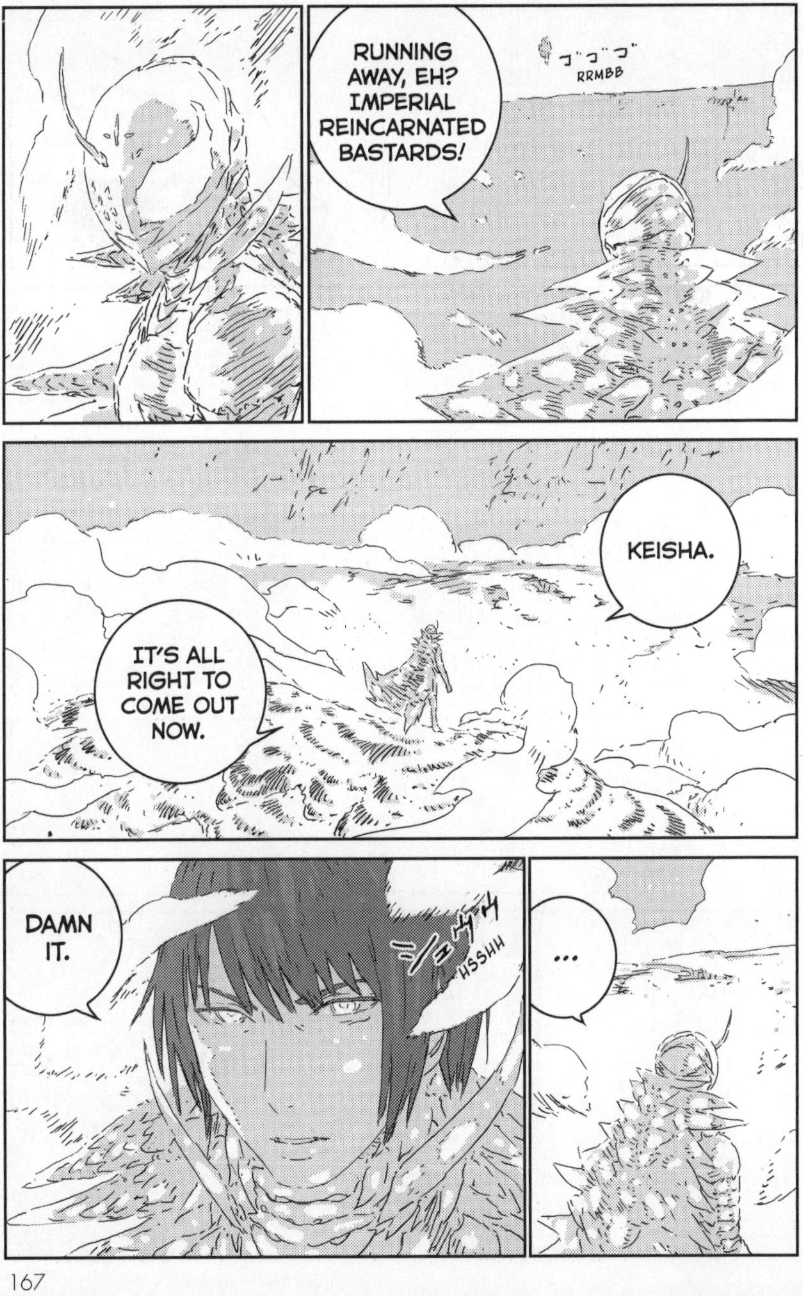
RUNNING AWAY, EH? IMPERIAL REINCARNATED BASTARDS!
RRMBB
KEISHA.
IT'S ALL RIGHT TO COME OUT NOW.
...
DAMN IT.
HSSHH

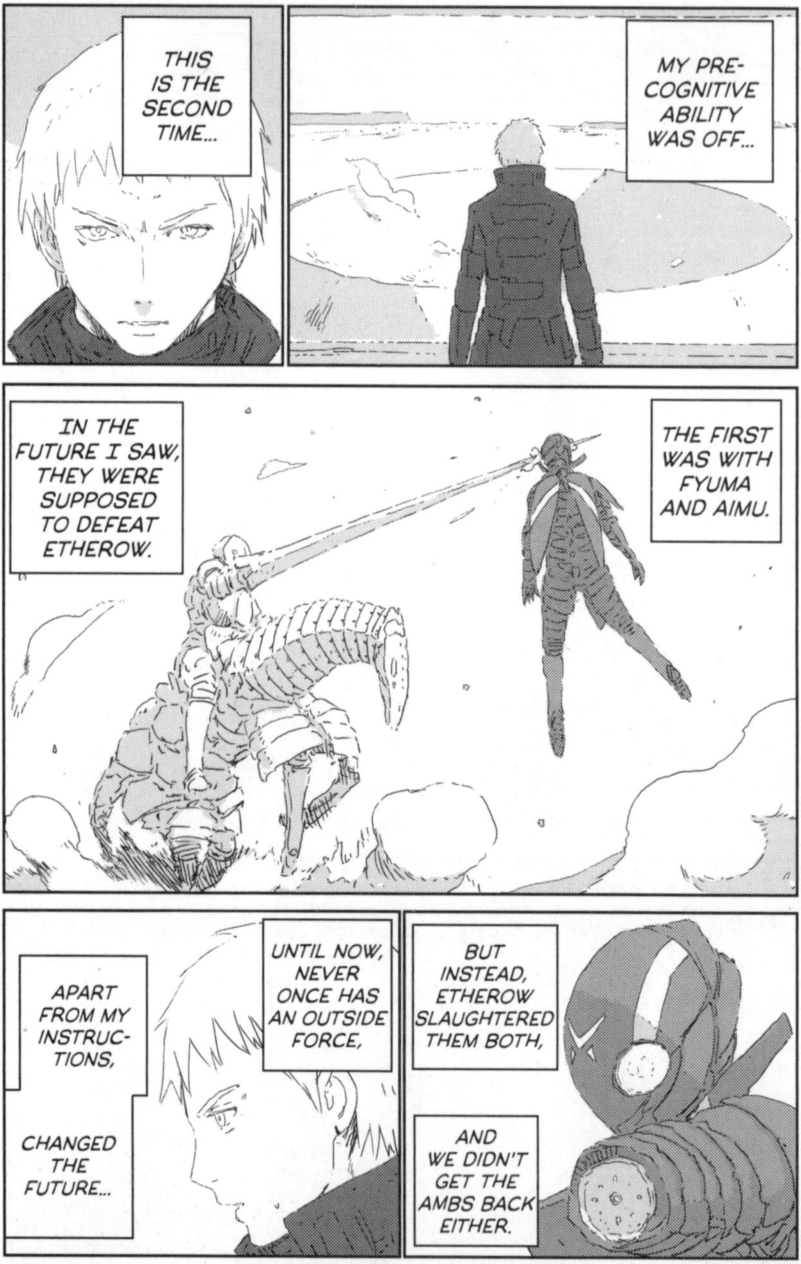
MY PRE-COGNITIVE ABILITY WAS OFF...
THIS IS THE SECOND TIME...
THE FIRST WAS WITH FYUMA AND AIMU.
IN THE FUTURE I SAW, THEY WERE SUPPOSED TO DEFEAT ETHEROW.
BUT INSTEAD, ETHEROW SLAUGHTERED THEM BOTH,
AND WE DIDN'T GET THE AMBS BACK EITHER.
UNTIL NOW, NEVER ONCE HAS AN OUTSIDE FORCE,
APART FROM MY INSTRUCTIONS,
CHANGED THE FUTURE...

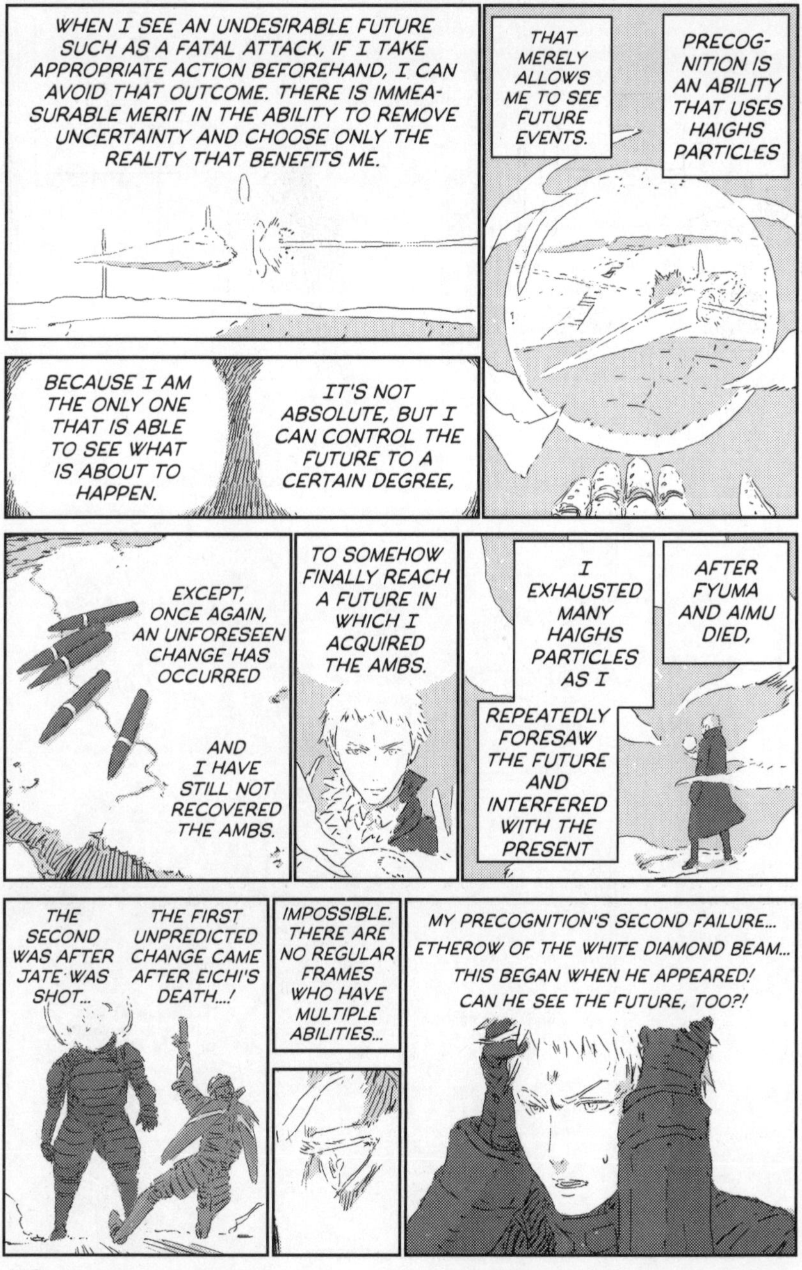
PRECOGNITION IS AN ABILITY THAT USES HAIGHS PARTICLES
THAT MERELY ALLOWS ME TO SEE FUTURE EVENTS.
WHEN I SEE AN UNDESIRABLE FUTURE SUCH AS A FATAL ATTACK, IF I TAKE APPROPRIATE ACTION BEFOREHAND, I CAN AVOID THAT OUTCOME. THERE IS IMMEASURABLE MERIT IN THE ABILITY TO REMOVE UNCERTAINTY AND CHOOSE ONLY THE REALITY THAT BENEFITS ME.
IT'S NOT ABSOLUTE, BUT I CAN CONTROL THE FUTURE TO A CERTAIN DEGREE,
BECAUSE I AM THE ONLY ONE THAT IS ABLE TO SEE WHAT IS ABOUT TO HAPPEN.
AFTER FYUMA AND AIMU DIED,
I EXHAUSTED MANY HAIGHS PARTICLES AS I
REPEATEDLY FORESAW THE FUTURE AND INTERFERED WITH THE PRESENT
TO SOMEHOW FINALLY REACH A FUTURE IN WHICH I ACQUIRED THE AMBS.
EXCEPT, ONCE AGAIN, AN UNFORESEEN CHANGE HAS OCCURRED
AND I HAVE STILL NOT RECOVERED THE AMBS.
MY PRECOGNITION'S SECOND FAILURE... ETHEROW OF THE WHITE DIAMOND BEAM... THIS BEGAN WHEN HE APPEARED! CAN HE SEE THE FUTURE, TOO?!
IMPOSSIBLE. THERE ARE NO REGULAR FRAMES WHO HAVE MULTIPLE ABILITIES...
THE FIRST UNPREDICTED CHANGE CAME AFTER EICHI'S DEATH...!
THE SECOND WAS AFTER JATE WAS SHOT...

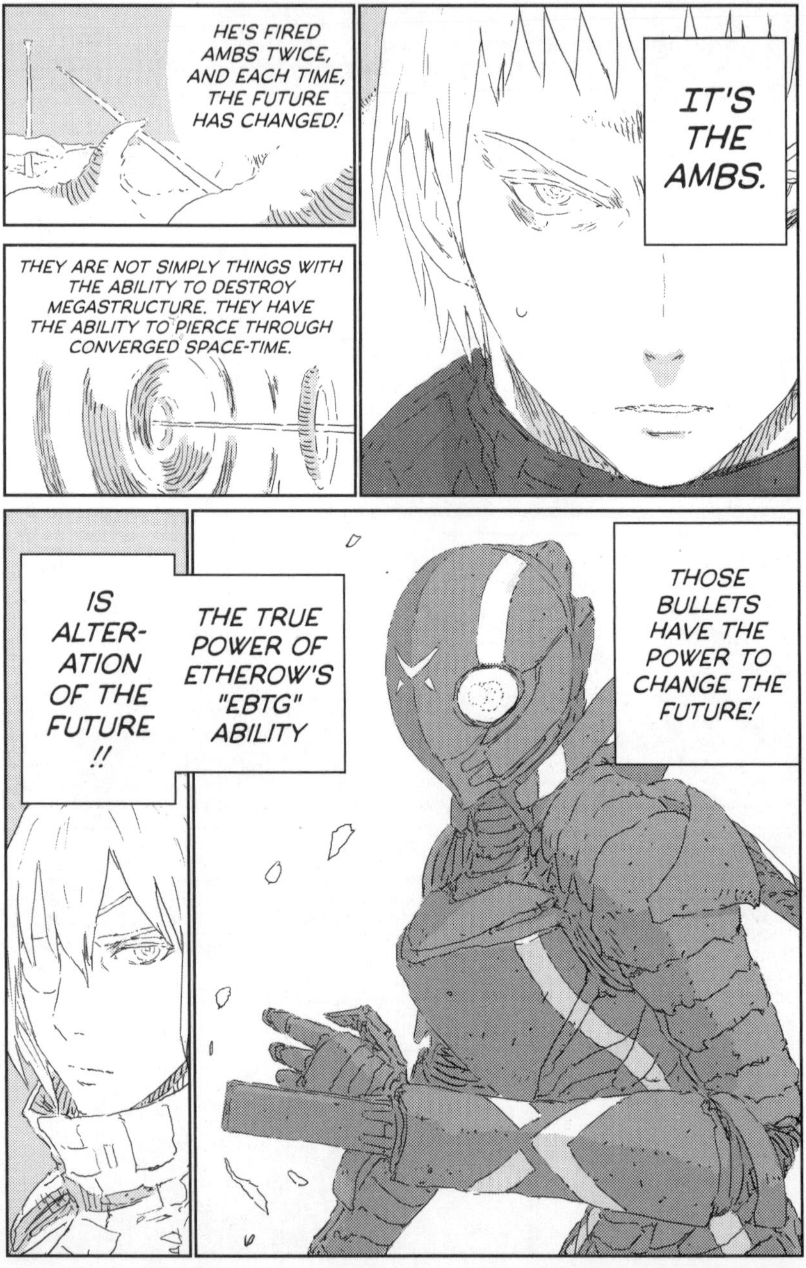
IT'S THE AMBS.
HE'S FIRED AMBS TWICE, AND EACH TIME, THE FUTURE HAS CHANGED!
THEY ARE NOT SIMPLY THINGS WITH THE ABILITY TO DESTROY MEGASTRUCTURE. THEY HAVE THE ABILITY TO PIERCE THROUGH CONVERGED SPACE-TIME.
THOSE BULLETS HAVE THE POWER TO CHANGE THE FUTURE!
THE TRUE POWER OF ETHEROW'S "EBTG" ABILITY
IS ALTER-ATION OF THE FUTURE !!

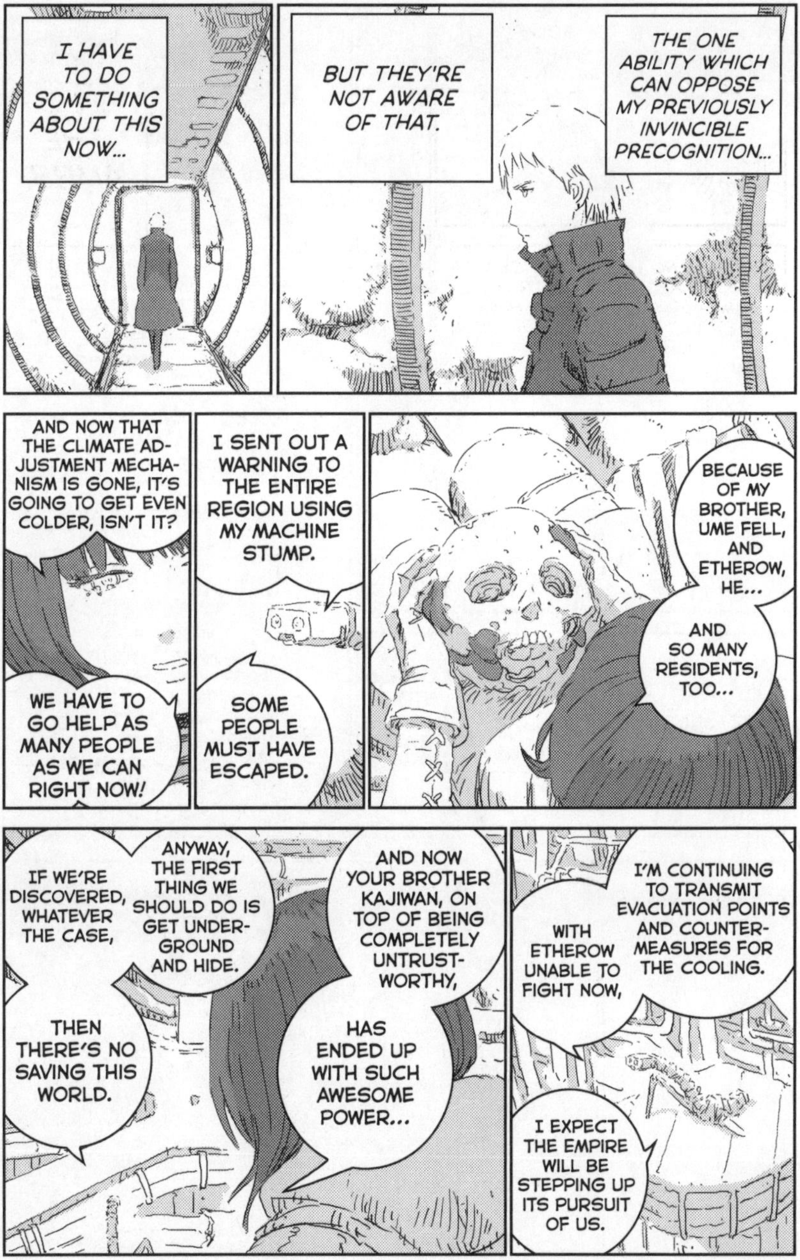
THE ONE ABILITY WHICH CAN OPPOSE MY PREVIOUSLY INVINCIBLE PRECOGNITION...
BUT THEY'RE NOT AWARE OF THAT.
I HAVE TO DO SOMETHING ABOUT THIS NOW...
BECAUSE OF MY BROTHER, UME FELL, AND ETHEROW, HE...
AND SO MANY RESIDENTS, TOO...
I SENT OUT A WARNING TO THE ENTIRE REGION USING MY MACHINE STUMP.
SOME PEOPLE MUST HAVE ESCAPED.
AND NOW THAT THE CLIMATE ADJUSTMENT MECHANISM IS GONE, IT'S GOING TO GET EVEN COLDER, ISN'T IT?
WE HAVE TO GO HELP AS MANY PEOPLE AS WE CAN RIGHT NOW!
I'M CONTINUING TO TRANSMIT EVACUATION POINTS AND COUNTERMEASURES FOR THE COOLING.
WITH ETHEROW UNABLE TO FIGHT NOW,
I EXPECT THE EMPIRE WILL BE STEPPING UP ITS PURSUIT OF US.
AND NOW YOUR BROTHER KAJIWAN, ON TOP OF BEING COMPLETELY UNTRUSTWORTHY,
HAS ENDED UP WITH SUCH AWESOME POWER...
ANYWAY, THE FIRST THING WE SHOULD DO IS GET UNDERGROUND AND HIDE.
IF WE'RE DISCOVERED, WHATEVER THE CASE,
THEN THERE'S NO SAVING THIS WORLD.

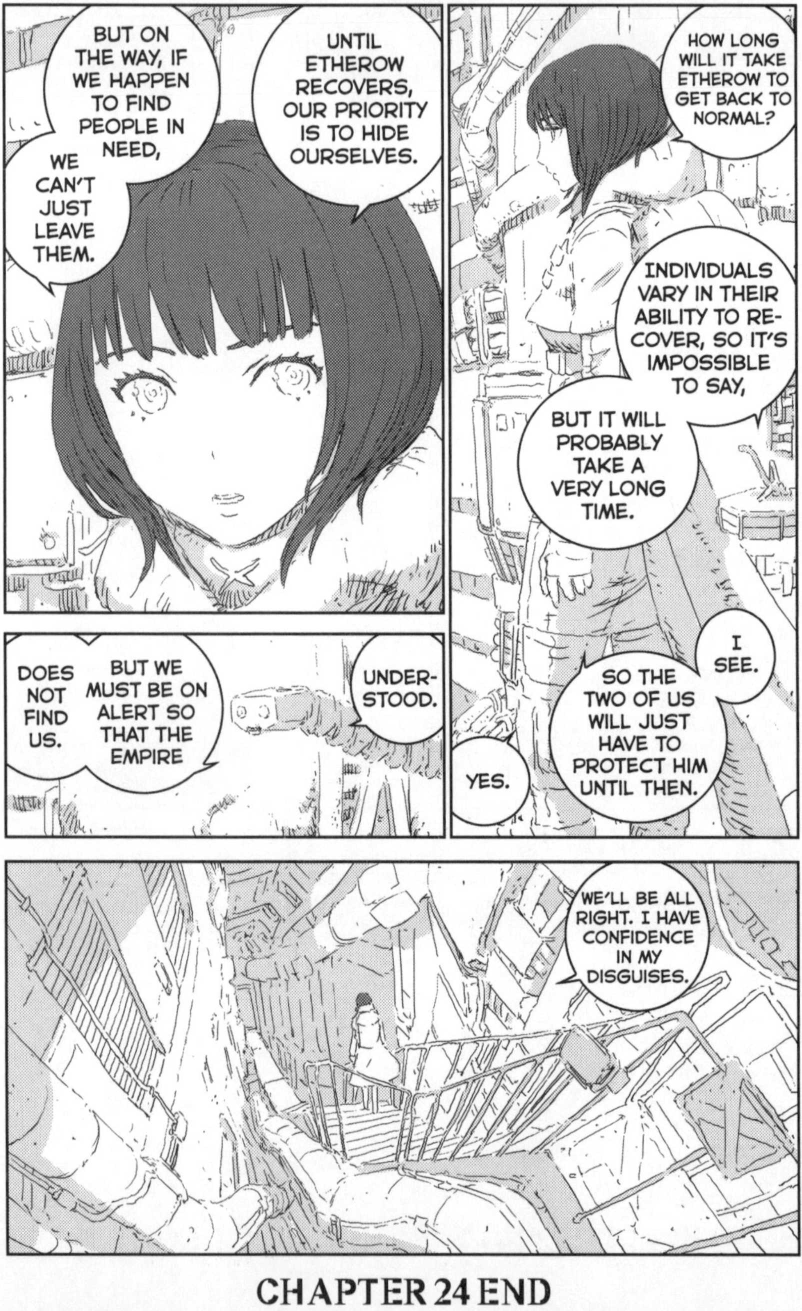
HOW LONG WILL IT TAKE ETHEROW TO GET BACK TO NORMAL?
INDIVIDUALS VARY IN THEIR ABILITY TO RECOVER, SO IT'S IMPOSSIBLE TO SAY,
BUT IT WILL PROBABLY TAKE A VERY LONG TIME.
I SEE.
SO THE TWO OF US WILL JUST HAVE TO PROTECT HIM UNTIL THEN.
YES.
UNTIL ETHEROW RECOVERS, OUR PRIORITY IS TO HIDE OURSELVES.
BUT ON THE WAY, IF WE HAPPEN TO FIND PEOPLE IN NEED,
WE CAN'T JUST LEAVE THEM.
UNDERSTOOD.
BUT WE MUST BE ON ALERT SO THAT THE EMPIRE
DOES NOT FIND US.
WE'LL BE ALL RIGHT. I HAVE CONFIDENCE IN MY DISGUISES.

CHAPTER 24 END

CONTINUED IN VOLUME 5

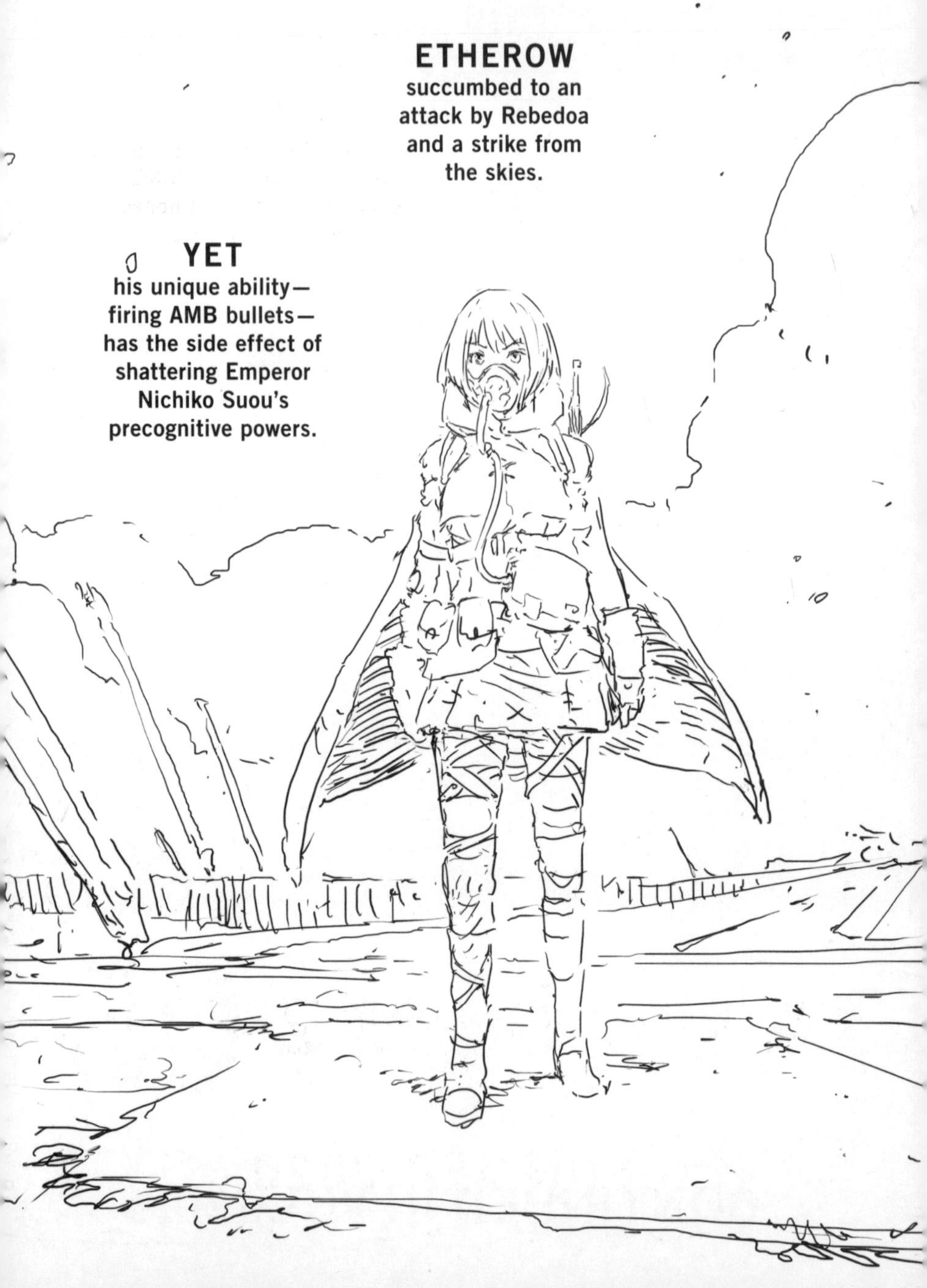
ETHEROW
succumbed to an attack by Rebedoa and a strike from the skies.
YET
his unique ability—firing AMB bullets—has the side effect of shattering Emperor Nichiko Suou's precognitive powers.

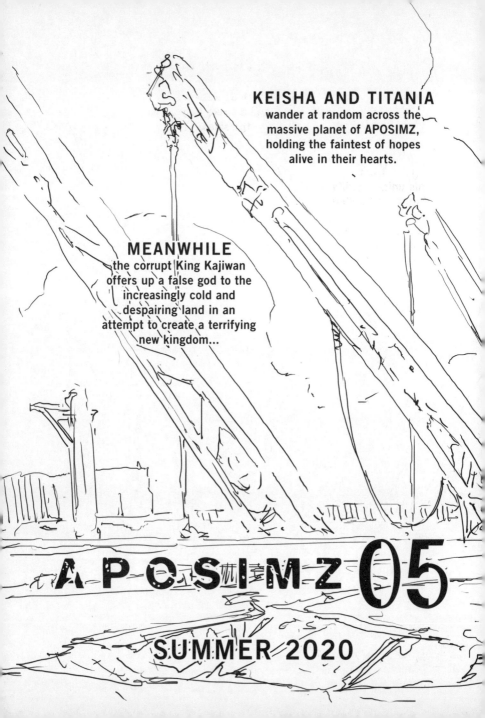

KEISHA AND TITANIA
wander at random across the
massive planet of APOSIMZ,
holding the faintest of hopes
alive in their hearts.

MEANWHILE
the corrupt King Kajiwan
offers up a false god to the
increasingly cold and
despairing land in an
attempt to create a terrifying
new kingdom...

APOSIMZ 05

SUMMER 2020

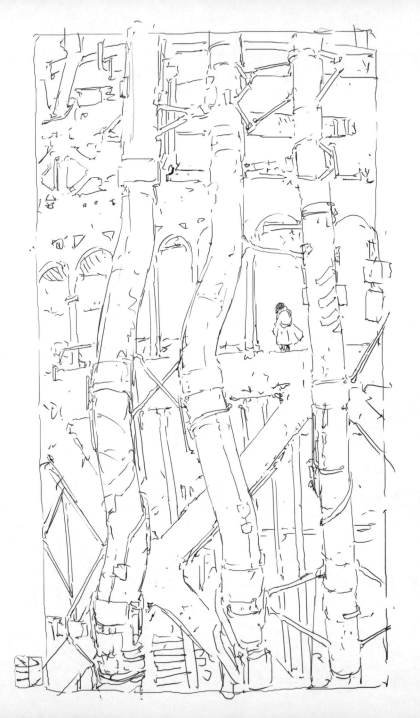

APOSIMZ

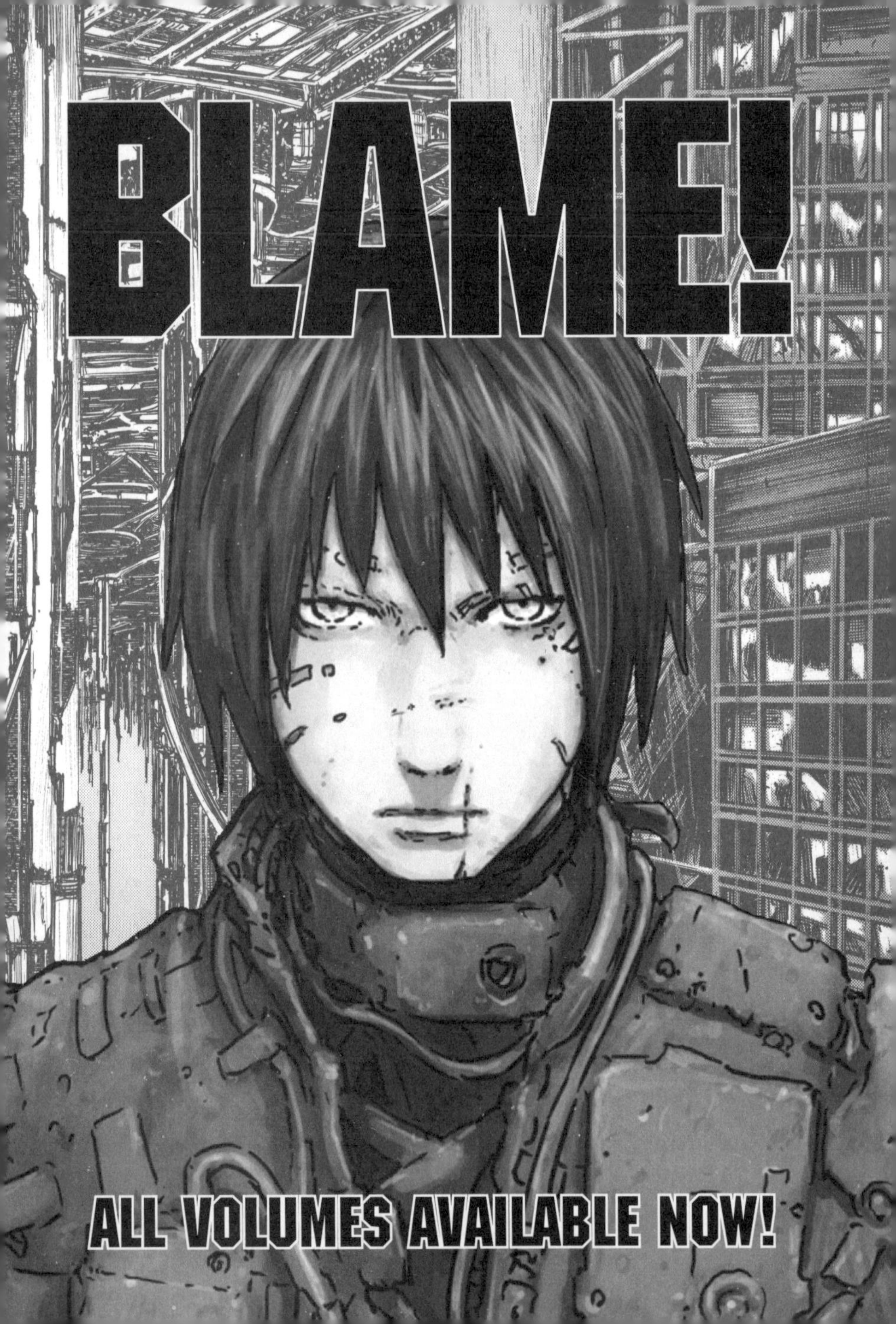
BLAME!
ALL VOLUMES AVAILABLE NOW!

IN A FUTURE VERSION OF EARTH, THERE IS A CITY GROWN SO CHAOTICALLY MASSIVE THAT ITS INHABITANTS NO LONGER RECALL WHAT "LAND" IS. WITHIN THIS MEGASTRUCTURE THE SILENT, STOIC KYRII IS ON A MISSION TO FIND THE NET TERMINAL GENE—A GENETIC MUTATION THAT ONCE ALLOWED HUMANS TO ACCESS THE CYBERNETIC NETSPHERE. ARMED WITH A POWERFUL GRAVITON BEAM EMITTER, KYRII FENDS OFF WAVES OF ATTACKS FROM FELLOW HUMANS, CYBORGS AND SILICON-BASED LIFEFORMS. ALONG THE WAY, HE ENCOUNTERS A HIGHLY-SKILLED SCIENTIST WHOSE BODY HAS DETERIORATED FROM A LENGTHY IMPRISONMENT WHO PROMISES TO HELP KYRII FIND THE NET TERMINAL GENE, ONCE SHE SETTLES A SCORE FOR HERSELF...

"WHETHER IT BE THE GREAT PACING AND LAYOUTS TO THE FRENETIC ACTION THAT OCCUPIES THE PANELS IN THESE SCENES, EVERY ONE OF THEM ALWAYS PACKS A PUNCH. THESE ARE ALL EMPHASIZED BY SOME GREAT DESIGNS ACROSS THE BOARD."

—THE TURNAROUND BLOG

"NIHEI'S MOODY MASTERPIECE FINALLY RELEASED IN ITS FULL DREADFUL SPLENDOR."

—UK ANIME NETWORK

APOSIMZ volume 4

A Vertical Comics Edition

Translation: Kumar Sivasubramanian
Production: Grace Lu
            Darren Smith

First published in Japan in 2019 by Kodansha, Ltd., Tokyo
Publication for this English edition arranged through Kodansha, Ltd., Tokyo
English language version produced by Vertical Comics,
an imprint of Kodansha USA Publishing, LLC.

Translation provided by Vertical Comics, 2020
Published by Kodansha USA Publishing, LLC., New York

Originally published in Japanese as *APOSIMZ 4* by Kodansha, Ltd.
APOSIMZ first serialized in *Monthly Shonen Sirius*, Kodansha, Ltd., 2017-

This is a work of fiction.

ISBN: 978-1-947194-96-0

Manufactured in Canada

First Edition

Kodansha USA Publishing, LLC.
451 Park Avenue South
7th Floor
New York, NY 10016
www.vertical-comics.com

Vertical books are distributed through Penguin-Random House Publisher Services.